Acclaim for *Vagabonds*

Short-listed for the Wolfson History Prize 2023

"Evocative, personal and moving. This book uses first-hand accounts to evoke the streets of 19th-century London. Richly woven with the voices of the city's poorest and most resilient residents."
—**Wolfson History Prize judges**

"Gives these past lives a monument, a dignity and recognition they deserve . . . Jensen is the real deal; I've never encountered a historian quite like him. . . . For two exquisite days, this book was my best friend." —**Gerard DeGroot, *The Times***

"Rescuing these diverse individuals from both the condescension of their contemporaries and the silence of so many historians since, *Vagabonds* narrates their lives with a sympathy and sensitivity that is often moving."—**Matthew Beaumont, author of *Nightwalking: A Nocturnal History of London***

"Compellingly written, utterly captivating . . . Jensen's book is stuffed to bursting with original voices and sources alongside his well-crafted expert analysis . . . every page of *Vagabonds* rings with the thrum and bass of a city that saw itself as the centre of the world." —**Fern Riddell, *BBC History***

"A vigorous and necessary account made timely by the widening chasm between obscene wealth and dire poverty in our contemporary metropolis." —**Iain Sinclair, author of *The Last London***

"The stories . . . make for fascinating and sometimes disturbing reading. Jensen weaves them together into a tapestry of pain and misfortune." —**Ana Alicia Garza, *Times Literary Supplement***

"Rich in research . . . a telling account."

—Martin Chilton, *The Independent*

"Social history as it should be: fascinating, well-written, passionate, revelatory, and deeply humane. Terrific."

—KJ Charles, author of *The Secret Lives of Country Gentlemen*

"A very readable and historically well-researched picture of the nineteenth-century poor."

—Gareth Stedman Jones, professor of the history of ideas at Queen Mary University of London

"With great sensitivity and scholarly rigour, [Jensen] ensures that, once again, we hear the lived experiences of those who lived and died on the margins of metropolitan life."

—Sarah Wise, author of *The Italian Boy: A Tale of Murder and Body Snatching in 1830s London*

"An elegantly written and vivid account . . . Jensen doesn't just present these hitherto marginalised figures on the page; like a delightful sorcerer, he brings them back to life."

—Tomiwa Owolade, author of *This Is Not America*

"Warm, vertiginously wide-ranging, and eloquent all at once, with the breadth and intensity of an academic study but the light touch of a skilled, sympathetic writer who lets every character in it speak for themselves."   —Niamh Campbell, author of *This Happy*

Vagabonds

Vagabonds

Life on the Streets of
Nineteenth-Century London

Oskar Jensen

THE EXPERIMENT

NEW YORK

The Experiment, LLC
220 East 23rd Street, Suite 600
New York, NY 10010-4658
theexperimentpublishing.com

THE EXPERIMENT and its colophon are registered trademarks of
The Experiment, LLC. Many of the designations used by manufacturers
and sellers to distinguish their products are claimed as trademarks. Where
those designations appear in this book and The Experiment was aware of a
trademark claim, the designations have been capitalized.

The Experiment's books are available at special discounts when purchased
in bulk for premiums and sales promotions as well as for fundraising or
educational use. For details, contact us at info@theexperimentpublishing.com.

Library of Congress Cataloging-in-Publication Data available upon request

ISBN 978-1-891011-42-9
Ebook ISBN 978-1-891011-43-6

Cover design by Beth Bugler
Text design by Danny Lyle
Cover photograph by Oscar Rejlander, courtesy of the George Eastman Museum
Author photograph © Andy Aitchison

Manufactured in the United States of America

First printing February 2024
10 9 8 7 6 5 4 3 2 1

For my family

Oscar Rejlander, *Costermonger* (*c.* 1860). Courtesy of the George Eastman Museum.

Contents

A Note on the Text

All dialogue quoted in this book is reproduced verbatim from primary sources. I do not expect my first-hand sources to be entirely accurate in recording direct speech – though we might suppose a trial report to be more faithful than a memoir, for example – but including this dialogue directly from the sources brings us closer to the spirit of the time than we could ever come if we excluded it altogether. While I have, at times, attempted to recreate or infer a thought process or emotional response, I have not invented any direct speech. Although I have occasionally modernised punctuation, I have not corrected or updated spellings, which also extends to place names: where a historical and a modern spelling differ, I have favoured the former.

Introduction

Saturday, 26 March 1859, and David Wire, Lord Mayor of London, is presiding over a Petty Session, ready to dispense justice. These court appearances are not easy for him: he is pushing sixty, double-chinned and far from well. Still, the case before him promises to be a swift one. Mary Ann Donovan, aged eighteen and (as is so often the case) Irish, is charged with attempting to sell combs on Cornhill.

It is not the combs that offend the law so much as the selling: Cornhill is a major thoroughfare in the City of London's financial district, and any act that causes an obstruction – by creating a crowd of comb-buyers, for instance – is punishable by a fine. Besides, the constable who arrested the girl reports that she used 'the vilest language' and threatened to '"smash"' him. She denies it, of course, but it is her word against his. This will not take long.[1]

Yet the trial does not go according to plan. Donovan defends herself, claiming that, if anyone has employed violent and threatening language, it is the constable.

Lord Mayor Wire sits a little straighter and addresses the prisoner directly. 'Well, you must not come into the City to sell your combs. That is often only a cover for immodest purposes; and, besides, you are liable to a fine of forty shillings, or one month's imprisonment, for hawking your things in this way.'

Unabashed, Mary Ann Donovan asks in reply, 'Then, what can a poor girl do?'

'Why you must try and get an honest living,' he says.

This only provokes the prisoner further. 'Why, I do try, and you stop me. I often stay about the streets all day to do so by selling my combs, and only gain a few halfpence; but I suppose you think I might go upon the streets, but that I'll never do.'

The journalist recording the proceedings makes a note that she utters these last, defiant words 'vehemently and with great natural eloquence'. As well she might – since 'go upon the streets' is a euphemism for prostitution.*

Lord Mayor Wire is taken aback. 'There's no occasion for that; there are many means of getting an honest living.'

'Then, Sir, tell me how,' says Donovan. 'I can't take a shop, and if I sell in the streets you say I am liable to [a] forty shilling fine or a month [in prison]. If I beg, you'll give me three months, perhaps; and if I steal, I don't know what will become of me. So tell me, if you can, what a poor girl can do?'

But Wire has heard more than enough from this Irish girl. 'At all events, you must keep out of the City, and as you have been here [in court] before, I must send you to prison for fourteen days.'

And so her fate is sealed.

~

Wire's verdict is neither the start nor the end of Mary Ann Donovan's ordeal. During the weeks that she is locked away, the papers publish

---

* I employ the terms 'prostitution' and 'prostitute' in preference to 'sex worker' in line with a general preference for historical usage over anachronisms in this book; I would use the latter in a modern context.

their reports of the trial, made notable by her eloquent self-defence. Wire comes in for heavy criticism; many readers send in money, to be given to Donovan on her release. In an effort to dam the tide of public opinion, Wire makes a statement, asserting:

> that if the whole of the case had been published there would have been no sympathy and no contributions. It is well known that the girl had been here before, and that she and those with whom she associates have been long in the habit of assembling together and annoying the passengers in the streets with the most disgusting language; and, in fact, she proved what a mistress of foul language she was while she was awaiting her examination in this house.

He goes further, initiating enquiries into the girl's early life. It emerges that, aged twelve, Donovan had been taken from a life of street selling and housed in King Edward's School of Industry – a children's home for paupers in Mile End. The school's secretary, Henry Williams, comes forward to taint the girl's reputation further:

> She was publicly expelled by the committee for inciting some six of the inmates to run away. Naturally she is a shrewd clever girl, with a plausibility of manner and expression as to deceive the most experienced ... The depravity which her education upon the streets had fostered exerted an influence generally which I hope never to see again in that institution, and I have no hesitation in saying that she is now a most abandoned and dangerous girl.

Picking up on his use of the word 'abandoned', and on Wire's unfounded speculation during the trial, prurient letter writers begin arguing in the press about the likelihood of Donovan already being a prostitute. Undeterred, barristers and radical journalists take up her cause. The *Illustrated Times* points out that Wire contravened the penal code by imprisoning rather than fining her, but adds, 'The illegality sinks into insignificance, in comparison with the injustice and the moral wrong of sentencing a girl to prison for endeavouring to sell combs in the street.' A month later, this paper is still trying to clear her name. On her release, Donovan refuses 'to enter an institution for the reformation of abandoned females' – presumably, the *Illustrated Times* points out, because she is *not* an abandoned female – but because of this, the Lord Mayor withholds the money that has been sent in on her behalf. Instead, he entrusts the funds to a clergyman, who refuses to give them to Donovan.

The reason for all this harsh treatment, the paper suggests, comes back to Donovan's conduct at the trial. 'The worthy Lord Mayor had been rendered angry by the girl's boldness and readiness in her replies to the judicial perquisitions – replies in which the girl clearly had the best of it.'

And this is why Mary Ann Donovan's case matters. Faced with all the might of the City of London, with a man in furs and a golden chain, she has the courage to speak up, to answer back, to give her side of the story. This is a remarkable and exceptional act by someone in her position. Eighteen, impoverished, unenfranchised. An Irish girl in London. Undaunted and unbowed, she has her say. And though things go badly for her, people listen. Many of them agree with her. For once, her voice is heard.

~

In this book, I want to listen to the voices of people like Mary Ann Donovan. Voices that have rarely been heard and taken seriously, both at the time and in the histories we write about our society. These voices – which cried out their wares, services, wants, or simply sang a song to buy – belong to those who lived and worked in London's streets between the 1780s and the 1870s. This was a period in which a great deal was invented, won, lost, overturned – but when, in practical terms, very little really changed for those on the street. It was the age of the great chroniclers of street life: writers like Charles Dickens and Henry Mayhew,[2] artists like John Thomas Smith and Gustave Doré. Until now, we have had to make do with their perspective: dazzling in its way, often moving, sometimes censorious and always faintly theatrical. It's from them that we inherit our impressions of urchins and prostitutes, pickpockets and sweeps, beggars and ballad singers. They in their turn had inherited a vision of street criers and scoundrels that went right back to the birth of printing: to the *Cris de Paris* published around 1500, and the *Cries of London* and other cities that followed soon after.

These were sets of illustrations sold to amuse and charm the middling and upper classes, organised either as collections of individual prints, or as a single page featuring dozens of miniature figures, each caged within their own little box (see Image 0.1).[3] Each image was a picturesque representation of a different street crier, often accompanied by a caption that either gave the words of their cry itself ('Milk below!', 'Buy a broom!'), or named their occupation with a dehumanising definite article: this is not *a* knife-grinder, but *the* knife-grinder, *the* dustman, *the* oyster girl, their singular identities eclipsed by their occupations.[4] Like Mary Ann Donovan, these street sellers have been imprisoned by the authorities that spoke for and over them: it is not their individual voices that we hear in our histories, but those of the wealthy, learned men (and the occasional woman) who have reshaped their stories, put them in boxes, sensationalised and exoticised their lives as dirty and disreputable – as vagabonds in the most unreconstructed sense of the word.

I want to set all that aside. Instead of inheriting the eighteenth century's compulsion to exhibit and the nineteenth century's compulsion to enumerate, might we not make more of the eighteenth century's other great urge – to sympathise, or better yet, to *empathise?* Because I don't want to look *at* people like Mary Ann Donovan. I want to look *with* them – and to hear, to smell, above all to feel. I want to stand with the people who made sense of the London street, not as a place to pass through in anxiety or wonder, but as somewhere to work – play – suffer – live. The streets themselves were almost infinitely variable: from broad thoroughfares to narrow back alleys; congested with traffic or practically deserted; gaslit or dark; open onto fields or hemmed by houses, shops, workplaces; new or old; surfaced with dirt, cobbles, flagstones, tarmacadam or even wood; dustbowls in summer or ice rinks in winter. But they all shared this common quality: while respectable London saw them as places to pass through, conduits for capital and traffic, the people *in* the street saw them as places to *be* – and it's this perspective I want to understand. This means closing our ears to the well-known chroniclers, turning our backs on Dickens and the rest. But it might compensate us with something else: the ability to recognise 'the' gutter child, 'the' crossing sweeper, 'the' milkmaid as a fellow person. One with a name and a perspective. Looking through their eyes, feeling through their skin, we might find a very different Victorian London to the one we thought we knew.

~

In the terrible winter of 1861, John Hollingshead – one of those literary chroniclers, a protégé of Dickens – finds himself in the Potteries, an infamous slum in Kensington. Collecting material for his articles, he interviews a man who trains pigs in the street.[5] This man, to Hollingshead's surprise and disappointment, launches into an attack on all interfering journalists:

'We're not swine,' he said; 'we don't lie in that there mud. We train pigs and we train children. There's a hut yonder that doesn't look fit for a donkey to live in, according to the editor of the *Bayswater Chronicle*; but let me tell that man ... that the old woman as has lived in that hut for forty years has brought up as large a family of nice spoken boys as any woman in the Potteries ... People as call theirselves Christians ain't got no right to come here and write books about us, calling us a lot of pigs...'

'Look at that brick-field,' he said, 'A brick-field ain't a drawing-room. Well, a gent comes down here and takes a pictur' of that brick-field, and makes it look a hawful place. He puts in such a hut as I never see, and makes out that all the roofs of our cottages is covered with cow-dung. Now that ain't the way to go and talk about people, and show people up. We're sure to see these things now, because a working-man goes to his coffee-shop, reads his newspapers, and is not such a fool as he's often made out.'[6]

To his credit, Hollingshead has the decency to publish the man's tirade – albeit without including his name, and with a censorious commentary that concludes, 'there is no help for [people like] them'. But he is clearly taken aback to find one of these slum-dwellers so articulate, enraged, and conversant with what respectable journalists are writing about his neighbourhood.

These are the voices I want to listen to: the ones that answer back, that overturn our assumptions. They have been here all this time, most of them in print, but so scattered and obscure that no one has ever gathered together more than a handful: mere scraps when set against famous tomes like *London Labour and the London Poor*.[7] Now, for the first time, a revolution in how we access and search sources in both physical and, increasingly, digital archives has released a host of these forgotten voices – many of them are abbreviated, constrained, heard only in passing, but together forming an astonishingly eloquent collective. They call from the margins: from unread memoirs and the proceedings of obscure trials, from short-lived periodicals and the reports of scandal-ridden societies. The stories they tell are a revelation, drawing us into worlds of tenderness, horror, shame and triumph that we never knew existed.

These voices fall into one of two camps. The first camp, which might include the irate pig trainer, actively sought to bring their own experiences to light. These were the life writers, the very few who were emboldened to think their own selves worth setting in type. In seeking a readership for their words, they were asking to be taken seriously by the wider public; they were staking claims of belonging to the nation, to the modern world and the things it cared about. That was a rare and astonishing thing to do at the time, when such a gulf existed between the written and unwritten worlds. Some of them wished to join the ranks of the bourgeoisie; others to issue a rebuke to that more complacent world, to challenge or to change it. Either way, they wanted to be heard. For the most part, these were exceptional people, who had either risen or fallen further than most, and as such they are tricky sources for social historians to draw on: the insights they offer are fascinating, but they cannot be trusted as representative of their class or station. Happily, in this book I'm more interested in them as representative only of themselves.

The second camp is a sadder one, for it consists of those, like Mary Ann Donovan, who found themselves caught in the machinery. The people who became entangled in that written system without asking for it, and had their voices forcibly extracted by the tools of the press or the judiciary. These are the lives that leave their traces, not in memoirs, but in trial accounts and the records of severe institutions like the Mendicity Society, which we will encounter many times in these pages: victims, put plainly.

'Victims', because the odds were so stacked against them. These sources make clear that self-styled charities of the time had very different missions to those we might assume today. Organisations like the Mendicity Society, dedicated to ending street begging, were motivated not by concern for the people living in poverty but by the drain on the public purse; they tackled the symptoms rather than the causes of penury, and they often did so by force or coercion. Convinced of their moral superiority – as confirmed by their own wealth, comfort and learning – men like Henry Williams, the secretary of the children's home that had been responsible for Mary Ann Donovan, saw no reason for self-recrimination in pronouncing their erstwhile charges as 'abandoned'.

These private institutions shared their assumptions with the public enforcers, the judiciary and the police, and drew their men of power from the same stock. The law was neither impartial nor professional: we have already seen the Lord Mayor presiding over a court – a man generally elected from a mercantile guild rather than a legal background. From the magistrates sitting until all hours at the many lower courts right the way up to the Old Bailey, justice was dispensed in an alarmingly arbitrary fashion. And though various laws were passed during this period, from the Vagrancy Acts of 1824 and 1838, to the various Street Music Acts, to the Poor Law of 1834 – and though, from 1829, London moved from a parochial system of watchmen and the Bow Street Runners to a formal police force – very few officers on the ground seem to have had a firm or accurate sense of those laws, operating instead on more rudimentary impulses.

Faced with such imbalances of power, I find myself compelled to favour, or at least to prioritise, the testimonies of those on the receiving end. I am not so naive, however, as to imagine that first-hand accounts provide us with the unmediated truth. As with all history writing, I am seeking to pin ghosts on to paper – yet these ghosts are always composed, or *de*composed, at least as much from printer's ink and parchment as from flesh and guts. The memoir writer leaves a select, filtered narrative, written for a purpose, often long after the events described.[8] The scribe in the courtroom is less than punctilious, and his record too is abridged and edited before we read it.[9] Some of the lives we will look at remain as seen through the mesh of middling institutions, from the newspaper to the reform society. But I hope that, if we cock our ear the right way, even these compromised voices will ring true.

~

Taken together these voices tell, not the architectural or legal story of London, city of bricks, of smog and statutes, but the story of its people. Though there are big historical themes that will emerge – about the march of modernity and capitalism, and those who resisted both; about movement and stasis; about the negotiation of racial and gendered stereotypes and identities; about the effects of a global system of empire and armies upon those at its metropolitan centre; above all, about power – this book aims to keep individual lives at its heart. The currents that pulse through this book are all too human: the desire for freedom at any price; an open-handed and -minded interest in and acceptance of one's fellows, however different their skin colour or culture; the vital ways, however small, in which people carve out their own space and story in the margins.

Vagabonds is not organised thematically, nor does it tell a story of change over time. As I have said, this was an age when, for those in the street, far less changed than stayed the same. This being the case, it often matters surprisingly little whether we are in 1787 or 1878. Bounded by two devastating wars – the Napoleonic and the Crimean – and witness to rapid alterations, it is a period that nevertheless feels coherent, and it was perhaps the last great age of London's streets. A generation later, there was an underground metropolitan railway; a concept of social welfare; a burgeoning sense of cross-class community that extended the vote to the majority of adult men. The seeds of that progress were planted earlier – but it's hard to see them at street level. So instead, this book is structured around a more fundamental narrative of human life, from birth to death. It is, in a word, a biography.

Each chapter takes for its subject a significant life stage, the street version of the 'seven ages of man'. Infancy. Young boyhood. Adolescent girlhood. The first experiences of newcomers to the London street. The professional peak of the street seller. Persecution. Finally, old age and death. For each of these seven 'ages' I focus on the experiences of a few individuals, supported by the more fleeting stories of many others. As this many-headed, patchwork life progresses, we'll encounter familiar faces, or see events for a second time through a fresh pair of eyes. My hope is that, by the end, we will have come closer to appreciating what it means to live on the wrong side of history – but to live nonetheless, to work and, against the odds, to belong.

This is, then, a book in which human interest is unashamedly the motivation, not the by-product. Writing it, I kept thinking about three sentences by Jane Humphries, one of our most eminent social and economic historians. In her mighty *Childhood and Child Labour in the British Industrial Revolution*, Humphries reads more than 600 working-class autobiographies in search of data. After 370 pages of rigorous, revelatory, but undeniably dry history – there are a lot of charts and tables – she reflects in her very final paragraph:

Sceptics will remain unconvinced. However, even doubters will be haunted by the images. Who could forget William Arnold, cold and lonely little farm worker, weeping for his mother, or Edward Rymer, without food, shoes or light in his first shift in the mines, finding solace in the words of an ancient hymn?[10]

Not Humphries, clearly, who chooses these images to conclude her magisterial study – but alas, she is writing the big history, and William Arnold and Edward Rymer have to take their anonymised places among its charts and statistics. Not here. In this book, that's the level I want to keep to: intimate, affecting, raw. The people we will meet on the street laughed, blushed, and cried. I hope that you will do the same.

1

The Infant

Our story starts, like every record of human life, with a birth. November 1787: 'a deserted, solitary, and otherwise unoccupied chamber in the neighbourhood of Gray's Inn'. It is half-past three in the morning and in London's legal district, the lawyers are asleep. All the same, doors are being knocked on. One is that of a disreputable actress, Charlotte Tidswell. Shaken from the arms of her lover, Moses Kean, by one of his brothers – Aaron? Edmund? – she is summoned to the aid of her friend Mary Ann Carey in Chancery Lane. 'Nance Carey is with child', the father-to-be informs her. 'With child' is putting it mildly – Carey's waters have broken. Years later Tidswell recalls, 'We asked if she had proper necessities, and she replied, "No, nothing;" whereupon [my aunt] Mrs Byrne begged the loan of some baby clothes'.[1] Armed with rags and blankets, the two women help Carey up Gray's Inn Road, where Carey's father has an empty room. It is bare and dank, but it will serve. It is not as if the women have a choice.

Mary Ann Carey is a hawker, a vagrant. Born into a talented if hapless family of theatre-makers – her father is a jobbing playwright; her grandfather wrote some of the most acclaimed songs of the eighteenth century – she ran away from home at fifteen to try her luck with a company of strolling players. Luck is a rare commodity in the Georgian street, however, so she spends rather more of her time selling flowers, powders and pomades, going door to door. Seduced and abandoned by one of the Kean brothers, she is still in her early twenties when we find her in childbirth in a bare room on Gray's Inn Road. You can imagine the cries carrying, stirring solicitors snugly abed – cries that mingle, come the morning, with others at a shriller, more startled pitch. How long and arduous the labour, we have no idea. But Carey survives, and so does her boy.

Carey is lucky: she has people to help her, a network. This is less unusual than you might think for a street seller, many of whom were woven into their local communities. But then again, she is a travelling hawker, not tied to one place, and within months – perhaps as soon as she has recovered – she is off again, 'into the country to resume her wanderings', leaving her baby Edmund in the care of Charlotte Tidswell and Moses Kean. According to one story, he will be lost and found again before she returns, 'left in a dark doorway, cold, hungry, and desolate', starving in Soho in 1789. But the boy is a child of fortune. We will see him again.

~

This book tells the story of life in the street. But even in Georgian London, children were not born *in* the street, even if they were the children of vagrants. There was always a room, a bed, a cellar, a workhouse. The birth of Edmund Carey, later known as Edmund Kean, is straight out of a melodrama* – the desperate mother in the November night, the knock at the door. Perhaps even a baby on a doorstep. But the door opens. The infant's first glimpse of the world is an interior one.

---

* Ironically, a good fifteen years before the conventions of that genre were established.

This raises three questions that I hope this chapter will answer, as we follow these infants from birth through to self-aware childhood. First: if those who lived and worked on the streets were not born there, where were they born - and what conditions marked out the early days of their existence? Second, by what strange or sorry paths did they come to the street, from an indoor world of rooms and roofs? Third, and most perplexing of all - remember, we are still talking of very small children - what on earth did they do once they got there?

~

Almost a century on from Kean's birth in 1787, the already famous philanthropist Thomas Barnardo interviewed an anonymous mother of three girls - albeit through a handkerchief, as 'the dreadful odour or lodging-house *foetor* exhaled by the group was so overpowering that, inured though I am, I became after a few minutes actually unable to continue the conversation.' He did at least find breath to ask where the children had lived. '"Lived, sir!" and she smiled drearily, "nowheer! the girls never had a 'ome all their lives!"' With her husband, 'Cripple Jack', this mother travelled the country singing ballads, sometimes working on farms, and sleeping in barns or beneath hedges. Even so the mother had, she admitted, resorted to temporary accommodation on three occasions. '"I used to go into the work'us [workhouse] then," said the woman, "and come out agin with the babby in a fortnight or three weeks."'[2]

How this couple not only coped on the open road with a month-old child, but successfully managed to repeat the process twice more, is unknown: their powers of parenting must have been remarkable. Many other travelling parents - like Mary Ann Carey - opted instead to leave their children behind, with relatives or friends if they could, or with institutions if they could not. The most famous of these was the Foundling Hospital in Coram's Fields – an elegant ensemble of Georgian buildings on what was once the northern edge of the city, between the lawyers' lodgings of Gray's Inn and the fields of Islington. Despite the rhetoric of the period, in which every child was a waif or stray, most foundlings were not actually orphans.[3] In the early nineteenth century, the Hospital would foster children under two months old – sometimes stretching up to a year old, or five for the children of fallen soldiers and sailors.[4] Despairing mothers had to argue their case on overcrowded 'reception' days, their life stories raked over by a row of gentlemen, bewigged and forbidding, before their baby would be taken in. Logbooks record the questions these men put to the women in an open court. 'Where did you reside when you were seduced and what led to your seduction? Was the criminal intercourse repeated?'[5] Imagine the mothers' internal struggles – to be asked such things in public; to have to answer. Worst of all: which is the *right* answer – are they more likely to take my baby if I sound more, or less, immured in sin?

The governors' conditions were exacting:

> Their sincere penitence, the prospect of their reestablishment
> in virtue and industry by the concealment of their shame,
> and the circumstance of the death of the father, or his escape
> beyond the reach of justice, are the chief objects of investigation
> [before] the order is made for admission.[6]

The successful few left their newborns in rags, often with a scrap of cloth pinned to their swaddling things as a mark of identification. Many of these scraps still survive, outlasting by centuries the wriggling little bodies to which they once were fixed.[7]

From the age of four, these foundlings were housed in the Hospital, fed and schooled – and marketed as a visitor's attraction for more affluent Londoners, who came to gawp and get their dose of sentiment. Indeed, in its early years:

> so many Londoners found a visit to the Foundling Hospital an irresistible pleasure that they even came to see the children after they were in bed. This disturbed the children's sleep, and the Committee soon put an end to it by ordering that a bell be rung at 7pm for the children to go to bed and that the wards be cleared and locked up half an hour later.

Even this reform leaves us with a vision of well-to-do strangers cramming in for their half an hour of bedtime, brooding over rooms full of small, breathing bodies – with motives presumably ranging from the charitable to the perverted, to the heartbreakingly poignant.

For the children, this must have been a profoundly disconcerting experience. But during their early infancy, the foundlings were not kept on site. Instead, they were farmed out to nurses across the Bloomsbury, St Giles's and Holborn parishes, each nurse receiving three shillings per child per week. This pittance was hardly conducive to good childcare – nurses could only turn a profit by effectively neglecting the babies – and for at least a century, the Hospital was dogged by scandalous reports of the fatality rate of these infants. In 1805, it was taken as a minor triumph that only one in six babies entrusted to nurses died in their care.[8]

Mass deaths notwithstanding, authorities spent most of the nineteenth century determinedly separating babies from their families. While the Foundling Hospital was swamped with applications, other institutions actively sought out their infants.

Barnardo tells the story of Nancy, a three-year-old orphan girl cared for by an aunt in 'a common lodging-house of the worst class'. He continues:

> A Bible-woman had discovered the child here ... She had offered, on the clergyman's behalf, that the girl should be admitted into an orphanage. To his and her great surprise, however, they found that the people who had possession of the child were unwilling to allow her to be removed.

Barnardo seems just as bewildered as the two missionaries that a family might resist its forcible separation.[9] Then, as now, it is hard for those who run institutions, utterly certain that they are doing good, to conceive of the horror they may inspire in those they are trying to help.

~

Our second story is a case in point. It takes place in 1850 – or thereabouts – in Marylebone, after midnight. Women are crowding into a low 'den' to hear the young John Weylland preaching. There is warmth from a fire, from bodies, there is free tea and coffee, even bread, but these are meant to be merely incidental to the real attraction of the Word. Among the listeners is Nellie, a child of so few years you would think she'd be able to count them. We must suppose that she welcomes the press of warm bodies, the relief from the cold that seeps up between her bare toes, insinuates itself through the rents in her frock. Intent on the needs of her body rather than her soul, she hopes to go unnoticed as she works the room, emptying each cup of its rapidly cooling dregs, sweeping crumbs straight into her little mouth. But the preacher has spotted her, and later, he will write all this down.

Perhaps she is too slow to clear out when the sermon finishes; perhaps she has not been paying attention. Above the elbows, shawls, tabletops, a face looms over her. It is plump, bearded. And it speaks, this time, to Nellie alone. Overawed by this voice of power, she tries to 'slink away', but a strong hand seizes her wrist. Compelled, she lays bare the scraps of her existence. Her mother? Dead of cholera. Her father? 'Bolted.' She has no home but begs a sleeping-place in dark passages or old omnibuses. Weylland will record that, in her words, '"nobody knowed" her', which seems like a contrivance: why would Nellie use the past tense?

But she is in his power now, and he can do more than adjust the words in her mouth. Nellie is to be 'rescued', with the complicity of the den's owners. At seven o'clock the next morning, Nellie is awoken, taken, dragged along by the landlord and propelled by his wife. '"You *shall* be reformed, you hussy!"' he declares. Nellie can only scream, with 'youthful vigour, "I won't! I won't!"'

Her spirit is fierce. Taken to one of the children's reformatories lately founded by the philanthropist Lady Ross, she makes a bid for freedom. She is thwarted. Her keepers label her 'both wild and cunning', 'an awful child' – they lock her in when they can and haul her back when she tries to scramble over the wall of the yard. Weylland and Lady Ross congratulate themselves on a job well done – in his words, 'We then laughed together over my night adventure'.

Nellie will conform in the end, becoming a model servant girl. Weylland has, in all probability, saved her: decades later, she is still writing to him in thanks. Unarguably he is on the side of the angels. But none of this wipes out Nellie's very real trauma, or the sobering reality that, given a choice, the infant Nellie would have chosen freedom to starve over salvation by force.[10]

~

Already we are forming the impression that, for many of London's poor infants, life in the street might seem preferable to life in an institution. A sense that, as soon as they are old enough, many will choose the freedom of the unknown over the drudgery they have been born into. In 1796 at Saint Pancras Poorhouse – which is still described, remarkably, as being 'near London' – Robert Blincoe, four years old, stares out from an upper window. Outside he sees children scarcely older than himself, begging from door to door or, in lip service to the laws against mendicancy, offering matches for sale. One boy cries his distress aloud, the plaint rising to where Robert sits. These are 'the poorest of the poor' – homeless, destitute. Looking down at them, Robert feels – what? Compassion? Pity? Far from it. Robert, 'so weary of confinement', knows only envy.

Decades later, set up as a grocer in Manchester following years of hardship and abuse, Robert Blincoe chooses to narrate his life story to John Brown, an unstable journalist who will take his own life before Blincoe's memoir makes it into print. Though rich in sentiment, Blincoe's life story is short on the usual opening details of biography, such as parentage or place of birth. The officers of Saint Pancras poorhouse kept no record of either of his parents. According to Brown:

> In one of our early interviews, tears trickling down [Robert's] pallid cheeks and his voice tremulous and faltering, Blincoe said, 'I am worse off than a child reared in the Foundling Hospital. Those orphans have a name given them by the heads of that institution, at the time of baptism, to which they are legally entitled. But I have no name I can call my own.'

Blincoe, reflecting on his earliest memories, speaks of the 'wall of brass' that cut him off from the rest of humanity. He was fed and cared for, but 'it was liberty he wanted ... He was cooped up in a gloomy, though liberal sort of a prison-house.' Depressed, the little boy stops eating or playing, and takes to standing before the poorhouse wall, working out his chances of escape – and concluding, gloomily, that they are nil.

So extreme is his condition that, a generation before *Oliver Twist*, he actually volunteers to be selected as a chimney sweep. In the weeks before the master sweeps come to pick, he puts himself through a programme of his own devising, walking on tiptoe and suspending himself from 'rafters and balustrades', hoping to stretch out his infant limbs, the better to recommend himself to their gaze. When the fateful day comes and any number of weeping, terrified children are singled out ahead of him, he is inconsolable. Such is his desire to escape the confines of the poorhouse. You would call his a lucky escape, were it not for the horrors of the factory that await him.[11]

~

The infant Robert Blincoe never gets his shot at freedom. Others do. It is the late 1810s. We are in, variously, the Old Kent Road; St Giles's Workhouse; St George's Workhouse. Josiah Basset, a very small boy, is getting his first taste of a life of vagrancy. Scouring the streets for cherry stones, he and his brothers stray north over London Bridge.

The streets are strange round here, unknown, and somehow the youngest of the brothers gets lost. Josiah and his remaining sibling begin to search for him – they roam as far as Shoreditch – and, splitting up, lose each other in the crowd. Josiah, alone, frightened, cannot find his way home. Come midnight, he is still in the street, still the wrong side of the river.

Not being able to find my way to my father's house, I began to cry. A woman that sold fruit in the street gave me some apples, and kept me till the watchman came round. Having told him that I had lost myself, he took me first to the watch-house, and from thence to Saint Giles's workhouse. When the porter opened the door, he said: 'I have brought you another young one.' After giving me some food, they put me to bed. In the bed lay a little child fast asleep – it was my lost brother! He awoke: we embraced each other. The next day we were sent home.

A happy outcome. At this stage, the brothers still have a home to be sent to. But their fortunes fall further. His father suffers from fits, his mother dies, and before long, they are in the workhouse for good. One brother is sent to sea. Josiah and the youngest, left behind, grow restless and, unlike Blincoe, actually manage to run away.

For a few days we gathered bones about the streets and sold them, earning in this manner about three pence per day. This sum supplied us with bread, and at night we lay down between some logs of timber in the York-road. The nights were cold and frosty, and sometimes our clothes stuck to the ground: not liking our quarters, we came to the resolution of walking the streets, hoping the night constable would take us up, and that we should be sent to the poor-house again.

Thereafter, Josiah is in and out of institutions. 'I ran away several times, but after enduring a few hardships, made my way back again.'[12]

Josiah Basset cannot choose between two evils. No fool, he feels the street's hardships, and returns to shelter when exposure threatens. But despite pain, poverty and danger, he runs the risk time and again in preference to a childhood of coercion.

The street and the poorhouse make for a simple – if sometimes perplexing – contrast. One offers a precarious kind of freedom, the other safety at a steep cost to pride and liberty. It is easy to see why an infant in an institution might long for the life of the street. But what of the home itself, of the domesticity so central to the thinking of the period, eulogised in 'Home, Sweet Home', the century's most famous, most influential song? There's no place like home! Surely, for an infant above all, home is the place to be?

~

George Godwin is a man of substance, a Fellow of the Royal Society. As editor of the *Builder*, which is promoting a campaign to improve domestic sanitation among the poor, he has taken it upon himself to go knocking on doors as a sort of Social Worker General. He is under no illusions as to whether he is welcome:

> To investigate the condition of the houses of the very poor in this
> great metropolis is a task of no small danger and difficulty: it is
> necessary to brave the risks of fever and other injuries to health,
> and the contact of men and women often as lawless as the Arab
> or the Kaffir: in addition to these obstacles, there is amongst the
> very poor a strong feeling against intrusion: few persons venture
> into these haunts besides the regular inhabitants, the London
> missionaries, the parish surgeon, and the police.[13]

Godwin is evidently about as racist as one might expect from a man of his time and class. But for all his faults, it is hard not to sympathise with him as, uninvited, he enters 'a miserable room in the neighbourhood of Gray's-inn-lane' one day in 1854. We are back in the streets where, almost seventy years earlier, Mary Ann Carey gave birth to Edmund Kean.

At first glance, he sees the usual squalor to be found when a large family lives entirely in a single space. The children are pressed to the walls, sullen, wary of this big man with his cape and stick. They appear to have no mother – at least, she is not present. There is, at least, a storage cupboard, which is suggestive of good order.

Godwin lays a hand upon the latch. Perhaps his nostrils twitch: above the usual odours, to which he is not yet inured, he detects something else, worse, something that he cannot place but that tugs, insistent. Something is wrong. With a creak, the cupboard door swings open. Godwin, we can only assume, swallows back a retch.

Later, remembering what he has seen, Godwin strives for detachment; even manages a touch of writerly pathos. He 'found, shut up with the bread and some other matters, *the body of a child*, without a coffin, but decently disposed. The child had been dead a week: on one of the shelves was its little mug, marked "Mary Ann," with some broken crockery.' Mary Ann must have been very small, for her corpse to be stowed on a shelf. But she is one of the family: she has her own mug.

Hers was not the first death. Godwin is informed by the father that 'The man's wife had died a few weeks before, and had been kept in the same room fourteen days amidst a family of children.'

Back among his books and papers, Godwin can breathe more easily. But traces of feeling remain. He writes, 'We had prepared a sketch of the closet, but its aspect was so painfully repulsive that we have withheld it.'

He has seen things like this before; he will see them again. His book, *London Shadows*, does include a somewhat less traumatic illustration, drawn in the area of Bishopsgate Street, of:

> the coffin of a dead child in the midst of the sleeping living. In a
> single room the family sleep, work, eat, and perform the various

duties of life in company with the dead, and the evil is increased by the length of time the poverty of parties obliges them to retain the corpse until what they consider proper preparations have been made for the funeral: this seldom takes place in less than a week; instances have been known of the interment having been put off for twelve days or a fortnight. This is a difficult matter to deal with, for the prejudices of the uninstructed are strong against the removal of the bodies until they are taken to the graveyard.

What he has seen humbles Godwin a little; he strives for understanding. 'The feeling which prompts [this practice] is a holy one', he writes. 'Far be it from us to depreciate it, still less to scoff'.[14] Indeed, in his attempts to weave for these little dead corpses a veil of custom, of context, he almost makes it sound a matter of little consequence to the families involved.

Other accounts are less dispassionate. On an August day in 1811, at No. 4 Rose and Crown Court, St Catherine's Lane, Tower Hill, we meet the Harforths. They make for a pitiful couple: she a new mother for the fifth time, he a disabled veteran lately invalided home from the Peninsular War. And now the sickness has come among the family. Some well-wisher, perhaps a neighbour, gets a note to the Benevolent Society, who send one of their Visitors* to Rose and Crown Court.

On entering the room, the first thing presented to the eye of the visitor was, the corpse of a child laid on an old box, which stood on a broken chair, covered with a piece of cloth. – On the bed

---

* 'Visitors' performed voluntary social work – they were those who, in the more cavalier language of the society's annual report, 'cheerfully take, as it were, their lives in their hands, and without fee or reward, explore cellars and garrets'.

lay another child dying in convulsions, – and on the side of the bed sat the mother, weeping over her dying infant, whose looks indicated the anguish of her mind, together with the weak debilitated state of her body. She seemed almost dying herself thro' want; – at the foot of the bed sat the father, (for indeed he was not able to stand) having lost the use of his limbs, and in excruciating pain with the acute rheumatism; – two small children were sitting in one corner of the room, – the other child was out.

It is the facts, not the feelings, that cut deepest here. With five children to provide for, this wounded soldier deserves a pension to supplement the three shillings a week the parish will begrudge him, but the Board of Ordinance has rejected his petition. It takes time for the helpless father to explain all this to the patient Visitor; the cries of wife and child must surely distract them both. By the time the details have been noted down, the convulsive child has died. Together, they move it to lie beside the other on the box. His strength exhausted, the father has no choice but to take its place in the bed, 'whereon it had so lately died'.

Writing up the account for their annual report, the Visitor appends a postscript, 'When the parish officers heard the children were dead, they stopped half the allowance'.[15]

~

The third of these reports from impoverished homes is the most vivid of all. One night in April 1859 – smallpox season – near Rose Street, Covent Garden, a mother hastens to the local mission house, where a bell pull outside offers some kind of lifeline. Frantic, she jerks the rope. Again, again, 'sharp, repeated rings'. Something of her urgency communicates itself to the sleeping residents, and eventually two Sisters of the mission are roused – Sister Mary, an old hand, and a young novitiate. To them the mother tells her 'very great and terrible distress'.

'There is nothing for it but for us to go,' says Sister Mary. Sending the mother ahead of them, the Sisters fetch matchbox and tapers, before hurrying into the 'still, dark night'. The young novice keeps a record of her experiences:

> The public-house across the street was within a quarter of an hour of closing, and the din of voices inside rose and swelled most audibly, mingled with here and there a piercing shriek or laugh from some poor wretched girl. Outside, on the kerb, a faded-looking woman, thin, haggard, wrapped in a ragged shawl, was singing plaintive songs in a rich contralto voice, for which she might get a few pence ... When we turned into Rose Street, all was quiet, and inside the open doorway of No. –, everything was pitch dark. We lit our coil of wax and stumbled up the shallow, old-fashioned stairs to the top floor, from whence proceeded a sickening odour of chloride of lime. Inside the room everything was splashed with and steeped in it. A bit of candle burnt feebly in a tin candlestick, showing a tub, half filled with a heap of clothes in chloride of lime; a bed, a mere heap of rags, in one corner on the floor, containing two children, thick out with small-pox; in the other corner a bedstead...

On this bedstead, they find a 'little dead child', three years old, the family's first casualty to the disease. There is no stoicism here, no acceptance of loss: the detail that has brought the two women running is that 'the husband declared he would cut his throat unless it was taken away, as the child had been dead five days'. And here he is:

> Crouching over the fire, [w]rapped in a shawl, was a gaunt-looking man, his face so seamed and scarred with small-pox, and his bleared eyes glancing every now and then with a half-fierce, half-frightened look at the form on the bed. The wife was moving up and down, wringing her hands and crying wildly.

Due to some technicality, the parish will not remove the body, and the room is become a place of nightmare. Sister Mary, taking charge, sends the mother in search of a coffin. Now follows 'ten minutes waiting, with the children wailing on the floor, the man shuddering and insisting that he would destroy himself unless the body went out'. The only helping hand the mother can find is a drunken bricklayer, who will protect the Sisters from the worst St Giles's has to throw at them. With his aid, they find and fetch a coffin – but neither he nor the parents can bring themselves to touch the body, so the Sisters 'wrapped the little body in the sheet, put it in, and tied down the lid with a piece of old list.* We could not trust the man to carry it downstairs, but managed it ourselves, and along as far as Greek Street'. Here the group is challenged by an officious individual who turns out to be an undertaker and is 'therefore naturally attracted by the sight of a coffin'. Things begin to calm down, and they get the child's body to a mortuary.[16]

For a time, the night came away from its hinges, but now the door can close. Still, to be a part of that night – and of the five days that led up to it! To be sibling to that 'little body', yourself sick with fever, and to see in your moments of lucidity the corpse of your dead brother or sister across the room. You have, perhaps, little sense of time or its passing. It is a boundless eternity you spend here, in

---

* 'List' in this instance meaning a strip or border of cloth.

16

a mass of rags, beside the body. You cling to your still-breathing sibling. Which of you is to be next?

~

I do not want to speak here of the lurid crimes that spattered the pages of ballads and newspapers – of babes beheaded with kitchen knives – nor of the everyday kind of violence meted out to children in the home. Abuse was common to all parts of society: the nineteenth century was one in which adults hurt children as a matter of course. This had been happening for centuries – though it was newly exacerbated by factory work, by overcrowding, by systematised schooling from Eton downwards, and given an aftertaste of hypocrisy by the century's sentimental obsession with childhood innocence. Yes, the homes of the poorest infants harboured pain within their walls, but this was not exceptional. The peculiar horror we have just witnessed, however – of growing into consciousness with a dead sibling lying still beside you – was particular to this class. Home! Sweet Home! The song is starting to sound a little shrill.

There is something about witnessing these grim events that borders on the distasteful: like George Godwin, editor of the *Builder*, we trespass in people's homes, intruding on private tragedy. But if we are to understand the stories that follow in their proper perspective, it is important to realise that there was no simple line to be drawn between domestic security and danger out of doors, and that not every infant who made her or his way outside was necessarily worse off for the change. As we emerge with these children onto the streets, we should do so free from illusions. Sometimes the dreadful thing isn't out here, in the open, but back there, behind the closed door.

~

How does a baby, an infant, a toddler even, come to find itself on the street? And what on earth is it expected to do once it gets there? Our next episode offers startling answers to both questions. 25 October 1817: a sunny Saturday morning in Duke's Place, Pimlico.[17] Mary Moseley's young daughter, just two years old, is playing in the court. This 'court' is a gloomy enclosure framed by the backs of the buildings, in one of which the girl lives with her mother and her father John, a chimney sweep. No one has bothered to record her own first name: let us pretend, as if in one of the newspaper reports where 'names have been changed', that it is Susan. 'Susan' has, perhaps, a vague sense that the word 'court' might also mean something different, because just a skip away is a big palace where the king lives, and soldiers stand to attention. Her little court, however, is open to the world outside, and now a lady has come in from the street and is smiling at her, offering her hand. Susan Moseley is decently dressed in her frock and pinafore and, there-fore, presumably not ashamed to go with the lady, whose name, she tells the little girl, is Ann. Susan, we must suppose, smiles back up at her, quite oblivious to the fact that she is being kidnapped.

As you may already have anticipated, this is an incident that ends in a trial. Being neither old enough nor important enough to be asked, we have no account of 'Susan's' experience of the events of this Saturday. Nonetheless, I would like to reconstruct the day, as far as the facts allow, from her perspective. Somehow, the strange lady – Ann – wins the girl's confidence: does she spin her a tale? Make promises? It is unlikely that she simply carries her off. Too heavy, too loud. So perhaps, she proposes an adventure.

At first it must be exciting, but before long, Susan starts to tire. She is dragged at speed through parts she knows, Duke's Row, Eaton Street, her short legs awhirl to keep up with Ann's deter-mined stride. At the next corner comes a busy crossroads, traffic blurring the high wall of the palace park, the rows of houses, and the King's Road itself, stretching off into open country. By now, Susan may be beginning to regret her decision. But somehow, Ann placates her. After all, it's not every day you get to see the world.

An eternity later – half an hour, maybe – they are back among tall houses. Ann carries her sometimes and keeps up a commentary on the places they pass: Bloody Bridge, Sloane Square. There is a tall, forbidding building with a crocodile of little boys going in at a gate. At last, they turn off the big road down a tree-lined avenue. There is a vastness of cropped green grass ahead, infinitely larger than her own court: any two-year-old would long to roll on it. But they are almost at Ann's chosen destination, and this is no time to be dawdling.

The Royal Hospital public house dominates the corner of Franklin's Row and Jew's Row, its big bay window above the door overlooking the grounds of the Chelsea Hospital. The building is incongruous here: with its ship-like appearance, you think automatically of Greenwich. A popular watering hole though, for Chelsea's industrious poor: servants, porters, gardeners, builders. By midday the place is heaving: the food is good, but the beer that washes it down is better. The landlord's name is William Pitt – no relation, he must be tired of saying, to the late statesman. Into the smoke and the steam, the haze of cooking and bodies, comes Ann Lee, dragging little Susan; Ann has stuck a couple of crumpled song sheets in the child's sticky hand. The infant surely shrinks from the press and the noise, but Ann is working now, striking up a song: a song of the late war, of the widows it has made. Come all, come buy, she calls between verses. Who'll give a halfpenny to relieve a wretched widow?

People all around. One, a stout woman, comes up to Susan. The woman smells of the laundry. Perhaps Susan finds this comforting; what's more, the woman holds out a shiny halfpenny for the girl to take. Emboldened by her sudden riches, Susan edges towards the door. Ann is looking at her though, and not a nice look either: she comes up and snatches away the girl's money. On the point of protesting, Susan is swept up and into the air by Ann, who resumes her song. The infant stays quiet, hoping, maybe, that Ann will use the halfpenny to buy her something to eat.

Meanwhile, Susan's family has not been idle. Mary Moseley has called her little daughter in for dinner, only to discover her missing. Uproar. The neighbours can tell her nothing. John comes home, hungry, to the dreadful news. All they can do is ask everyone to spread the word and start the search. Few can spare the time to help: the parents' best hope is that the chain of news will grow into a net wide enough to gather up their girl and bring her home.

They scour the nearest streets in vain. Perhaps they screw up courage to ask the sentries who stand outside the Royal Mews: nothing. John, thinking that maybe the girl is hiding, or stuck, goes poking round the court's privy. Here he meets Tom Chittle, their neighbour, a waterman come home for his own dinner. Tom has heard something, down Chelsea way. He is a good man and can lend a hand: within minutes, he is off in the direction of the Hospital. The hunch pays off: he catches sight of the girl on College Walk, hand in hand with a frail young woman, all over rags. But it would be dangerous to tackle them alone: the passers-by might side with the woman. He turns, looking for an officer, a constable. When he turns back, the pair have gone. Chittle hurries back to the Moseleys with his information.

Ann is cleaning up: she has chosen her spot well, and the combination of the pitiful song and the little infant are working as never before. Almost too well – people are in and out all the time, and though she has put a mile between herself and the girl's home, she is still drawing too much attention. Time to clear out. But the infant is wilting; it will be hard to move on. Shifting the girl in her arms, Ann starts the song again. For the hundredth time, the door swings open.

The Infant

Mary Pearce stands close by, finishing her beer – ironing is thirsty work. All the same, she is cursed with a tender heart, and couldn't help but slip that little babe a halfpenny when the mother started singing. And now she looks up, as the door clatters open, and three people rush in. A waterman, a constable, tall and uniformed, and a ball of fury that resolves itself into the shape of a woman, shaking with emotion as she accosts the singer. 'You wretch! What do you do with my child?' the woman manages, before fainting clean away.

~

All this takes up little more than an hour – though perhaps it seems half a lifetime for John and Mary Moseley – and the case, being open and shut, takes just four days to come before the Old Bailey. Chittle and Pearce both appear as witnesses for the prosecution. Ann Lee, twenty-six years old, is accused on two counts. The law has no provision for the emotional distress she has wreaked, it deals only in tangibles, which means, mostly, property: she is charged with intending to deprive the Moseleys of possession of their child, and – on a second, lesser count – of only attempting to steal the infant's pinafore (value: four pence) and frock (tuppence). The court does not deign to place a monetary value on the child herself.

Ann Lee is incoherent, cowed by the occasion, by the judge, by her nights in gaol. Her only defence – 'I found the child at the top of Church-lane. I am innocent' – makes little sense: Church Lane is half a mile further west even than College Walk; she is asking the court to believe that the little girl has strayed nearly two miles from home of her own accord. Found guilty, she is sentenced to transportation. Seven years in Botany Bay. Yes, the Moseleys are reunited. But it would be a stretch to call it a happy ending.[18]

~

21

Ann Lee may have been desperate. But her actions in kidnapping the Moseleys' infant were wholly rational. (The same cannot be said of Emily Lewis, another young kidnapper whom we will meet in Chapter Three.) Lee was impoverished, homeless, a singer in the streets: she appears to have spent the last of her capital on a small stock of songs. More than likely they were songs written to solicit pity and charity from listeners: tales of love and loss, of husbands fallen in service overseas. This was 1817, two years on from Waterloo, a cataclysmic and tragic event – itself the culmination of a generation-long conflict – that had an unprecedented impact upon the psyche of ordinary Britons. For much of the nineteenth century, Waterloo would remain *the* cultural reference point for death and destruction, and it brought in its aftermath a disastrous economic crash and a wave of unemployment that saw begging in the capital soar out of control. Many of these people had been disabled, traumatised or orphaned by war; many others had lost their jobs with the advent of peace.

We don't know why Ann Lee found herself on the streets, but in the moral climate of 1817 one of her chief misfortunes was, almost counterintuitively, that she had no child to provide for. She would do far better as an object of pity if she had a picturesque infant in tow – and a two-year-old would be best of all: the perfect age for Lee to have been left, pregnant, by a soldier husband ordered off to Belgium in the spring of 1815, never to return. In the Moseleys' little daughter, she found the ideal accessory or support act for her singing, and Mary Pearce's testimony confirms it: 'I gave the child a halfpenny, seeing the woman in distress'. For all we know, Lee was planning to return the child once she had made enough to get her through the day, no harm done. But the fact that she was willing to commit so serious and hazardous a crime is harrowing evidence of her total desperation – and testament, too, to the value of a pitiable infant to a woman in the street. To a destitute mother (genuine or otherwise), a baby was not merely a burden: it was an asset.

Nineteenth-century morality was a strange thing. You might expect respectable London to disapprove of a single woman with one or more babes, reduced to poverty: to mark her down as improvident, wanton, probably a prostitute. Some did cleave to this severe code. In 1858, aged fifteen, Constance de Rothschild accompanied her mother, Baroness Louise, on a series of philanthropic house calls. That evening, she recorded in her diary:

> We went into one cottage where a young woman sat with a baby of about four months in her arms. Mamma asked the unlucky question 'How long have you been married?' 'A half year' was the answer. Mamma hurried out of the cottage and was determined not to give her anything. If Mamma practiced this upon [all] the people there would be few to whom she would give presents.

Constance shared the anecdote with her governess, who 'did not look very much shocked ... She said the scandal in London was worse than in any village and that [even] if you condemned a fashionable lady you must pity a poor girl.'[19]

It is the censorious Baroness de Rothschild who stands out as the exception here, not as the archetype. Consider too that this was forty years later than the Moseley case, and though there had been another recent war, this time in the Crimea, there was no question of a tragic explanation, since the father was still around. Even de Rothschild might not have been so puritanical if faced with a widow. In this brave new age, there were so many ways for men to die. Since a distressed single mother might very reasonably claim to have lost a husband through service overseas even in peacetime, or through a factory accident, public sympathy could generally be counted upon in 1858 as in 1817.

There was, therefore, nothing shameful about walking the London street with a babe-in-arms. If anything, it was more respectable, as well as more lucrative, to be with one than without, since a visibly dependent infant allayed any suspicion that the woman in question might be soliciting. If she had a baby with her, then she was substantially less likely to be having sex.

~

Ann Lee's desperate search for a useful infant was therefore far from unique. Saturday, 20 November 1824: midday, and as usual, it is raining. Joey Skinner, twenty-one months old, sits in his chair. There is, perhaps, a grubby pane on which the water hammers, relentless. His mother Mary, a street seller of fish and vegetables, is with him, and though the room is far from warm, it is at least dry.

A knock at the door. A woman Joey knows – Sarah Lafoy – and he hears sharp words exchanged, their voices raised. A third voice calls, and his mother goes off to answer: it is their landlady's daughter, not someone to be left waiting. Sarah Lafoy is still in the room, however, and now she stands over Joey, blocking the light. Hard hands grasp him around the middle, lifting him from the chair. Perhaps he kicks or tries to cry out – but her hand is over his mouth now, her lips shushing in his ear.

Just as in the Moseley case, Sarah Lafoy absconds with young Joey and goes out begging. But she roams further afield than Ann Lee, and for longer: it is several days before the searchers catch up with her, some miles beyond St Albans. Again, a man and woman give evidence – Ann Simpson of Rosemary Lane, Edward Clayton of Whitechapel. Yet Sarah Lafoy is not sent to Australia. She is not even found guilty. It turns out that she and Mary Skinner have a standing arrangement, so that she often borrows Joey for half an hour's begging. It was only the wetness of the morning that the mother objected to on this occasion. You would think the time and the distance would count against her – but Joey looks well, they apprehend her in the act of giving him bread and milk, and Sarah Lafoy is more eloquent than Ann Lee when speaking in her own defence:

> She [Mary Skinner] frequently gave me the child ... and said, 'When you are going up the street you can get a [hat] for the child.' I have frequently taken it into a cook shop, and fed it, and have taken it off the floor when she [Skinner] has been beastly drunk; she gave it to me, but not to take into the country – I have had six children, and am in the family way now, it is not likely that I should steal a child.[20]

By her own account, Lafoy had no permission to abscond from London with the child. But Skinner is a drunk, and Lafoy a good parent. The case is dismissed.

Babies, it seems, are hot property, their ability to engage the consciences or affections of passers-by much in demand. For two days in October 1814, Catherine Cremer, mother of six, sits begging with her latest pair of twins in St Paul's Churchyard, a prime location. A woman gives her a penny and admires her 'two fine babies', before observing that 'you do not seem to get much money here; if you will go along with me, I will take you to a fine lady that will give you half a guinea'. Cremer, who is maybe not the sharpest of beggars, thinks this a fine plan, and so begins a kidnapping saga that runs for six weeks, taking in a thwarted escape to sea and a sham pregnancy – a tale well worth reading, though at this point it ceases to have anything to do with life in the street.[21] Still, even credulous Catherine Cremer knows one thing: it is her babies that will get her alms.

Summer, 1817: the reformer Henry Barnet Gascoigne quotes a begging widow, who describes her youngest child as 'worth thirty pounds to me' as reckoned in 'the shillings and half-crowns – ah! and the gold too' in alms the little one will extract from impressionable gentrywomen.[22]

July 1818: Hannah Hall, who sells fruit in the streets near Horse Guards, has her ten-month-old boy, Thomas, taken from her by the same trick that deceived Catherine Cremer.[23] 1824: a boy known only by his surname, Macher, goes missing for seven whole months when he is lured away from 'his playmates' in Knightsbridge by a notorious beggar named 'Thomas Wood, *alias* Buxton, *alias* Cox', in order to join him in his begging. Macher comes from a prosperous home. Yet when they are finally caught in Russell Square, the boy gives his name as 'John Smith', and 'strenuously denies' his real identity, apparently preferring Wood's company to life at home.[24]

Sixty years later, a commission investigating the abusive practices of Italian barrel-organists finds that 'sometimes, in order to excite compassion, a child of a few months old is carried about on the top of an organ placed on a barrow' – an experience that, compared to the cases we have just heard, may have been something of a delight for the baby in question.[25] Nonetheless, the commission frowns upon it, as well they might, all these cases being pretty bald instances of infant exploitation.

~

Though these cases all display some degree of cynicism, they were all motivated by genuine distress and need. It is important to remember this when confronted with the most outrageous examples from these decades. On 25 March 1831 in Christchurch, Spitalfields, parish officer Thomas Brushfield is dispensing poor relief.* On the

---

* So influential was this officer that, in February 1870, nearby Union Street was renamed Brushfield Street in his honour.

advice of a doctor, he has just given sixpence to Kitty Daley, whose infant has the smallpox. A short time later, he finds himself doing the same for a second woman. Then another, then another.

> Each brought in her arms a child, which she said had the small-pox. The child was muffled up very carefully. One woman showed me the arm of the child; the other showed me the face of the child which she had; the third gave me a glance of the face of the child which she had. It appeared to me strange that there was so much small-pox about; but when I saw the face of this third child it immediately struck me as being the same child that had been shown to me before, though it was now in a different dress.

The game is up, and the three unknown women make themselves scarce.

> But on visiting the residence of Kitty Daley, there I found the very same infant I had last seen, and it was dressed in the same dress. She did not deny the fact, that it was the same child that had been brought that morning in three different dresses by three different women. I accordingly gave her no relief.[26]

Of course, we are led by the evidence: it is only the most shocking instances that anyone bothers writing about. There were, I suspect, a hundred honestly distressed and loving mothers for every confidence trickster. And we should be wary of passing judgement even in these rare cases.

In 1849 a certain Mr Branch, attending a Missionary Meeting, spoke of his recent encounter with a woman in the street, a dying infant in her arms:

She seemed to be in great distress, but after some questions she said, 'What shall I do if the child dies? - when she is gone I shall have to give ninepence a day for another, while this one costs me nothing. Unless I do so I'll earn nothing, - it's the children that moves compassion.'[27]

Branch's point, apparently, was that this mother was selfish, devoid of real human feeling and thus a cautionary example of the ungodly, undeserving poor. I am not so sure. In that eloquent explanation - 'it's the children that moves compassion' - we find both cynicism and its justification. When you are starving - when your children are starving too - the ethics of how you make use of that child are scarcely foremost among your concerns.

In the very worst of circumstances, want and depravation could create a cruel cycle of abuse. The year 1848, which will see regimes toppled across Europe, begins with a whimper in the streets of Holborn. It is January, and Mary Ann Murray, aged thirteen, is out singing, begging, generally making a scene. She has her sister, eleven, in tow, and in her arms is her young brother, getting too heavy for her scrawny muscles now his second birthday is coming up. The girls' song, pitiful as it is, does little to stem the flow of passers-by, and they leave off singing entirely once the infant starts to bawl: small as he is, his lungs are quite capable of drowning out the two girls.

Though Mary Ann must wince at the noise so close to her ears, it is somehow expressive of their total abjection in a way the words of the song, written by another, could never be - and indeed, it seems to be working. People are stopping, coming closer: first one, then a trickle, and now the crowd has its own momentum, drawing others in, solicitous, grimacing, fumbling for pennies.

Quickly, Mary Ann rearranges her features, the better to take advantage of this sudden interest. She lavishes a particularly

grateful smile on an elderly lady, who is close now – too close, even, peering at the infant in a way that makes Mary Ann feel decidedly uncomfortable. Leaving her sister to gather the small change, she keeps her gaze on the old woman as the latter backs away – turns – calls over a constable. And now the policeman is walking towards Mary Ann. Hastily, the girl drops the incriminating evidence: with luck it will be lost in the gutter. Either way, the game is up.

In the event, it takes only seconds for Mary Ann's sharp practices to be revealed, for the wicked object glinting in the gutter, red-tipped, is a large pin. As the journalist who attends the trial at Bow Street will later report, 'it was instantly discovered upon examining the child, that his sufferings had been caused by [this pin's] continual incision in the lower part of the body, while being carried in his sister's arms'. Mary Ann has been stabbing him in secret, the better to make him writhe and scream.

The babe will probably recover: quite apart from 'the punctures and lacerations caused by the pin', the boy's health is judged to be 'deplorable', and he is immediately placed under the care of the medical officer of St Giles's workhouse. Mr Justice Hall, shocked by the case, dispatches the sharp-eyed constable – Dodgson of the F Division – to go after the 'inhuman parents' behind it all, and he tracks them down to 4 Tyndall's Buildings, on Gray's Inn Lane – the same street, in fact, where Mary Ann Carey gave birth to Edmund Kean, and where George Godwin will find the corpse in the cupboard six years hence.

If we believe what is written in *The Times*, Mr Murray senior is a shameless drunk, forever refusing the shelter of the workhouse, preferring to send his children out to sing and spending the proceeds entirely on drink. For his part, the father claims ignorance of his daughter's malpractice, and insists he has no parish to fall back on for aid, having been born at Edinburgh Castle – for his father was a soldier in the 92nd Foot, the Gordon Highlanders.[28]

The journalist neglects to inform us of the outcome – since the police went after the parents, it is unlikely that Mary Ann and her sister were sentenced themselves – but it is clear with whom we are meant to sympathise: the concerned forces of paternalism, the old woman, the constable, the judge and the beadles of the workhouse. The father is a liar and a reprobate, the evil stems from his wilful rejection of the help on offer. We, the educated *Times* reader, are sophisticated enough to seek a greater cause behind the young girl's apparent malevolence, rather than damning her outright. But having found a villain in the father, we can stop there, our conscience satisfied, and mildly titillated by the horror of it all.

Such is the difficulty with these cases, in detaching the rhetoric of prejudice from our appreciation of ambiguous moral circumstances. The infants themselves, of course, are the innocent victims – but at what point in the chain do those making use of them become truly culpable? At the time, it was easy enough to demonise the parents. This was a constant throughout the period. Three decades earlier, in the immediate aftermath of Waterloo, and following years of apathy towards the issue, the House of Commons, no longer preoccupied with bringing down Napoleon, had been forced to take interest in Matthew Martin's public-spirited enquiries into mendicity – meaning begging. In 1816, a full parliamentary committee was convened to hear the evidence of upstanding citizens. Here is the Reverend Henry Budd, Chaplain of Bridewell:

> Do you know that the children of the poor are sent out begging? ... I believe it is a common thing, and is probably known to many persons, for the children to be sent out, and not be permitted to return to their mother at night without obtaining sixpence. It is not very long since in going to see a friend in Gower-street, I saw a [girl] child sweeping the way in Bedford-square: I said, 'What have

you got to day; have you almost got the sum?' 'No, Sir,' the child said. I asked, 'How much are you short of it?' 'I have got five-pence, and only want a penny.' 'Then if I give you a penny, you may go home out of the cold?' 'Yes.' I believe that is a very common thing.

Next up before the committee is Sampson Stephenson, an iron founder in Seven Dials, and overseer of St Giles's parish. Mostly he watches beggars from the comfort of his own home: they have a 'den' not eight yards away. You might call him an armchair investigator.

> There is one person of an acute nature, who is practised in the art of begging, will collect three, four, or five children from different parents of the lower class of people, and will give those parents sixpence, or even more per day, for those children to go begging with; they go in those kind of gangs, and make a very great noise, setting the children sometimes crying in order to extort charity from the people ... [These children] are sent out as soon as it is possible for them to extort relief, and distributed about; one perhaps takes a broom, and if they do not bring home more or less, according to their size, they are beaten for it; a family is the greatest resource of such persons.[29]

That final phrase bears repeating: 'a family is the greatest resource of such persons'. As long as men like Sampson Stephenson placed the moral emphasis upon 'such persons' – and were understood to do so by the assembled parliamentarians – then the odds were stacked against the babes in the street. They had the sympathy of the great and the good – but if it was used merely to denigrate their parents, this counted for nothing. Until the emphasis fell on questioning why these 'persons' had no more secure, tangible resources, society would continue to fail its youngest and most vulnerable.

Vagabonds

~

The decades that followed the parliamentary enquiry of 1816 saw the abolition of child chimney sweeps in 1840, the birth of the Ragged School Movement in 1844, crusades against child prostitution, and any number of committees and enquiries aimed at improving the lives of the smallest and poorest in Victorian London. Yet the impulses of pity and paternalism that motivated many of these efforts also held them back from succeeding, with the result once again that relatively little actually changed across these years in the streets.

Nineteenth-century London led the way in inventing the idealised child – innocent, picturesque, a creature to pity, to protect, to fetishise – and it also excelled at enforcing the old saying that children should be seen and not heard. As such, the received wisdom of Victorians with regard to children typified the wider relationship, which we will see time and again in this book, between those in the street and those who looked at them.

Infants in the street were constantly being looked at. As the historian Carolyn Steedman has observed, they stood out by reason of their very incongruity from among the mass of industrious adults: their faces at a lower level, their patterns and speed of movement, the register of their voices, their actions, so different from those around them.[30] But the encounters that resulted were all one way. The infant had little power to speak, to surprise, and the capacity even to trouble the conscience of the man or woman looking at her or him was channelled down pathways of conventional sentimentality. Evidence of malnutrition was viewed as tragic rather than criminal – sad, to be sure, but predictable, a confirmation of something intrinsic to the underclass rather than an accusation prompting a call for change.

Here is Joshua Stallard, describing the street children admitted to pauper wards in the late 1860s:

The children are not like other children; they are puny, pale, and pot-bellied; they are listless, shy, dull, and do not even care to play. They have frequently a positive distaste for wholesome food which often makes them ill, because the stomach cannot digest the unaccustomed meal. The circulation of the children is so feeble that they are not permitted the use of cold water, and it is found necessary to warm their bedrooms; whilst in winter they suffer from chilblains, which the warmest clothing scarcely prevents.[31]

Stallard was a campaigner, a reformer; there are glimmers within his words of recognition of a system broken. Even so, these sentiments jostle with loaded phrases - 'puny', 'feeble', 'a positive distaste for wholesome food'. Stallard was aware that these qualities were the result of social deprivation and was struggling to do something about it. But the language he used was still drawn from a moral code that saw the weakness, the physical failings of such children as both inevitable and intrinsic. For many of his contemporaries, this was the way of the world: to be pitied and managed through charity and even (limited) education, but not to be addressed on a more fundamental level.

~

Of all the symbols associated with street infants, reinforcing their status as meek little victims, the most potent was undoubtedly their ragged clothing. Observers endlessly recycled descriptions of these children's 'naked' or 'almost naked' condition, and no account was complete without an itemisation of rags, holes and bare feet.[32] I have been doing it myself. Rags were essential stage-dressing for charitable exchanges, prompting numerous tales of parents who tore their own children's clothes before sending them out begging. Inevitably, this emotionally fraught combination of peeping, submissive flesh, exposed to the gaze of the powerful onlooker, led to the ragged child figuring heavily on the spectrum of Victorian sexuality. The literature on this sordid but significant topic is extensive; its legacy remains with us today.[33]

Famously – and with profound implications for the infant in the street – this combination of charity, voyeurism and the techniques of pornography coalesced into scandal around the photography organised by Thomas Barnardo in the 1860s and 1870s. Barnardo used elaborately staged photographs in his campaigning and fundraising, dressing his children to make them appear more 'authentic'. These photos were spectacularly successful yet supremely artificial: the mechanical limitations of early photography could never hope to capture a genuine portrait of the streets even if Barnardo had wished it. A crowning example of this duplicity may be seen on the cover of this book: a photograph of a young 'costermonger' taken by Barnardo's most famous collaborator, Oscar Rejlander – but created not only in a studio, but a studio in Wolverhampton!

In 1876 things came to a head: the mother of Florence Holder took her complaints to Thames Police Court, outraged at seeing a published image of her young daughter as a barefoot, 'savage'-looking newspaper seller, when in reality Florence had been 'clean and comfortable' when she was sent to Barnardo's Home – a shelter-cum-training centre that had grown out of the Ragged School movement.[34] Holder protested to the judge that her third daughter, meanwhile, 'is called "a little waif of London, rescued from the streets, six years old." They were never on the streets, your worship.'[35] The following year, a court of arbitration heard the complaint of Samuel Reed, another of Barnardo's poster-children. Reed testified:

The morning after I entered the Home, I was taken to Mr Barnes's to be photographed. I was taken upstairs into a room with Dr Barnardo. He took out his penknife and tore my clothes to pieces. After he had disfigured me, I was taken downstairs, and laid upon the floor, and in this position was photographed, as you may see me on the cover of 'Rescue the Perishing' ... In consequence of Dr Barnardo having torn my clothes in pieces I was ashamed to walk through the streets to the Home.[36]

The great villain here is not so much the fraudulent Barnardo as the society within which he operated, which insisted on rags and dirt – in a word, abasement – if it was to condescend to charity.

~

These were the children the city spat out: seen and not heard in the profoundest sense possible. And here we find the answer to our two earlier questions. Effectively helpless, infants were taken to the street, often against their will, in order to be looked at, in the hope that they would provoke sympathy. Indeed, in this time period, and in our sources, this was the condition of almost all of those on the street, whatever their age: looked at, drawn, described, catalogued and categorised – absolutely and overwhelmingly *seen*, visible, in a way that is rarely true of the poor in twenty-first-century post-industrial cities. But not heard. Not listened to.

~

I would like to end in 1890 – two decades after the date this book is meant to stop. Nonetheless, this example crystallises everything we have encountered so far. The artist Dorothy Tennant has made a career out of exploiting street infants: she is a well-known painter, an illustrator of stories for middle-class children, and she specialises in life-drawings of her young readers' poorer counterparts. Reflecting on her work to date, her advice for artists is refreshingly candid:

A good supply of rags is essential (carefully fumigated, camphored, and peppered), and you can then dress up your too respectable ragamuffin till he looks as disreputable as you can wish. If you have no rags to start with, and shrink from keeping them by you, the best way is to find an average boy, win his confidence, give him sixpence, and promise him another sixpence if he will bring you a boy more ragged than himself. This second boy must be invited to do the same, and urged to bring one yet more 'raggety.' You can in this way get down to a very fine specimen, but the drawback is the loss of time.

Sometimes, she writes, you have to give your borrowed urchin a good telling off. 'He will probably weep, but that helps to make his face dirty, and is therefore to be slightly encouraged.'

Tennant is an at times hilarious exemplar of her century's tendency to objectify and to 'other' its street children. But she also listens. As we move from infancy to childhood, we gain a sense from Tennant's conversations with her sitters of the world these children are growing into. Here are four of the 'definitions' she records as evidence of 'how difficult it is for us to understand them or be understood by them'. It is worth digesting each in turn: they articulate a humanity that, far from being difficult to understand, makes an all too bitter kind of sense.

I asked Harry Sullivan to define a *gentleman*. He replied, not without some fervour, 'Oh! a fellow who has a watch and chain.' I suppose he read disapprobation in my face, for he hastily added, 'And loves Jesus.'

This same boy had a very hazy idea of Old Testament history. He had heard of Adam and Eve – 'They stole apples and were turned out of the *gardin*, and then they had to work for their living till the sweat poured down.'

A girl of eleven told me how she wished to live in the country, 'because then I shouldn't see a lot of people having a lot of things I can't have.'

A dear little boy of six told me he loved Christmas Day because on Christmas Eve he hung up his stocking, and the next morning he found a present inside. 'What did you find last Christmas?' I enquired. 'A halfpenny,' he said, smiling with pleasure at the recollection. 'But,' he added truthfully, 'I put it in myself overnight.'[37]

2

The Boy

Easter 1824, on Brick Lane in the East End: John James Bezer, aged seven and three-quarters, is eyeing his tea tray full of hot cross buns and wondering how it ever came to this. His mother expects him to sell these? Here, in the streets around his home – outside his Sunday school? But people will *see* him!

His mother sets down her own borrowed basket of buns; puts her hands on her hips. Well, yes. 'If people couldn't buy buns without seeing the seller, it *was* strange,' she says, straight-faced, the irony hitting home in spite of the double negative.

John James realises he has no choice but to do as she says. He turns away, hides his face. She mustn't see him crying. And so, as he sets off 'with aching heart, and scalding tears, and scarlet face', he wonders again, how is it he has come to sell buns in the street?

Twenty-seven years later, he will tell us. Bezer, now a minor celebrity of the waning Chartist movement for political reform, serialises his memoir in the *Christian Socialist* under the title 'The Autobiography of One of the Chartist Rebels of 1848'.[1]

His is a story fit to make anyone question the state of the nation. His father had served in the Royal Navy, triumphant against Napoleon but beaten time and again by both rum and the lash. In Bezer's words:

Father was a drunkard, a great spendthrift, an awful reprobate. Home was often like a hell; and 'Quarter days' – the days father received a small pension from Government for losing an eye in the Naval Service – were the days mother and I always dreaded most; instead of receiving little extra comforts, we received extra big thumps, for the drink maddened him ... Father had been an old 'man-o'-wars man,' and the many floggings he had received while serving his country, had left their marks on his back thirty years afterwards; they had done more, – they had left their marks on his soul. They had unmanned him; can you wonder at that? Brutally used, he became a brute.

Bezer's is the first of many fathers and father figures we will encounter in this chapter, and far from the worst of them. Freud would have had a field day raking through these father–son relationships, and especially so in Bezer's case, which is halfway to being Oedipal: they are united by a disability, his father losing an eye at sea and John James losing the sight of his left eye through smallpox as a baby.

For his naval service and sacrifice, Bezer's father received a meagre pension which, supplemented by his income as a barber, was enough to support his wife and son. Disaster struck, however, on 15 November 1823, through the unlikely means of a sermon given by Mr Isaacs at Gloucester Chapel, Hackney. Persuaded to attend by his wife, Bezer senior saw the light. But though he sobered up, he also stopped opening his barber's shop on a Sunday – the keeping of the Sabbath was a hot topic at the time – and as a result, he became a pariah among his former customers and drinking companions.

He and his business having dried up together, the old sailor petitioned for an increase in his pension, and from there things went almost as badly for the family as they did for poor Mr Harforth, whom we met in Chapter One. The pension was stopped, and

Bezer's father ordered to Greenwich Hospital to be 'looked after' in-house, rather than left in the community. As John James recalls, 'Our little home, which though humble, had become precious to us, was broken up, the persecuted saint went to Greenwich [Hospital], and mother and I became out-door paupers to a parish in the City.'

By Easter 1824, John James's mother is getting four shillings a week from the parish; cotton-winding brings in another two. It covers rent and bread, but barely. She gambles everything on three shillings-worth of hot cross buns – the sum being borrowed from a friend – and gives her shy, underweight, stunted son a third of the stock. They are to split up, sell their hearts out, make a profit. It's Easter, the buns are hot. How hard can it be?[2]

Looking back from a distance of decades on the five hours that followed, Bezer can afford a wry smile at his failure:

> I walked up and down the by-streets, and *whispered* so low that nobody could hear me,
>
>   'Hot cross buns!
>
>   One a penny, two a penny, *hot* cross buns,'
>
>   till, all the gods of Homer will bear me witness, they were as *cold* as the corpse of a Laplander; still I called them *hot* from seven till twelve, and took the magnificent sum of Twopence!

All the same, the total agony of the situation, so burnt into his memory that it forms a major episode in his life story, has not left him even in 1851:

> I say to any philosopher of *nine years old*,[3] – cry hot cross buns for the first time, for five hours, till you are as cold as they are, and hungry enough to eat the 'stock,' and then if you don't talk of giving up, you are a noble little fellow. I went home – folk had

laughed at me, had rejoiced when I wept, but only two persons had bought.

His one consoling thought – for, young as he is, he is well aware that this failure *matters* – is that his mother, though she may be disappointed in him, will nonetheless make amends.

> I went home, I say, determined most dutifully to present my mother with the remains of my merchandise, thinking, of course, she had sold out, and would be ready to sell mine too, when lo! my venerable and courageous parent had sold none at all; having met a person she had known years before when she was better off, her courage failed, and she came home again almost directly ... I was right glad of this, [in] spite of our desperate circumstances – it prevented her finding fault with me; so after we had had our soiree of tea and buns, mother moved, and I seconded, a resolution, to the effect that we would never go out with buns any more, hot or cold.

It sounds rather like a punchline, and there is something comical about the whole anecdote, but what is patent is that Bezer is unfit to be a street seller. He is small even for his age, sickly and visually impaired. Though he makes light of it, his partial sight is a major hindrance in the busy London street:

> [O]ften have I been nearly run over through having a 'single eye' towards the road; and often have I knocked against a dead wall ... I've had many a blow through giving half a look at a thing! How many times since I became a costermonger has a policeman hallooed in my ear, 'Come! move hon there, vill yer! now go hon, move yer hoff!' while I've actually thought he was on duty in some kitchen with the servant girl.

But it is less his body that handicaps him than his overmastering sense of shame. He is a respectable boy, he attends Sunday school: the thought of meeting anyone he knows is mortifying – and his mother feels it too. For the churchgoing Bezers, it matters not that the father is first a drunk, then a pensioner, at all times debilitated: they are *not* street folk, and they cannot bear to cry out wares.

Shame is an important part of street life, the 'social emotion' defined by Samuel Johnson as 'the passion felt when reputation is supposed to be lost'.[4] We have already encountered the implicit social contract where the guilty passer-by is shamed into stopping and sparing some change. But this shame works both ways. In 1851, Mary Carpenter, the famous reformer, reviewing new proposals for especially humiliating punishments to be exacted upon young offenders, writes, 'The sense of shame, so keen in noble natures, is not even extinct in these, though often manifested in ways little understood by persons who think those only entitled to respect whose exterior commands it.' To her, shame is a very proper feeling, as it implies morality and self-respect – and she knows the street boys have it.[5]

In 1847, one ten-year-old boy recounts how he is tempted into playing the bones for an organ grinder. He is a natural; it pays well. Still, he'd rather be beaten, rather be thought a thief, than confess to his parents that he performs in the streets:

> I didn't like to tell the old woman or father what I was up to. I felt kind of ashamed of it, and I used to bring home such a lot of money – six and seven shillings a-day sometimes – and I wouldn't split how I came by it; and the old woman thought I had gone wrong – thought that I went out priggin' [stealing], you know, and they used to whack me orful; and before they went out to work in the morning, they'd lock up my clothes, right down to my shirt.[6]

Almost a century earlier, Thomas Holcroft works with his father in the streets. On market day, 'my father, thinking me almost perished with the cold, gave me a pint of ale to drink, which so far inebriated me, that I was quite ashamed'.[7]

At every turn we hear from authorities that street folk are shameless, which is meant as an accusation. But no one enters the street innately shameless; quite the reverse. Though we are born without self-consciousness, shame and pride are acquired young, and children in particular feel these emotions acutely. How many of our childhood memories are excruciating moments such as Bezer's bun-selling nightmare? To triumph over that – to put yourself out there amid a multitude, or worse, among your own neighbours, and to cry out the mark of your own degradation – is an act bordering on the heroic. It requires either rare courage or total self-abandonment to make a spectacle of yourself in the streets of London. If a boy is to succeed, his first task is to conquer this shame, and put himself out there.

~

Back to Bezer in 1824. It is 'the very next Monday' at a warehouse in Newgate Street, and from some unknown part of himself, little John James Bezer summons the courage to ask for work. Glancing up at the giant in the doorway, he spills his words in a rush.

'If you please, Sir, do you want a boy? My name is Bezer; mother winds cotton for *you*, sir; father is in Greenwich College, and we are in great distress – almost starving, sir; I'll be very willing to do anything.'

Palpably desperate, he's aware he's not exactly selling himself here. Repressing a smirk, the master looks down. 'Why, you're so little! What's your age?'

'Past nine, sir, and I'm *very* strong!'

John is lying on two counts, but the man doesn't particularly care. Still... 'What wages do you want?' he asks.

'Anything you please, sir,' says John James, well aware he has nothing to bargain with, wanting only to ingratiate himself.

A pause. The family fortune hangs in the balance.

'Well, come tomorrow morning, six o'clock, and if you suit I'll give you three shillings a week; but bring all your victuals with you – we have no time for you to go home to your meals.'[8]

So Bezer is hired – on trial – as an errand boy. Elation. He's still in the streets, but it's gainful employment. An errand boy is practically respectable. And so it begins. He is contracted to a fourteen-hour day that is in practice seventeen. Six o'clock finds him outside the warehouse door, wet and shivering, waiting half an hour for admission to a 'damp freezing cellar' where – once he has cleaned the other workers' cutlery and footwear – he can wolf down 'a hunk of bread, *perhaps* buttered, and a basin of water bewitched, called tea'.

Nominally, his role is deliveries, and he is dispatched with a parcel to Whitechapel, two miles east. Returning, he is given another bound for Piccadilly, two miles west, and told to 'make haste'. Then, for light relief, some housework – cleaning and polishing – before dinner, or rather: 'Dinner! God help me! a penny saveloy … or bread alone at the latter end of the week.' Thus fortified, he is sent 'over the water' – that is, to the south bank – and back via Blackfriars and the City. Just in time to make for Islington (again, nearly two miles in each direction) before the evening round to 'the "West," which meant haberdashers shops up Holborn, Soho, Oxford Street, Regent Street, Piccadilly, over Westminster Bridge to two shops near the "Broadway"' – yes, another two miles distant.

He is allowed to go straight home with the empty sack, rather than return it to the warehouse. But since home, in Spitalfields, lies a mile and a half further east than the warehouse – which he passes en route – it's not exactly largesse on the part of his employer.

Returning to bed almost at midnight, 'foot-sore and ready to faint from low diet and excessive toil', he walks barefoot, too blistered and raw to endure his boots any longer. But he puts them on again before reaching home, because his mother is up and waiting, anxious every night. He tries 'to laugh it off ... saying, "never mind mother, I don't mind it, you know I'm getting bigger every day."' One suspects his mother is not deceived. But it is in both their interests to remain silent and accept the situation. No holidays for three years – but of course he gets Sundays off in order to attend school; his employer, like his father, is a God-fearing man. So that's something.

Looking back, a grown man, Bezer wonders how he stood it. He could, after all, have left at any time. But...

What then, should I have got another [place]? And if I had, that's not all – my master was my mother's master; and if I had discharged myself, he would have discharged her; he has told me so often ... so I toiled on, for father was as it were dead to me, and mother always ailing, and I saw no alternative but the workhouse, that worst of all prisons so dreaded by the poor, – so I toiled on, I say, till I was about eleven years of age; then typhus fever laid me prostrate, and for weeks I was to all appearance dying. I was glad to hear that the parish doctor gave me up, and the farewell of my teachers and my fellow Sunday scholars I loved so well, and my poor dear father who crawled on crutches to see me, was, though affecting, happiness to me. I felt an ardent desire for death – but it was not to be. I at last recovered. Still was I thankful even for my illness, inasmuch as it gave me a respite[.]

As an adult, Bezer writes, 'May God forgive my tyrant master for the acute sufferings I then endured'. Because *he* certainly isn't going to. But though he is eloquent on his despair, on the injustice of the situation, and on its physical consequences, he tells us little of the street itself. However, John James is not the only errand boy to stagger under the weight of a heavy load.

~

1866: a spring morning in Kensal New Town, a part of northwest London on the make, and Frank Bullen, nine years old, steps into the warehouse of a chandler. He's heard there's a job going. For a moment, he is taken aback by the sheer multiplicity of stock – how does it all fit, and how to remember where anything is? – and by the heady cocktail of scents: paint, soap, paraffin, glue, dog-biscuits… and under it all the fresh waft of newly cut pine.

Nostrils flaring, Frank straightens his back. The job, it seems, is his. If he has second thoughts about submitting to the 'stout, stern, dark man, who appeared to me like the dread arbiter of my fate', it is too late now.[9]

In some ways his job is better than Bezer's. His hours are seven a.m. until ten p.m. – a mere fifteen out of every twenty-four! – and the bread he gets has dripping on it. And although he is 'so willing and eager that my employer forgot my pygmy size and put me to tasks absurdly beyond my strength', at least 'he never struck me, nor even abused me'. In other respects, however…

A salesman took my order, looked at me, and said loftily, 'Ow yer goin' ter take it?' In reply I only stared dumbly, because I had no idea what 'it' was. He shrugged his shoulders and retired, presently bringing forward an iron drum full of treacle, which he plumped before me, saying, 'There y' are.' I looked at it helplessly for a moment, and then looked at him; but seeing no encouragement in his eye, essayed to lift it, and found that I could just manage to raise it an inch or two from the floor.

'Can't carry it,' I said.

'Nothin' to do wi' me,' he replied, taking it up oh, so easily, I thought – and putting it outside on the pavement. I did not need telling what that meant, and so calling my wits to work, I did the best I knew, that is, I turned it over on its side and rolled it! Yes ... until I came opposite Moorgate Street Station, where I halted, baffled by the width of that great highway. But a kindly costermonger came to my aid, and, finding what the trouble was, uttered many strange words about the behaviour of whoever had sent such a kid on an errand of this kind.

At this point, we leave the street: remarkably, with the coster's help, Frank gets the iron drum onto a train, alighting at Westbourne Park. It's the 1860s after all: they have trains now.

Arriving there, and being helped again by the tender-hearted guard aforesaid, I ... fled shopwards, pantingly explaining on arrival that I wanted the 'truck.' ... Now this truck, of which more anon, was one of those curiously shaped ones used exclusively by wine merchants at that time. It was curved and hollow, in order to take one barrel. It had a very long push handle, and no bottom. So you can imagine how difficult was my journey with that drum upon it, a veritable pilgrimage of pain. Let me pause awhile to solemnly curse that truck, and the evil chance that harnessed me to its awkwardness. Nevertheless upon this occasion I did reach my journey's end in safety, with the drum and its contents intact, only to be grumbled at because I had been so long!

On another occasion, he is given the same truck to transport a hundredweight of soap – that is, fifty kilograms or eight stone, considerably more than young Frank weighs himself – and his employer neglects to lash it down properly. Still, Frank:

succeeded fairly well too, until I came to a quagmire of a road where building was going on. Still I strove, the truck bumping horribly over the boulders hidden beneath the mud, until, when abreast of a church, which was just abuilding, the calamity which had been looming ever since I left the shop occurred – the box slid off the truck and capsized in the mud. The bars of soap flew in all directions, disposing themselves picturesquely as if planted in the slush, and I surveyed the awful scene in a sort of philosophic calm...

From that stupor or reverie I was aroused by the loud laughter of the bricklayers on the scaffolding near at hand, and I sprang with desperate energy to the task of righting the wrong ... By the time I had finished, and I had no help, a circumstance which even now I wonder at – it would have been hard to tell which was muddiest, the truck, the box, the soap, or myself.

Eventually, he:

arrived at my destination, overheated, unrecognisable for mud, but triumphant. I knocked at the door, and the laundress appeared, a comely figure in spotless print. She gave a little start back when she saw me, as if she feared I would soil her eyesight, but I said quickly—

'Please, 'm, I've brought the soap.'

You can imagine the sort of reception he gets. Nor is it his last such ordeal. Some months later, now working for a trunk-maker in the Edgware Road, Frank is sent to Hoxton on the other side of London to collect 'a full-sized leather portmanteau' – an item 'so large that I could almost have got into it, and it was correspondingly heavy. But I was six miles from home, and had to do something'. Four hours later he arrives back at the shop, 'dead beat but triumphant', having towed the portmanteau through constant rain with the aid of a begged yard of clothesline.

It is worse even than the soap:

> for that spruce portmanteau looked as if it had been subjected to years of the hardest wear, and was besides almost covered with mud. My employer gave one glance at it, uttered a sort of whoop, and sat down trembling ... 'If ever you come near this shop again, and I catch you, I'll break every bone in your skin.'

~

In Frank Bullen's epic struggles, we glimpse the new London that is coming. It's the same step taken by Bezer as he renounces hot cross bun-selling – an ancient custom, scraped together with shillings, sold in the street among a community – in favour of running errands. This new London doesn't run just on trains, it runs on the circulation of capital: goods stream through the streets, and the whole gigantic city is tethered down by a vast web of networks, like Gulliver in Lilliput. But though this new London is one of warehouses and haste, scorning those whose work is done at walking pace, it still depends on boys like Frank and John James: urchins, fleet of foot and disposable, incapable of unionisation and scarcely showing up in the ledgers. It is a city where the children sweat in the streets to support their figurative fathers.

Some of these fathers are literal – and often, these are worst of all. Thomas Holcroft's father is far from a model employer. 'My father one day whipped me very severely for [wanting] to go to a school in the neighbourhood ... He used to beat me, pull my hair up by the roots, and drag me by the ears along the ground, till they ran with blood.'[10]

When young George Acorn's father catches him, desperate with hunger, stealing redcurrants from a fruiterer's stall, it's the father who leads the cry of 'Stop thief!' Once home, 'the street door was closed, I was knocked down in the passage and kicked and punched, until almost senseless'. Their landlady, Mrs Potter, cannot help but overhear these beatings – but merely tells George that they will 'make a man of yer'.[11]

Yet even his experience is as nothing to Arthur Turner's, the son of a chimney sweep too ill to work. In 1838, when he is aged six, Arthur is sent out with his brothers, and nearly suffocates up his first chimney. Another time he is almost burned to death. His working day often starts at half-past two in the morning. Once a week, he and his brothers have a wash, and are allowed to sleep in the house. Six nights out of seven, they lodge in the soot warehouse 'in a place very much like a cupboard, where the dust was almost choking'. In the 1840s, London bans its child sweeps – at which point Turner and his brothers are forced out into the countryside, and carry on.[12]

1860: Charles Humphreys, aged nine, of Walham Green in southwest London, has known his share of outdoor labour. Until now it's been pretty picturesque: helping his landlord sell flowers from a donkey cart, 'for which he would give me a drink of beer and a piece of bread and cheese, and sometimes a penny', or going out harvesting in the summers, sleeping in barns. Coming home, he 'generally used to be put in a sack and carried over Putney Bridge to avoid paying [the] toll'. But now his father, out of work, has plans to hire him out.

Already, Charles is itching for independence. He is lent to their neighbour for 'one-and-sixpence a week, and twopence for myself if I behaved', and that first taste of his own tuppence is intoxicating. Immediately, the boy goes behind his father's back, hiring himself out to several other neighbours and cutting out the parental middleman. Meanwhile, his father sets him up with a friend, Mr Jones – a drinking companion, a drunkard:

> While Mr Jones was drinking with my father in a pub, he gave me a very bad character, and called me a very lazy young devil ... My father, being three sheets to the wind, told him that when he asked me again, and I wouldn't do it, to give me a b[loody] good hiding.
>
> He did ask me again ... and when he found that I wouldn't, he hit me full in the face with his fist. They carried me home, and my nose bled three days and two nights without stopping, but it opened my eyes and my ears to look out for a better job.

In the years that follow, Charles will never forget this moment, when his own father turns against him and calls for violence. It is a rift that will never heal.[13]

So common are these fathers, seemingly bent, saturnine, on feeding off their own sons, that they become the stuff of cliché. They even become useful. In 1854, James Lewis, aged ten, 'small of stature' and with 'an impediment in his speech', is begging in the streets. His clothes are in rags, 'his wretched conditions well calculated to draw forth pity and assistance'.

And – if we believe all that we read – 'calculated' is the word. Questioned by an officer of the Mendicity Society, James states:

> that he had been forced into the streets by his father to beg, who expected him to take home a shilling every night, but he had not collected that amount, and in consequence had not been home for several nights to avoid the beating his father would give him if he returned home without it.

The officer summons a regular constable to take the boy home, but he will not admit his address:

> The youngster commenced walking up one street and down another, avoiding that part of London where his father ultimately was found to be living. Having amused himself this way about three hours, he was taken to a Station House, when the fear of being locked up by the Constable obliged him to admit that his father was living at Bermondsey.

The outraged father protests: he has done nothing, the boy is a liar. If we believe the father, then James has been sharp enough to use the trope of the abusive, exploitative father as a story in his begging. If we do not, then the man is a monster indeed, and we must fear for young James when the door closes behind him.

What we are seeing, I think, is one of the uglier faces worn by paternalism. If the boy in the street wanted bed, board, security, then he was forced to submit to the total authority of a master – a father figure – who wielded supreme power by dint of pay, shelter, boot and fist. This was no kind of freedom. But for a boy without support, what was the alternative?

~

1800 (more or less): St George's Fields, Southwark, and the sounds of merriment spilling from the doors of the public house are surely a little out of the ordinary. People are streaming in and out, laughing. In the street outside, a woman – young, flustered, not *quite* respectable – turns her head. Stops. Decides to enter.

Inside the taproom, the press of men and women is thick. But at its centre, a patch of sawdust floor is left open, and within it cavorts – what can it be? It looks something like Jack-in-the-Green, but surely those are feathers, not leaves, that cover its whirling, tumbling body. The creature leaps again, and a few of the feathers come loose, flutter down upon the dust-strewn flags. It straightens, bows – the crowd applauds – pennies are thrown – and somewhere in the centre of a grimy face, a smile breaks forth like the sun from heaven.

The woman knows that smile. It is Edmund Kean.

Edmund Kean, the baby born in Gray's Inn Lane a dozen years before, and now a limber, twisting, fantastical thing sprung out of a mythical bestiary. He grins around, asks what'll they have next? His 'orrible knife-grinder, perhaps? The famous dancing monkey that so astonished the good folk of Lisle Street last week? They've heard of the monkey, they want the monkey, and his smile widens – only to fix in a rictus of horror as he sees the woman, her face set, shouldering her way to the front. It's Charlotte Tidswell, his mother's friend – his joint guardian, no less – and she's holding a formidable-looking rope.

Hoots from the crowd as this new play begins: the resolute, well-dressed woman grappling with the sticky, feathered boy. Caught between the desire to escape and to gather his pennies – and perhaps unwilling to let the curtain fall on even this humiliating new act – he is no match for her. In minutes, she has the rope secured around his waist. They exit the pub to a chorus of cheers, cat calls and wolf whistles, and, young Edmund still struggling against his bonds, they begin their long and highly conspicuous journey north, back to Leicester Square.

He does this sort of thing a lot. If it's not St George's Fields, it's Vauxhall, where he sings to the pub-goers. If he's not tarring and feathering himself for the sake of spectacle, then he's off into the country, tumbling and juggling at wayside inns. Sources describe him as 'wilder than the quagga' – a bucking sort of zebra, bound for extinction, but just then becoming legendary for its temper and antics. His uncle Moses Kean – his other guardian – once finds him 'sleeping on a dunghill, in a state of exhaustion, ragged and foot-sore, and altogether in squalid disorder'. It's in his blood, of course – this couple are only his guardians at all because his mother has gone off again with the circus – and it's infinitely preferable, thinks the wild young Edmund, to thrashings and boredom at his day school in Green Street.

Kean chooses to go wandering, to perform in the streets – to go without shelter or protection – rather than submit to authority. And perhaps he has a point. In later years, Kean will apparently remember of Charlotte Tidswell, 'She did not like me; or, if she did, she didn't appear to do so. She kept me, indeed, but she used to thump me often enough, and tie me to the bed-post; and at last, she put a collar round my neck, as though I had been a dog.'

A collar? Yes indeed – a brass collar, and etched upon it the words: 'This boy belongs to 9, Lisle-street, Leicester-square; please bring him home.' When Edmund finds he can conceal the hated collar with a handkerchief, and continues to abscond, she takes to locking him in a secure room during her absences from home. Most curiously of all, at one point he is lodged for safekeeping with a Mr and Mrs Duncan, and the husband goes on to recollect, 'He used to sleep with me and my wife in the irons, *and they hurt us.*' No wonder Edmund prefers the freedom of the streets.[14]

In one sense, Edmund Kean's is a common story. Driven out by ill-treatment, he fends for himself as best he can – which is better than most. In 1831, John Munday, aged ten, is left an orphan when his parents – a carpenter and a laundress – die in quick succession. 'As soon as the funeral was over my mother's brother took my two brothers to the [Chelsea] Workhouse ... And then my uncle came back after me, but I was too cute for him. I ran down the docks at the bottom of the street and away to Cremorne through the mud.'

For Munday, the workhouse is a fate worse than death, and his uncle is a rank traitor. Life on the streets is infinitely preferable – a sentiment Edmund Kean certainly shared.[15]

Kean differs from our other boys, however, in one crucial, overwhelmingly important respect – he has connections. The people who shake their heads in concern over the wild boy include Charles Incledon, the foremost tenor of his day, and Henry Angelo, the legendary fencing master. Though of humble stock themselves, these men are now celebrities, they know royalty, and Kean's networks will see him right: next time he escapes, it is to join Abraham Saunders' company of travelling entertainers and reprise his role as a monkey. We'll meet him again at Bartholomew Fair.[16]

~

Without such connections, freedom can be desperate. 'One December morning' in the 1860s, Harry – who will eventually settle on the name Henry Warren Kelly – is queuing outside Drury Lane Theatre with his best friend Millie and 'a couple of hundred other children'. Pantomime season is coming – this year it's *Cinderella* – and they've heard the theatre is hiring children for chorus parts. Decades later, after he has chosen his name and, at the age of forty, finally learned to write, the incident is still burnt into his memory:

> I remember that most of the children wore tidy clothes, and very few were without boots and stockings, which made Millie and me think our chances small. It came my turn to be questioned.
>
> 'Your name?'
>
> 'Harry.'
>
> 'Surname?'
>
> 'Ain't got none.'
>
> 'Where do you live?'

That finished it. When I replied that I had to live here, there and anywhere, I was ordered off the premises. Poor Millie fared no better. I remembered this as the first time I considered my lot a hard one. Why couldn't I have a home like other boys?

Unlike Edmund Kean – who first appeared on stage at the age of two – Harry is *outside* the door when it slams in his face and the key turns. Presuming himself an orphan, he has no home from which to escape. Instead, he sleeps where he can. Under the dark arches down by the Adelphi:

I, with others, required no light to find every recess and corner. I could not have been more than five years of age. There, many a time we would huddle together in the night for warmth and shelter, till the shout of 'Copper!' or the flash of the policeman's bull's-eye would make us scamper.

Or, less pleasant, beneath Hungerford Bridge, 'where we would huddle and shiver under its sinister arches till the first sign of daylight'. What little shelter could be found was liable to be snatched away; he describes 'myself with those others running for dear life along the Thames Embankment in the early hours of the morning, drizzling sleet falling the while, the cold penetrating our bones to the marrow'.

A lucky morning: 'we might run into a good-hearted workman, his lunch tied up in a handkerchief, lingering outside a coffee palace. "Hello, boy. You look cold! What? Out all night? Well, here you are – I'll walk to work this morning."' A workman's cab fare is turned into a meal.

An unlucky morning: 'The thieves – "nobility", we called them – from the Dials ... knew where we could be found', and descend in search of supple, small accomplices, who can easily be left in the lurch if the job goes wrong. 'We knew that if we were not to be shut up [in prison] for months at a time, we had to clear off and start the day on an empty stomach.'

Harry's London is one governed by a fickle clockwork, in which machinery greater than himself turns the cogs by which its elements – bed, work, safety – are shifted in and out of place. Its built surfaces are cold and hard, unforgiving.

To compensate, he and 'other children of equal poverty and homelessness' clump together. They form a functioning herd or tribe, taking turns to watch for enemies, huddling for warmth and softness. They are gregarious; Harry is not lonely. The girls 'mostly sold flowers made up into buttonholes', in an operation masterminded 'by an old woman we christened "Granny"', while 'the boys sold matches, hawked the daily and weekly papers, and eked out a living in those hundred and one ways known to the great underworld'.

His existence is far from anonymous. Viewed from outside, he is one among a litter of grubby, interchangeable faces, to be called Arab, urchin, or simply boy. But Harry's survival depends on personal connections just as much as Edmund Kean's does – it is only that Harry's are of a humbler order. He is devoted to one girl, Millie – and with good reason:

> When I was about eight years of age I was troubled with severe inflammation of the eyes. Whenever I awoke of a morning my eyes were, so to speak, hermetically sealed, and a flower-girl we called Millie would lead me to the Hungerford Steps on the bank of the Thames, or to the nearest fountain, and bathe them until I was enabled to open them. The result was that I became deeply attached to her, depending greatly upon her assistance.

These fierce bonds, formed early, are mutually beneficial. Harry recalls how, thereafter, he saw himself as Millie's protector.

> One afternoon I was selling papers at the corner of Waterloo Bridge, and Millie was standing in the gutter with her flowers laid out on a cardboard box, when a boy called Pongo, a hooligan of high repute, and terror of our young lives, launched a ferocious kick at Millie's box of flowers, scattering them in all directions. Without a moment's hesitation, I flew at him, determined to teach him a lesson. We had hardly begun to square up when the shout 'Police!' was raised, and we disappeared at a bound. But that same night at the back of the Savoy we finished what we had started in the afternoon, and the redoubtable Pongo slunk off defeated and dejected. From that day, in the eyes of others as well as myself, I became a person of importance.

But a reputation can only stretch so far:

> Millie, myself and a few more decided to shift our quarters to Tottenham Court Road. I may say it was a difficult task to earn a livelihood in fresh pastures, as strangers were regarded with suspicion and dislike, and although we struggled on for a few weeks, we eventually had to return to our old haunts.

However vast it grew, London remained divided into a myriad little territories, communities of knowledge and belonging. Even the homeless had their own place, and suffered once out of it.[17]

If he is allowed, a boy can sleep almost anywhere. 1831: John Munday again, fled to Cremorne - not far at all from Chelsea, but distant enough to evade his uncle and the threat of the workhouse.

I got another boy for a mate, and we used to sleep where we could find a quiet place ... [W]e lay on a barge for several nights under a tarpaulin opposite the 'Cage and Stocks,' and then in a water cart at the corner of Swan Lane, and then my mate got tired of it and went into the house, and so the next night I lay on poles under the covering next to the house ... and I had not long been there when a policeman told me to come down or he would fetch a ladder and get me down, but I lay breathless and he went away, and I stayed there till morning waiting for an opportunity to get down.[18]

Around 1870: Billy Tagg, aged 'nine and a half', proudly informs social investigator James Greenwood that 'I lives in Playhouse Yard in Whitecross street'. Although, he concedes, this may give a false impression. 'It ain't a house, at least it ain't a house what you goes indoors to.' In fact, it's a barrow. '"A baker's barrer," poor little Tagg hastened to explain – "one of them with a lid. The baker lets me sleep there, and I watches out for the cats."'[19]

Tagg fares better than Munday in his barge and water cart, as he has come to a working relationship with his landlord, but they are both wholly dependent on the transformative action of time: at night, a moving vehicle – part of the productive circulation of London capital – comes to rest, and is repurposed by the savvy street child. For the space of a few hours' sleep, London is a world turned upside down. Come sunrise, these homes vanish.

1869: nine thirty p.m., and a winter meeting at the Ragged School run by a young Thomas Barnardo, not yet the titan of philanthropy he will become, is winding up for the night. Jim Jarvis, 'a little lad' of ten years who will become unwittingly immortalised by the good doctor as 'My First Arab', is loath to leave the comfort of the warm room. Querulous, suspicious, Barnardo corners him:

'Please, sir, do let me stay. I won't do no 'arm.'

'Well, but had you not better get home? Your mother will wonder what kept you so late.'

'I ain't got no mother.'

'Haven't got a mother, boy? Where do you live?'

'Don't live nowhere.'

'Now, my lad, it is of no good your trying to deceive me. Come here and tell me what you mean. Where do you come from? Where did you sleep last night?'

… 'Down in Whitechapel, sir, along o' the 'aymarket in one of them carts as is filled with 'ay; an' then I met a chap as I knowed this afternoon, and he told me to come up 'ere to school, as perhaps you'd let me lie near the fire all night. I won't do no 'arm sir, if you let me stop.'

Jarvis, too, has become expert in making his bed from those moments of stillness between industrious movement. He thinks he can do better still, and sleep by a fire. But the price is a steep one: he must show Barnardo his haunts. Under sufferance, he leads him to a hay loft in Petticoat Lane. As Barnardo recalls:

This loft was closed, but a good deal of straw had dropped from it into the gutter, and was put into use by the lads, whom we saw lying there asleep. With their heads upon the higher part of the roof and their feet somewhat in the gutter, but in a great variety of postures, lay eleven boys huddled together for warmth – no roof or covering of any kind was over them[.][20]

This proves to be Barnardo's Damascene moment, and he dates his efforts to 'save' homeless children from this night. A year later, before dawn, and he is on the prowl in Covent Garden – a place he describes with breath-taking levity as one of his 'happy hunting grounds'. Every inch the colonial explorer, he has a native guide – a small boy – to point out features of this exotic terrain, strange in the shadow of the dark side of the clock. The boy draws Barnardo's attention to a nook, high upon the market's western wall:

'That's a fine *lay* up there, Sir,' said my young companion, pointing with his hand. 'It 'ud just fit a young feller like me first-rate once't I was up, for no bobby'd ever get up there, I'm sure, and I don't think many of 'em would think of lookin' at it.'

Someone has abandoned an empty orange box, and it is lodged almost out of sight, accessible only by a rickety assemblage of scaffolding. Its positioning protects a sleeper from the officious attention of the new beadle, an energetic man who has driven most of the homeless children from the market. Anyone who has made a home here can only be admired for their ingenuity and daring, and has surely earned a good night's sleep. But no: Barnardo and his helper tear down the scaffolding, toppling the orange box to decant a bruised and startled boy.

Barnardo is delighted, 'He was just such a child as I was in search of'. By which he means 'one, in short, who lived *on* the streets and *by* the streets'. His name is George, and his mother is a Southwark thief. Like many of his peers, he has been subjected to 'such a succession of unmerciful beatings, that, when only a little past his ninth year, he fled from the wretched room which he had hitherto always called *home*, and betook himself to a street life'. And of all our rough sleepers, he is perhaps the canniest, for he stays 'chiefly about the meat market, the fruit and vegetable markets, and the fish market'. George makes his bed where, at the close of the day's trading, he has immediate access to any boy's most important consideration: food.[21]

~

Anatomists may disagree, but among the street poor, the thing closest to a boy's heart is his stomach. At a street market in the mid-1830s, young John Hollingshead, eight or nine years old, has his eye on a bargain. 'I knew how much more was to be got for a penny when I bought the stale pastry from the tea-tray placed at the side of the doorway.' A penny can also get him two regular apples – 'ribstone pippins' – or four 'little red apples, several seasons old'. He speaks with relish of the *cucina povera* available for small change at these markets:

> Good, greasy Yorkshire pudding was a favourite, sometimes plain, sometimes with an occasional raisin stuck at rare intervals on the surface – always on the surface. Next to this stood baking potatoes, brown and crisp; and, after this, peas[e]-pudding, in warm and heavy lumps upon a cabbage-leaf.[22]

A good meal like this could change the course of a life. James Greenwood, the journalist and self-styled 'social investigator', often used food as a lure when he wanted to interview urchins. Here he is tempting ten-year-old Ginger, a blacking seller and young Billy Tagg's best friend, to talk:

> Ginger's delight when the landlord brought in, along with a big loaf, the half of a huge Cheshire cheese, was a sight to behold; his amazement when the landlord left the room, leaving the half cheese behind him, I will not attempt to describe.
>
> 'He's forgot it, ain't he?' he said ...
>
> 'No, he hasn't forgotten, my lad,' said I, 'he'll fetch it away when we have done with it.'
>
> 'When we have done with it! What, are we going to eat as much as we likes on it?'

It is a long time before Greenwood can get Ginger to talk, so determined is the boy to consume a cheese weighing 'probably thirty pounds' – that is, thirteen and a half kilograms. But his hunger is eloquence enough.[23]

In 1830, John James Bezer, despite his brush with death, is still working as an errand boy and attending Sunday school on his only day off, and he shows such promise as a scholar that the superintendent makes a suggestion. In these ad hoc, inner-city forerunners of the Ragged Schools, it is common for the brighter pupils to teach their less able classmates, and Bezer is now offered:

> a place at 1s a week and my victuals, and didn't I close in with the offer without hesitation! The word *victuals* decided me at once, for Mr. A. [the Sunday school superintendent] kept two Ham and Beef Shops, and the bare idea of becoming a 'beef-eater' was so agreeable a novelty that without a moment's warning to my Newgate-street master, I went to my new situation ... I was led into temptation; – Ham and beef, after bread and potatoes! Oh! 'Twas a consummation devoutly to be wished![24]

Clearly John James has learned his *Hamlet* at this Sunday school. Indeed, it is the making of him – and the promise of ham and beef is enough to take him out of the streets... for now.

Our other errand boy, Frank Bullen, is similarly preoccupied with getting a decent meal. He rejoices in securing a job delivering milk because he gets a pint to himself twice a day – but soon finds that his non-stop working day (four thirty a.m. till nine p.m. in summer, with a five thirty a.m. start in winter) leaves no time to eat. In the end, he has to give up most of his earnings to his landlady so that she will agree to 'subsidise a local coffee-stall keeper to the extent of one cup of coffee and one slice of cake, price together one penny, every morning. This I bolted at the street corner, often scalding my mouth'.[25]

As Frank moves on through new jobs and new streets, he becomes more resourceful, not altogether within the bounds of the law:

[I]t is an incontrovertible fact that the stomach of a young human being that has never known pampering can assimilate food that should, theoretically, derange the digestion of an ostrich. For instance, Fresh Wharf, Thames Street, was the rendezvous of many steamers from Spain, laden with dried fruits, nuts, oranges, etc. In the handling of cases, sacks, and other packages, there was a good deal of breakage, and I could often snatch a few handfuls of currants, nuts, raisins, etc. I always ate of them ravenously, in spite of their copious admixture of dust and dirt, but even after devouring a couple of pounds of currants I never remember feeling the slightest ill effects.

But when he can afford it, his preference is for pease soup – the thick, porridge-like pudding made with split peas – and ideally as made in one particular cookshop opposite Billingsgate Fishmarket:

It was sold at twopence a basin; but the half basin for a penny, not being carefully measured, lacked very little of being full. Moreover, to the initiate, there were degrees in the quality of this soup. It was freshly made on Monday, and even then was good. On Tuesday, however, the thick residue at the bottom of the tank remaining unsold was left, and the usual ingredients for a fresh mess were added to it, making it much richer and more substantial. On Wednesday, this process was repeated, with the result that Wednesday's soup was a thick purée in which a spoon would stand erect, and he who could buy a penn'orth and eat it with a ha'penny hunk of bread, could go on the strength of that meal for twenty-four hours without any inconvenience.[26]

For all his hard-won knowledge of how best to game the system, Frank Bullen is still never quite full. His account is all the more affecting for its pragmatism, its attention to detail; the way he talks of soup and bread will be chillingly familiar if you have read Solzhenitsyn's short novel *One Day in the Life of Ivan Denisovich*. Frank is not just a hungry boy: he is an expert in survival.

Not every boy's constitution is as robust as Frank's. Out working for his father, Thomas Holcroft encounters a kindly servant who lets him sup from 'a large bason of rich pease-soup'. To his mortification, 'the moment I smelt it, and applied it to my palate, I conceived such an excessive dislike to it, that though I felt ashamed, and made every effort I could, I found it impossible to swallow a spoonful'. Roundly mocked, the familiar sensation of shame engulfs him. Years later, reflecting on the experience, he supposes that 'perhaps, accustomed as I had been from childhood to the plainest food, and empty as my stomach then was, this high-flavoured composition would unavoidably excite disgust'. The boy Holcroft is malnourished indeed if pease soup seems insupportably rich fare.[27]

But few can afford such delicate stomachs. 1870: Billy Tagg – Ginger's barrow-sleeping friend – spends the entirety of his meagre income on food. Forming a gang with a few other boys, he leads them at close of trading to Bermondsey skin market. Here they club together to buy:

Bits of meat what they scrapes off the insides of the skins and the ears of the bullocks; stunnin' stew it makes with an ingun [onion] and a few taters ... you buys it in lots. Them wots got the priwelege cuts 'em off, and makes 'eaps of 'em on the pavement, about a couple of pound [or just under a kilogram] for two pence.[28]

Billy doesn't make clear how they manage to cook this stew – perhaps his landlord the baker is generous with his premises. Most working-class Londoners, not only street urchins, had to buy their food ready cooked. Lack of access to equipment could defeat even the ever-resourceful Frank Bullen:

> I was ravenously hungry, and there seemed to be no possibility of getting anything to eat. So diving down into the shell-fish market beneath the main building of Billingsgate, I watched my opportunity, and filled the breast of my shirt with whelks from a mighty tubful ... but was immediately confronted with the difficulty of extracting the whelks from their shells ... I was fain [forced] at last to smash the shells, no easy task either. Then clearing the mollusc from débris I tried to eat it, but it was quite impossible, it was tougher than gutta-percha, and I realised that my whelks were unboiled![29]

Faced with such hurdles, it is all too easy to find yourself on the point of starvation. And as Bullen confesses:

> I was certainly not one of those wonderful children of whom we read in prize-books that they would starve rather than steal. I stole whenever I saw a favourable opportunity, and when found out and made to suffer therefor, only blamed my own stupidity in not taking more elaborate precautions.[30]

And though he speaks lightly of being 'made to suffer', a boy forced by hunger to turn pickpocket or thief was taking his life in his hands.

~

There can be something liberating in the act of – well, 'liberating'. Many boys seem to have been at their best when they were at their worst. Broad daylight in Westbourne Grove, the late 1860s, and Frank Bullen walks into a grocer's shop, bold as brass. What a difference from his first timid entry into a chandler's at the age of nine, overawed by the multitude of things. He is wiser now, he knows the layout of such places and how to turn them to his advantage.

As he has expected, the vast counter is 'laden as usual with samples of goods for sale'. In such a place, he is dwarfed, small and slight, a figure of no importance – which is what he is banking on. Without a second's pause, and right 'under the nose of the dumbfounded salesman', he seizes a large box of biscuits, and is gone 'before he had even attempted to clear the obstacles between us'.[31]

A boy's first taste of crime can be exhilarating. Bullen, who claims that there is 'nothing melodramatic' about theft, is far from the boldest of child outlaws.[32] 1795, and speaking of outlaws: William Brown, aged fourteen, is a country boy come up to town. But he's no bumpkin, and, young though he is, he already has a trick or two up his sleeve:

> Being one evening short of money, I hit upon a project to get some; the ballad singers of London were at that time singing with great éclat, the song called the Arethusa; I determined to take advantage of the circumstance, so getting a number of old newspapers, in the evening I took my station at the end of several streets, (having previously cut them into slips resembling songs) I began to sing the above, and so rapid was the sale, (in the dark) that in a quarter of an hour I had sold about forty at a halfpenny each.[33]

The boy is a scoundrel, but he's also a genius. Brown's takings – one shilling and eight pence – are clear profit, and almost twice what an average ballad singer might hope to earn in a full day by selling actual songs. It takes a special sort of cunning to note the similarity between newsprint and the ballad sheets known as slip songs – both being dense, narrow columns of crabbed-together text – and then turn that resemblance into a confidence trick in the dim-lit streets. Above all, for his ruse to work, Brown has to master 'The Arethusa' – a swaggering sea song built on the lines of an operatic aria, spanning nearly two octaves with a nasty leap in the middle.[34]

He manages to escape the scene before the watch shows up. And to cap it all, he reveals towards the end of his memoir that 'William Brown' isn't even his real name, just one of four aliases he has used over the years. Two hundred years on, it's never too late to be taken in by a consummate rogue.

1814: a boy known only as 'Master Demar', around ten or twelve years old, is also singing ballads in the street. Though in all other respects destitute, he does own a 'very sweet, strong, and flexible voice', and the act of drawing attention to himself in the street – so shameful to the seven-year-old John James Bezer – comes naturally to him. Demar takes readily to this much derided but surprisingly difficult trade; his young eyes and quick mind make light of the small, smudged, misspelt lines on the cheap paper before him, and his unbroken treble is the perfect instrument to carry his tunes clearly through the London hubbub.

In no time, he is talent-spotted. William Reeve, the in-house composer for Sadler's Wells, is a resident of the street where Demar sings. Confronted with this well-to-do, innocent-looking gent, Demar's eyes light up. He tells:

... with much *naiveté*, an apparently artless tale. His Mother was dead: and his Father, a journeyman Hair Dresser, had turned him into the Street; where by begging, he obtained money enough to buy a few Ballads, and between begging and Ballad singing he had supported himself from the time that he was deserted by his Father; sleeping at night under Sheds, or wherever he could hide his head.

Reeve is an easy mark. The story may be true or false – the point is, Reeve not only swallows it, but is moved 'to snatch him from what he considered would be his destruction' and takes him in to his own household.

At first, all goes as well as in any children's story: Demar, a cocksure, mercurial child, is not one to suffer stage fright, and does well as a 'vocal precocity'. London's theatregoers can still remember William Betty, the 'young Roscius', who made such a sensation a decade before, and they lap up Demar, encoring his songs. 'But Master Demar also became more than pleased with many articles of Reeve's [silver] Plate, with which, one Morning, before anyone was up but the Servant, he absconded from Reeve's House, and we never heard any more of him.'[35]

Looked at one way, Demar's is a tragicomic experience, a promising career undermined by a short-sighted weakness for silverware. Looked at another way, Demar is a chancer *par excellence*, whose talent and charm help him get away with a series of ever-greater deceptions. Sometimes it pays to get better at crime.

Earlier we saw young George Acorn pilfering redcurrants, so flagrantly that his own father spotted him at it. A few months on, and he has fallen under the influence of Jimmy Braid, a self-proclaimed 'desperado', who teaches him the finer points of pickpocketing. Quite literally the 'finer points': Jimmy shows George how to cut the nail of your little finger at a sharp angle, to create the perfect tool for snagging silk handkerchiefs from passers-by in Bishopsgate – or, as he calls it, 'Bishigit'.[36]

In 1855, respectable London is appalled as thirteen-year-old John Reeves, an inveterate, masterful, yet convicted pickpocket, testifies against policeman and thief-trainer Charles King, a real-life Fagin in the ranks of the police, who taught Reeves how to size up a crowd, when to move on, how to throw off a pursuer. But for all this education, for all that he has an 'inside man' looking out for him, Reeves still finds himself in the Westminster House of Correction.[37] At a time when any ragged boy was assumed to be a potential thief, the odds were stacked against those who actually were.

~

1830: a little before John James Bezer is saved from the streets by the promise of beef and ham. 'Past nine o'clock' at night, and he is still working. He is 'trailing up Holborn-hill with my bag full of orders nearly dragging the ground behind me' when a policeman, suspicious of his sack, stops him. '"You sire, what er ye got in there, a?"'

Perhaps his recent brush with death has made the boy reckless; perhaps it is the onset of adolescence. But these are the 'new police', only recently formed: much resented and much mocked. Just the other day, a scandal rocked the force when one constable was found to have stolen a leg of mutton. So John James, who is 'not in the best of humours', decides not to explain. 'I answered promptly, looking at the gentleman as impudently as an embryo Chartist well could, "Legs o' mutton."

'"I'll leg o' mutton yer," says he; and off I was taken to the Station.'[38]

Amazingly, Bezer gets away with this cheek, and is soon back at the work that is ruining his health. Indeed, none of the boys we have come to know well is ever convicted of a criminal offence. Lucky for them. A boy far gone in cold and hunger might welcome a night in the cells: one child thief who went by 'many names' opined in 1850, 'I would rather be taken up at Brixton than Croydon, because there is a lot of hot pipes in the cell – they call them steam pipes'.[39] But if your case went so far as a trial – very often an open-and-shut affair with no jury – then things swiftly became more serious.

In 1849, in a rare touch of empathy, reformer Thomas Beggs imagines himself in the position of a street urchin:

It is a cruel mockery to see a child of ten or twelve years of age brought [as] a prisoner into a court of justice ... The child is bewildered by the appearance of the Judge, the pleading of counsel, and the charge from the Bench. The only part of it he understands is, that which condemns him to a certain term of imprisonment. He feels, too, that there are parties without, in the little world of which he is a denizen, who will inquire whether he bravely bore his part.[40]

Seen from this diminutive perspective, Mary Ann Donovan – with whom this book began – shows uncommon courage and comprehension. For a small boy, the situation is bewildering, while any sense of defiance, stubbornness, fear of what your peers will say, or indeed the firm conviction of innocence, is likely only to make things worse, when your best hope is to burst into tears or hang your head.

In 1834, another reformer, Edward Pelham Brenton, interviews little James Burke in Newgate Prison. To his horror, he realises that the boy '*had been tried, but did not know it*'. James has, of course, been convicted. Ignorance is no sort of defence.[41]

8 January 1850, and George Ruby, aged about fourteen, is not even on trial. But as he stands in the witness box at the Guildhall,

the judge becomes preoccupied with the boy's perceived idiocy. Their exchange will become famous:

> Alderman Humphrey: Well, do you know what you are about? Do you know what an oath is?
> Boy: No.
> Alderman: Can you read?
> Boy: No.
> Alderman: Do you ever say your prayers?
> Boy: No, never.
> Alderman: Do you know what prayers are?
> Boy: No.
> Alderman: Do you know what the devil is?
> Boy: I've heard of the devil, but I don't know him.
> Alderman: What do you know?
> Boy: I know how to sweep the crossing.
> Alderman: And that's all?
> Boy: That's all; I sweeps a crossing.

Infuriated with the boy's 'deplorable ignorance', the judge dismisses his evidence. George Ruby becomes a momentary *cause célèbre* – he sweeps the crossing outside Charles Dickens's house in Tavistock Square, where the great writer allegedly not only makes sure Ruby gets a decent meal but uses him as the basis for Poor Jo in *Bleak House*. Yet he is far from unique, and it is fortunate that he is summoned merely as a witness, or his reticence might well have landed him an exemplary sentence.[42]

Even for a boy inured to hardship by a life on the streets – indeed, perhaps *because* of that very fact – sentences are harsh. In 1852, Thomas Miller, aged twelve and four foot two in height, is whipped and imprisoned for two days. This is his eighth criminal conviction, including being twice sentenced to transportation (commuted both times) and imprisoned for spells of between two weeks and two years. His first sentence, of one month inside and a whipping, he received at Clerkenwell when aged just eight.

In 1849, Edward Joghill also receives his eighth conviction of at least a month in prison, including two whippings. He is more precocious than Miller; he has racked these up before the age of ten. But then, since he's never had a trial by jury, just a series of magistrates rattling through the open-and-shut cases, perhaps this isn't so surprising. This is going by the records of 'one prison only' – he's been inside elsewhere too; maybe one of the other institutions gave him a proper trial. Neither boy has done more than steal a scarf or coin on any occasion.[43]

As the details of Thomas Miller's size remind us, these are not strapping youths, but little children, cruelly malnourished. Incarceration aside, it is terrible to contemplate the reality of sentencing such a boy to a judicial whipping: the tiny child, shoulder blades raw to the birch; the uniformed policeman standing over him. It is the boy's whole plight incarnate in one bloody moment, braced against a world bent on doing him harm, both physical and psychological. And that world is not made up only of strangers. January 1848: Henry Tackrell, twelve, a 'diminutive urchin' with a record of prison and whippings behind him, is in the dock at Worship Street. His accuser and prosecutor? His own father.[44]

~

It is a terrible system that metes out such punishment to those so young. But in a way, youth brings its own resilience; a brittle ability to find pleasure in the most meagre of circumstances. As Frank Bullen reflects in later life, 'even if hungry and cold, young things will try to play'. William Brown joins in with the chimney sweeps' jig: the dirtiest boys in the capital 'adorn' themselves with paper gilt, and dance to the clatter of shovel and brush. Later, he plays pitch-ha'penny – a throwing game – and tricks another boy out of sixpence. Gaining another five pence for selling a catskin, he uses his stake to challenge grown men to the same game. But not just any men: the inmates of a venereal ward. So good is he at the game, that when 'I had half a hat full of copper at least, the men were so enraged on my leaving them, that they threw shoes, hats, &c., at me' – though he does not state whether he has the presence of mind to make off with these items too.

George Acorn's favoured pastime involves the hats themselves:

> Sometimes those of us who possessed caps placed them in a heap in the road, and then, forming a circle by joining hands, would pull this way and that until one of us was forced to kick the heap; whereupon the defaulter left the circle, which thus diminished until one was proclaimed victor.

John Munday knows a better game. At night, the streets are ill-lit, patrolled by beadles, a dangerous place for a child. All the better, it heightens the atmosphere:

> [T]he principal game we used to play at in those days was Nick, Nick, strike a light; one of us used to carry a flint and steel and had a little [head]start, and at the corner of every street he turned down he had to strike his flint, so that we could see which way he had gone and so be able to catch him if we could, and the one who caught him was Nick for the next game.

Easy to imagine the delicious terror of the game, chasing a red sparking will-o'-the-wisp down dark alleyways. Round the corner, you might catch your friend – or someone else might just catch you.[45]

Best of all is the life of the mind. Our boys are bright, and – unlike many of their fellows – they learn their letters quickly. George Acorn, whose abusive father drives him to crime and the streets, also finds his way to a much-thumbed edition of *David Copperfield*, which he reads aloud to his illiterate parents. 'The tears united us, deep in misery as we were ourselves. Dickens was a fairy musician to us, filling our minds with a sweeter strain than the constant cry of hunger.' It is a kind of reconciliation.

Frank Bullen, blistered and sore-backed from running errands, is feeling his way to a secret realm in which he can escape his:

> dull, hard, monotonous life ... I occasionally got hold of a copy of the 'Boys of England,' 'The Young Briton,' or the 'Sons of Britannia,' among the waste-paper we used for linings, and lost myself in the realms of romance with 'Caradoc the Briton,' 'Alone in the Pirate's Lair,' or the 'Young Centurion,' [which] supplied the place of pleasant companions and of kind words, and were in a great measure educational – at any rate, they were all the schooling in one sense that I had.[46]

Our boys are, strange to say, the lucky ones, those whose ready grasp of and greed for learning helps them not only survive the streets, but tell the tale. Bullen, no romantic, is ready to leave: he has tasted freedom, and found it bitter. 'I was like a homeless dog, ready to fawn upon any possible proprietor, and gladly give up my hated freedom for the certainty of continuous employment.' He is merciless in his self-analysis, clear that, for him, the only way is out – at almost any price:

> I felt that I could not hold my own in the rough and tumble life of the streets much longer, and I craved with all my heart and soul for a master. I know that there are boys who, even in good

homes, have the nomad instinct so strongly implanted that they cannot be contented anywhere, will endure, nay, embrace voluntarily all kinds of privation, so long as they may vagabondise, but I was not one of them ... I longed for a home, and to have some one in authority over me[.][47]

Thus exits Frank Bullen, to a life more ordinary – by the standards of the steady, respectable world he is ready to join. He will go on to become a ship's mate; a clerk; a successful travel writer and lecturer. For now, his choice is to submit to authority. But it is not a choice that many make. For others, their bodies a palimpsest of overwritten bruises, every encounter a lesson learned, their games and reading all good experience, the path is not submission. These boys are growing up. They are even flourishing.

~

Although – as George Acorn makes clear – our boys are familiar with Dickens, it would be wrong to take them for so many Oliver Twists. No accident of birth is going to save them, nor is their growth necessarily upright and upstanding. The lessons George Acorn learns from Jimmy Braid are uncompromising: 'You'll never be a man or the captain of a click unless you don't *blinking* well swear'. Charles Humphreys, last seen trying to shake off the influence of his hated father, is quick to learn obsequiousness in his new job attending a horse trough: he makes much of the cabmen's horses, he bows and scrapes, and 'very modestly' puts out his hand for tips. 'By this means I made money rather fast.' And if modesty is a form of performance, so is showing off. 1843, and Henry Jones, a boy accused of begging, is up before the magistrate at Marlborough Street. Not only does he get off, he is given a shilling in view of his extreme destitution. Eager 'to show his gratitude' – and, just as probably, to assert his talent as well as his poverty – Henry boasts there and then that he will:

> favour the worthy magistrate with a specimen of his performances and his vocal powers. No sooner said than done. In an instant he was standing on his head in the dock, striking his feet together, and had commenced [the American minstrel song] 'Jim along Josey,' when he was, amidst peals of laughter (in which the bench joined), removed from the court.[48]

Even the dread court room can be a temporary stage for a talented boy. But even so, Henry Jones is not a patch on young Edmund Kean. No one is.

When last we saw him, Kean was moonlighting in public houses. And now he's pulled another fast one, escaping his guardians for long enough to join Abraham Saunders' troupe as they visit Bartholomew Fair, held – as it has been since the year 1133 – in West Smithfield. Here, in front of the crowd that he has always known would be his, he is in his element. Twelve years old, he draws on everything the streets can teach a boy: to bend, to climb, to duck – but also to perform, to command attention. Here again is his monkey impression – his nightingale's serenade – his Tom Thumb. And at last, we see him teetering atop 'a ladder balanced on a man's chin, [from which he] surveys the spectators from the top with a countenance expressive of anything but a sense of the insecurity of his position'. As he leans out over London, master of the throng, I can't help thinking that he looks – a hundred years too soon – remarkably alike to Peter Pan.[49]

~

It is here that we leave Kean, bound for greatness (see Image 2.1). Thanks to his genius – and, let's be honest, his unparalleled theatrical connections – he will go on to be one of the greatest Shakespearian actors of the century, perhaps of any century. But for the boys who remain, there is business left unfinished.

Little Thomas Holcroft, bashful, beaten, weak of stomach, has been entrusted with a task. For some time now he has 'trotted after' his mother as she hawks gewgaws through the streets of London. 'I might at first perhaps feel some disgust at this employment: but use soon reconciled me to it, as the following anecdote will shew.' He has earned the right to tell it in his own words:

> I was either encouraged, or commanded, one day to go by myself, from house to house, and beg. Young as I was, I had considerable readiness in making out a story, and on this day, my little inventive faculties shone forth with much brilliancy. I told one story at one house, another at another, and continued to vary my tale just as the suggestions arose: the consequence of which was, that I moved the good ... people exceedingly. One called me a poor fatherless child: another exclaimed, what a pity! I had so much sense! A third patted my head, and prayed God to preserve me, that I might make a good man. And most of them contributed either by scraps of meat, farthings, bread and cheese, or other homely offers, to enrich me, and send me away with my pockets loaded. I joyfully brought as much of my stores as I could carry, to the place of rendezvous my parents had appointed, where I astonished them by again reciting the false tales I had so readily invented.

Gauche as he is, even young Thomas has found out how to make his way in the streets. A little learning and a glib tongue can combine to turn drawbacks – physical frailty, youth, shabbiness – into assets, props, like the mewling babies of the last chapter.

Yet Thomas's facility for falsehood is also troubling:

> My father, whose passions were easily moved, felt no little conflict
> of mind as I proceeded ... 'God bless the boy! I never heard
> the like!' Then turning to my mother, he exclaimed with great
> earnestness – 'This must not be! the poor child will become a
> common place liar! A hedge-side rogue! – He will learn to pilfer!
> – Turn a confirmed vagrant! – Go on the high way when he is
> older, and get hanged. He shall never go on such errands again.'[50]

Thomas, who obeys, remains touchingly (or troublingly, depending
on your perspective) loyal to this father throughout, defending
his mood swings and bouts of hypocrisy. This ability to forgive is
Thomas's victory. Others go further.

John Munday – fugitive, rough sleeper – has been his uncle's
enemy ever since the latter sent his brothers to the workhouse. Now
one of those brothers, 'the next youngest', has:

> ... died in the workhouse, and they sent me word that if someone
> did not come and own the body it would be sent away for dissec-
> tion. So I sent for an uncle that was living at Smithfield; I would
> not send to the one who ran after me, for I had done with such
> as him altogether.

At this ultimate moment, it is the boy, now a teenager, who takes
responsibility, and the perfidious uncle is disowned. He has lost
both parents and a brother (inside and subservient, remember,
while John has taken his chances on the streets), but within what
remains of his family, he has begun to take charge.

1862, and Charles Humphreys, now aged eleven, has left home
and his father's resented influence for ever. He has graduated from
flattering cabbies at the horse trough, and now makes a tidy profit
by stealing corn from stables and selling it on. One evening, he

runs into his father in a public house. Though one is eleven and the other a man, it is hard to tell who is the worse for wear – the working day is long, and each has had a drink or two. Charles's father, grown maudlin, asks, 'Don't you love your father?' Charles – if we take his word for it – replies:

> 'No blessed fear, and never shall again. A man who will tell another man to give me a b[loody] good hiding, I have no use for him as long as I live.' This sobered him, and he soon went off without saying good-night.[51]

Perhaps, in reality, Charles's eloquence was less pat. But the strength of feeling, the striking note of independence, rings true. Grown in mind and body, provoked beyond endurance, even the most timid may strike a blow for freedom.

I have said that these boys are not to be taken for Oliver Twists. But this final moment puts that resolution to the test. We are with John James Bezer one last time – as a child. Recovered from his illness and still working for his old master, it is now his mother who has fallen desperately sick. John James is at breaking point, while:

> Master's tyranny became more and more insupportable ... In the second week of Mother's illness, I was sent to Mile-end Road with a parcel, and as we then lived in High-street, Mile End New Town, close by, nature predominated over my fear of offending, and I came home; it was thought Mother would not live an hour. I stayed [with her] that hour, and yet she breathed – and I ran back with quick step but heavy heart.
>
> 'What has made you so long, sir?' [said the Master.] I told him the truth, and he *kicked* me! I never remember feeling so strong,

either in mind or body, as I did at that degrading moment; I threw the day-book at him with all my might, and before he could recover his presence of mind, sprang on the counter, and was at his throat. I received some good hard knocks, which I returned, – if not with equal force, – with equal willingness, crying, 'Oh, if my poor Father were here,' – 'I'll tell Father' – 'I'll go to the Lord Mayor' – 'I'll tell everybody.' The tustle didn't last long, and the result was that we gave each other warning; and I, nothing daunted, threatened to stand outside the street door, and create a crowd by telling every one as they passed all about it; – whilst he threatened, in his turn, to give me into custody for tearing his waistcoat and assaulting him, saying I should get into Newgate Closet [i.e. Prison] before I died.[52]

The similarities with Oliver, throwing himself at Noah Claypole for insulting Twist's mother, are hard to ignore. The surprise attack, the invective, the direful threats of a bad end. And clearly, the adult Bezer hands us his memory in Dickens's shadow. But if our memoir writers are indebted to fiction for their style, our novelists are the more indebted to life for their material.

Young John James, springing at his own 'tyrant' in the late 1820s, is a true Twistian hero *avant la lettre*, and while his literary counterpart is bested, locked up, thrashed, disgraced, Bezer comes out of his own uprising unbowed, appealing to a street full of witnesses: it is the making of him, and a fit start for a child who will become a rebel in the cause of democracy. What are a few 'hard knocks' to a boy who's been through what John James has been through, when set against the knowledge that he can answer back – that he can fight back? He might even win.

3

The Girl

December 30 1862: the last knockings of a grim year. Probably the date matters little to Margaret Cochrane, whose own relationship to time is an unstable one. She thinks – she *says* – she is fourteen, and the scepticism with which this claim is met must irk her. But most days are alike to Margaret, who, like George Ruby, knows a single job: she sweeps a crossing.

For hours at a time, her world narrows to a whirling tunnel, a constant churn of mud and dirt. Sisyphean, she sees her labours undone by the minute, so thick is the traffic in this most prestigious of crossing places. 'She sweeps a path from King Charles's statue to Spring Gardens; the densest part of the wide throng of hurrying carriages.' This is the heart of heaving Charing Cross, the southern apex of Trafalgar Square where the vehicles of the Strand and Cockspur Street funnel down to Whitehall – the point where, 160 years later, mass demonstrations bound for Parliament Square will continue to congest and stutter. A prime spot, this, and potentially lucrative because those who cross are *meant* to tip. But also dangerous.

The idea of a crossing sweeper might suggest monotony, drudgery, even idleness. But the reality is rather different:

She plies her daring broom under the wheels, which bespatter her with mire as they fly; she dodges under the horses' heads, and is ever ready to conduct the timid lady or nervous old gentleman through the perils of the crossing; she is wet through her thin clothing when it rains; she is in the street all day, the lowest and least protected of that roaring buffeting crowd.

Margaret not only cleans, but is lollipop lady, lifeguard – and all at great personal risk. The job requires keen senses, working together; good peripheral vision; sharp reflexes. Small wonder that, when asked if she intends to stick with this job that, already, she has held 'for several years', her considered response is, '"No Sir – I think I shall take to selling oranges when I grow up."'[1]

In earlier decades – and in some backwaters still – a crossing might be a job for life. But in the thrum and rattle of the Victorian city, it takes the nimbleness – and disregard for risk – of a child, girl or boy.[2] When she started out, Margaret Cochrane might as well have been either. Now, however, people are starting to notice that she is a girl. Her interlocutor for one.

Arthur Munby, whose diary is the only place in which Margaret's sweeping days survive, could not be more Victorian. He is respectable, opinionated, inquisitive – inquisitive, in particular, where lower-class females are concerned. I'd rather not give too much of the limelight to this undeniably fascinating man, who marries his housekeeper, and whose diary is bursting with descriptions of a certain kind of well-muscled, callus-handed woman. We will meet him in this chapter more often than coincidence allows, because his private peccadillo is so representative of a century that liked to look at girls and women. Right now, he is looking at Margaret Cochrane:

[S]he is a wellgrown and really pretty girl; with a delicate complexion and refined features and bright eyes: her mudstained frock and bonnet are neat, though shabby; and even in her dirt she is attractive, as she drops you a quiet curtsy and says 'Please Sir', holding out her hand and leaning on her wellworn broom ... She says she is but fourteen, but she looks much older – quite a young woman, indeed.

It is hard to read this without inferring a leer behind the words. Her features itemised, assessed. Her conduct, her deference judged. Margaret is an adolescent girl, working on the streets. The male gaze is becoming not merely an unwelcome aspect of her working life, but that life's first and ruling principle.[3]

~

On a wet November evening some years later, Bridget – a girl a year or two younger than Margaret Cochrane – is caught in the rain, an abject specimen, literally almost frozen in the attitude that best suits the sentimental literary stylings of Thomas Barnardo (yes, him again). Yet though he waxes lyrical on her soggy state – 'Her thin dress, showing great rents here and there, was as wet as though she and it had been dipped bodily in a pond and then allowed to stand up and drip' – Barnardo has to admit that Bridget is generally doing rather well. She is:

a bright-eyed, merry, independent Irish girl – Irish by blood rather than by birth, for, having been born in Whitechapel, of Irish parents, Bridget was really a Cockney. But she was a blithe little lass, and held her head as high as any of the numerous youngsters who tried to pick up a living upon the streets.

The Girl

Neither orphan nor newcomer to the city, Bridget is hardly crying out to be rescued. Yes, she has left home, her mother being violent, but she has made 'a home for herself in a common lodging-house in Wentworth Street, Whitechapel'. In fact, Barnardo seems to be struggling to make a case for even a soaking-wet Bridget as an object of sympathy – a difficulty that makes it likelier that 'Bridget' has a real existence beyond Barnardo's pamphlet:

> She loved what she termed her 'freedom,' she liked to go hither and thither, free and unrestrained. And after a fashion of their own, the acquaintances she made upon the streets were kind to her, perhaps won by her bright spirits.

These characteristics are real assets in her trade of selling newspapers:

> Bridget was a general favourite among those who knew her. Her pert, witty rejoinders, bright looks, and bold spirit won her many friends; and it was remarked that she generally got through her morning papers before any of the other girls or boys who stood about the same part of the city. I have myself seen her on a fine forenoon surrounded in Exchange Alley by a number of clerks and passers-by, who quickly purchased all the papers she had, and sent her off singing with delight and laden with the harvest of coppers so quickly reaped.

Curiously, it may be that Arthur Munby too has met Bridget, or at least a girl who is her equal. On 6 March 1860, he:

> bought a copy of the 'Standard' of a sharp dirtyfaced little girl who plies there among the boys, selling, as they do, the penny papers, running with her freight after the omnibuses, or calling

'Star!' 'Telegraph!' from the kerb stone. The creature is a perfect 'gamin', and carries off the trade from her male companions – rivals rather – by her superior quickness. With her bundle of papers under her arm, she rapidly counted out the halfpence into my hand, and then, saying 'Thankyer Sir', she did not curtsy, but 'touched her hat' smartly and made a leg [bowed], as the street boys do.[4]

Whether this second girl is Bridget or not, she knows her stuff, and prospers. But on the rainy day that Barnardo describes, he makes much of Bridget's unusual failure to sell her quota in the inclement conditions. Even so, it transpires that her good standing in the business allows her to obtain new stock on credit, so that one bad day is no disaster. "'Oh!" she explained, "some of the chaps about here as I knows on, lent me the ha'pence for half a quire"".* Bridget, in short, might rival for assurance and success any of the boys who made it through the vicissitudes of the last chapter. Only, she isn't a boy. And this is Barnardo's entire motivation.

Noting that Bridget rents a room in a 'common lodging-house', Barnardo launches into what seems at first like a digression, but in fact forms his entire argument for the need to 'rescue' her:

Often have I seen in such places, girls of fourteen, or even of barely thirteen years of age, who seemed to have long before begun an abandoned career, and who have explained in answer to my expostulations, 'What better could you expect, sir, brought up in a place like this?' A poor child of fourteen, whose younger sister I was fortunately able to save in time, assured me that *she*

---

* A 'quire' is a printer's term referring, in this usage, to a number of news-sheets – potentially twenty-four or twenty-five.

had been drawn into the practice of the worst vices when she was but ten years old.

For all his sensationalism, Barnardo is describing a genuine and pressing problem, a preoccupation of the second half of the century. What he fails to grasp is the extent to which he, Munby and all the others like them, are culpable, so long as they persist in looking at perfectly happy, self-reliant, competent young girls, and seeing only the problem of sex.[5]

The worst of it is that we must do the same. Or, put another way: we are incapable of hearing girls' stories as we do those of boys. Though both come down to us almost entirely as recorded by grown men, the crucial difference is that, in the case of boys, those grown men were often their later selves, writing their memoirs. We do not have those autobiographies where girls are concerned, and all those details of growing up, playing, learning, wreaking havoc, are lost, victims of historical indifference.[6] Tales of male adolescence are, interestingly, far scarcer than those of boyhood – having grown up fast, the teenage years of our boys are in some ways less distinctive, a simple coming into maturity, settling into the default social role of manhood. By contrast, the lives of girls suddenly begin to interest those on whom we are dependent for our sources when they reach the age at which we leave our boys – thirteen or fourteen, like Margaret Cochrane. But mostly, they are of interest for a single reason. The historical record *forces* us to engage with the street lives of teenage girls as circumscribed by gender prejudice.

This is an uncomfortable position to be in. Faced with an avalanche of prurient, prostitution-focused literature, the immediate response is to push back; to ask, what else? How good it would be to champion the unheard experiences of girls who were *only* cress sellers, crossing sweepers, singers, thieves. But we can't, because no one gave a damn. And it would be, in part, to miss the point – for in a world so in thrall to its sexist assumptions, not even the most innocent of occupations or the youngest of girls was free of that taint. Not the eight-year-old cress seller of Mayhew's *London Labour and the London Poor*. Not the six-year-old ballad singer M. McG (Mary McGrath?) who the Mendicity Society fear without foundation will be used by her mother 'for the worst of purposes'.[7] Not every single good-looking girl described euphemistically in one of a thousand charity reports as 'interesting'. Not the jolliest of flower-sellers – just try being a girl offering something sweet and beautiful for sale on the street, its nectar secreted within unfolding petals et cetera, et cetera. And certainly not agile Margaret or popular Bridget, both busy getting on with making their living while nosy gentlemen frown and squint, brows knitted in altruistic concern, as they guess at the curves beneath the buttoned-up jacket.

As the historian Carolyn Steedman writes of Mayhew, who interviewed that young cress seller, 'She puzzled him: she repelled him: he felt attraction towards her. For him she was a child, and not-a-child; and something else.'[8] So it was, not just for Munby and Barnardo, but for thousands of men encountering girls in public – men who could be customers, irritants, hazards, friends – but who could never, for a vulnerable girl, be merely insignificant.

Sex was not the only profession for a girl on the street – indeed, it was only ever a minority occupation – but it came into almost everything. So that, whether or not a girl's adolescence featured so much as the faintest brush with actual sex work, her teenage years were, by necessity, a story of coming to terms with the male gaze and with male judgement. It was a life of permanent exposure, encounter, negotiation. Whereas the young boy's journey is towards a place where he can fend for himself, the girl's is more a case of fending *off*; of learning how to move and speak under constant surveillance; of simply dealing with men. And, if nothing else, we can at least do justice to this journey, and try to keep up as these girls attempt to survive in a London that is made of a thousand eyes.

~

Already, we have felt the burn of three eminent pairs of eyes: Munby's, Barnardo's and Mayhew's. They are as nothing to those of Henry Spencer Ashbee, the probable (but disputed) author of an interminable collection of Victorian pornographic literature, *My Secret Life*, that presents a litany of purportedly real sexual encounters, spanning much of the mid-nineteenth century. This memoir is almost certainly fiction, but it seems cribbed from all kinds of more accurate material, and while none of its episodes are exactly real, they are unparalleled in capturing the sordid dilemmas of the moment in the street when a man looks at a woman – or, in many cases, at a girl.[9]

While few male gazes can have been quite so relentless as that of *My Secret Life*'s monomaniacal narrator 'Walter', his interior monologue makes plain the predicament faced by the girl in the street. Here he is among costermongers:

> As I passed I saw a small girl standing inside the door of a house, and thought I would like the little one ... She took no notice of me, I repassed, and there she still stood. 'Is she gay?* I wondered, 'she does not look it.' Lots of girls and women not gay stood in a similar manner in those streets.

---

* 'Gay' being slang for a prostitute – 'on the game' is a close parallel.

Here he is again:

> On a cold evening ... I saw a shortish, dark-eyed girl going along
> the Strand. She walked slowly, and looked in at almost every
> shop. I could not make up my mind if she was gay or not. She was
> warmly wrapped up, her style that of a well-to-do servant. I passed
> and repassed her, looked her in the face; her eye met mine and
> dropped, then she stopped and looked round several times after
> unmistakably gay women as they passed her, then went on again.
> Opposite the Adelphi she paused and looked at the theatre for a
> long time, a gentleman spoke to her, and seemed to importune
> her, she took no notice of him, and he left her. After walking on
> for a minute quickly she loitered and looked in the shops again.

And on a third occasion:

> One night towards the end of November in Leicester Square, I
> accosted a lass who looked between fifteen and sixteen years old.
> She was walking very fast, and I was not quite sure whether she
> was on the town or not, but know that girls out by themselves at
> that time of night more frequently than otherwise get their cunts
> filled for love or money, before they get home.[10]

When we are done shuddering, we can reflect. 'Walter's' gaze is
one of constant enquiry and assessment. The instant he looks at a
girl, any girl, a relationship is created that quivers with ambiguity.
While some prostitutes are 'unmistakable', young girls in particular
attract his attention, not because of conscious signals of attitude
or attire, but simply because they are young and female. Within
the frame of My Secret Life, the first of these three proves to be a
prostitute; the second, an honest but impoverished servant with

an ill mother, is nonetheless cajoled into sex for a sovereign (he promises to pull out, but doesn't); the third is allowed to pass by, molested only in thought.

While this is partly a self-evident instance of *plus ça change* – the dynamic remains a depressingly familiar one – there is a historical specificity here that intensifies the situation, and it is not merely the fact that prostitution was rife. It starts with dress. One might think, bearing in mind the depressingly persistent view that 'revealing' clothing is a signal of availability, that there is a historical corollary – pragmatic rather than ideal – whereby conservative attire might serve as protection from the male gaze. And yes, this was a society that was 'awash with clothing and "clothing aware" in a way that would not have been the case in, say, 1700'.[11] (On another occasion 'Walter' observes prostitutes who are 'so dressed that I could not offer them a small sum', their sumptuous get-up clearly signalling a correspondingly high fee.)[12]

But a girl could not simply choose her clothing in order to attract or deflect male attention. Partly, this was because there was no absolute line between respectable and suggestive appearance – the dictates of fashion and the desire to emulate others put paid to that – but more importantly, free choice over clothing was a luxury beyond the reach of the street poor. Theirs was an economy of the makeshift, dependent on the pawnshop. The clothes available might not accurately reflect one's trade or status; they might bear the cut – and the signification – of an earlier generation. For those on the streets, the weather was bad enough that the dowdiest, most durable of garments – dun-coloured woollens, leather, stuff, duttle – were in demand by all. And clothes were coveted, not merely for their present function, but for their future resale value: being portable, and infinitely less susceptible to theft than cash (because if you were in this situation, you probably had to sleep in your clothes), clothes were, to a large extent, the chief currency, capital, and petty savings of the very poor.

At the same time, even the poorest cared about their appearance – as we have already seen, it was both a social and a professional necessity – and thus any modicum of display you could afford, a trinket, a flash of linen or lace at cuff or collar, would bolster your self-esteem; and any shapeless, worthy clothing handed out by a charity (with the exception of a good pair of boots) might be scorned as a mark of shame and dependency.

All of which made the policing of modesty and sexual availability by means of dress a minefield of chance, confusion and interpretation, especially in the case of the poorest. A society that persisted in summing people up at a glance was dealing with an underclass incapable of conforming to those codes. While this affected men and women of all ages, it posed the greatest problem for adolescent girls, whose age, sex and looks were grounds for attraction, suspicion, interest on all sides, which they could not easily counteract.[13] And while the consequences of public encounters were of supreme importance for all of the street poor, it was the girl emerging from childhood who ran the greatest risks – to her person and to her reputation.

The streets of London were a dangerous place for a young girl, and prostitution in particular was a grim bargain to strike – it could be demeaning, even deadly. But if we go too far, we risk making the same mistakes as the better sort of Victorian writer. While some dismissed prostitutes as abandoned, wanton, deserving everything they got, others showed compassion and concern. But at the same time, they reduced the 'fallen' girl to everything that word implies: helpless, vulnerable, above all, a *victim*.

As Judith Walkowitz and many other scholars have argued so eloquently over recent decades, this is an idea we should resist.[14] Yes, the odds were stacked against them – but street girls were far from helpless. I want to follow four cases in particular when, with varying degrees of success, girls rose to the challenge of controlling their own narratives, reshaping the street as a place where they held the power.[15]

~

Monday, 10 June 1844, and once again, a child is missing. Elizabeth Meade, four years old, lives with her parents, Michael and Mary, and her aunt and uncle, Elizabeth and James, at 53 Eagle Street, an obscure alley just south of Red Lion Square, Bloomsbury, dominated by the malodorous Day and Martin blacking factory.[16] At least, she did until five o'clock this evening, when her aunt and namesake Elizabeth, who is on childminding duty, turns to the girl – and finds her gone. It will be five anxious days until the child is restored to them, more or less unharmed.

But this is not young Elizabeth's story. Instead, we follow the girl who takes her: Emily Lewis, herself aged just fourteen. That afternoon, Emily and an unnamed friend have trekked the three miles south from Chalk Farm Fields – a bucolic outskirt beyond Camden, nestling in the lea of Primrose Hill – into the heart of Holborn. She is clearly an intrepid girl: 53 Eagle Street is within earshot of the headquarters of the Mendicity Society, a mere fifty metres off around the corner, and why she should venture into this heartland of an organisation dedicated to the suppression of begging is a mystery; presumably, she knows no better.

Yet here she is, and she takes her chance. Seeing an unguarded child, and perhaps egged on by her anonymous companion, she lures away Elizabeth Meade, just as Ann Lee enticed the Moseleys' daughter a generation earlier. And it's back north, out of enemy territory, two girls with their prize, bound for the relative safety of Chalk Farm Fields. Past the kempt square lawns around University

College, and up along the new-laid railway route that leads out of Euston, the tracks on their right, the barracks and mansions that fringe Regent's Park at their left. By the time they cross Regent's Canal, the houses have thinned, giving on to open country, newly in the throes of being colonised by optimistic builders and railway companies. The air is clearer here, and the girls can breathe easy. The three of them bed down for the night under a hedge and rise with the dew, cold and nervous. Time for stage two.

Over the next few days, Emily Lewis makes the most of Elizabeth Meade. Though her friend, perhaps getting cold feet, abandons her at dusk on the Tuesday, Emily keeps hold of the little girl, and begins to weave her story. In fact, it is the runaway companion who starts the fiction, which Emily will keep up on her own. We are wise by now to the role that infants play in begging, as half-orphan of war or industrial accident— but wait. Emily is fourteen. It won't wash; no one will believe her if she claims to have been legally married and widowed at her age. She *could* claim to be the child's sister, but that's thin stuff, suggesting a parent in the background, it doesn't appeal to Emily's sense of the dramatic. No, the story they concoct is this: 'that she had been seduced by a gentleman living in Berkley-square [sic], and the child belonged to her'. It's a staggering lie to tell. And Emily runs with it for several days, trying it out on male servants and men of business. She takes her friend's desertion in her stride.

It is not until Thursday that disaster strikes. Emily has been hanging around Primrose Hill, presumably because its leafy villas and picturesque atmosphere, at the height of summer, attract the sort of affluent idler who might be moved by her tale. On Thursday, crossing a fence, she sees a woman she has met the day before – Jane Plumridge – and asks her to hold little Elizabeth while she hops over. As Jane recalls, the infant 'was then walking, and came to me – she smacked it – I said, "Don't hit the child, it don't know

any better" – she said, "It is my child, and I must teach it better"'.
Walking on, they meet a man, who comes up to Emily and says,
'"The mother of that child is looking after [i.e., for] you"'.

Jane does a double take. 'You told me that was your child', she
says.

Caught out and forced to improvise, Emily thinks of her friend,
who started the fiction. '"I said it was my sister's child"', is the best
she can manage.

The writing is on the wall – quite literally. James, the child's
uncle, has had bills printed and posted about town. Jane
Plumridge, who goes off lost in thought, sees one of these posters
and joins the dots. Her first action is to try and find Emily and
Elizabeth, who are nowhere to be seen. Curiously, Jane looks for
the girls in 'Church-lane, where I had seen her in bed with the
child in the morning', suggesting perhaps that Emily's takings
have been enough to rent a bed in a shared room – not exactly
luxury, but better than an open hedgerow. But Emily knows the
game is up, and – belatedly – has fled the area. Jane, mindful of
the poster, hastens to Eagle Street with her news.

On Friday, 14 June, Emily is caught, arrested by police constable
Thomas Vickers. Unaccountably, she has returned to Chalk Farm,
where she is known – but without the infant Elizabeth. As she is
empty-handed, she is confident enough to protest her innocence.
But as the constable, unmoved, escorts her to the station, her brittle
self-assurance crumbles. Coming clean, she admits to PC Vickers,
'"We took the child with the intention of stripping it of its clothes,
and pawning them, and going into the country, begging."'

Confronted with the child's uncle James, she begins to deny
everything once again – and then gives in, confessing that 'she
left it in Bury-street that morning'. Emily spends the night in the
cells, and next day, Elizabeth is found wandering the Tottenham

Court Road, taken to St Pancras workhouse (the grim prison, remember, of Robert Blincoe), and there she is finally reunited with her family.

When the case comes up before the Old Bailey a few weeks later, Emily sees where she has gone wrong. There is Jane Plumridge, telling all. And there too are the men she has attempted to hoodwink: William Scott, George Sinder, men who have spotted her with and without her companion, heard the inconsistencies in the story – which is the mother, which the sister? – and have smelled the rat. Defeated, Emily clings to her only possible defence – 'It was not me that stole the child, it was the other girl' – a girl who is neither present, nor even named. It looks bleak for Emily. Except that her *real* sister, Sarah Burlton, a respectable married woman, gives her a good character. And something about Emily – her youth, her personal charm, her sheer pitiable helplessness? – has moved the jury, who recommend mercy. The verdict comes in as Judgement Respited. To all intents and purposes, Emily has got off.[17]

~

Beyond its sensational headlines, it is the detail of Emily Lewis's case that is really compelling. It all hinges on that desperate, theatrical fabrication: the cad in Berkeley Square, then, as now, one of London's most salubrious addresses – the aristocratic deflowerer of a shockingly young maiden mercilessly abandoned to the shameful consequence. The strangest thing is that there is the merest possibility that the story was founded on a real experience: on the Thursday night, knowing she was rumbled, Emily fled Chalk Farm for Bury Street, which is in St James's, a stone's throw from Berkeley Square and a surprisingly genteel neighbourhood for a vagabond's refuge. In all probability, she knew of a den, brothel or cheap lodging house of the sort that crops up even amid exalted addresses, but there's just a glimmer of a hidden connection to a mysterious gentleman.

It is far more likely, however, that Emily and her erstwhile accomplice took their inspiration from what they had heard, seen on stage or – if they had received a basic schooling – even read. Mid-century London was awash with accounts of ruined maidens, decoyed and debauched in deceptively genteel surroundings. Many of these, and the most probable influences on young Emily, were fictional, and it is these stories that feature the most exaggerated plotlines, with West End addresses and aristocratic seducers. But there were more than enough true reports in circulation to make Emily's story, if not convincing, then at least halfway plausible.

1808: Mary Stansfield, eighteen, is dying in poverty in Church Lane, St Giles's. Her story gets out, and the Benevolent Society transfer her to the workhouse, before locating her estranged mother in Oldham, more than 200 miles away. Before mother and daughter can be reunited, Mary Stansfield dies 'in apparent tranquillity [sic]', leaving behind only her cautionary tale, for publication in the Society's annual report.

In service at sixteen, she is seduced by a gentleman and taken to Dublin, where she falls for good, losing her health and place, before begging her way to London, where she sells matches in the street, aided by her 'fine figure, but emaciated appearance', which 'excited compassion'. A cautionary tale to all young servant girls – one among many.

Indeed, by 1839, the Society for the Prevention of Juvenile Prostitution has its hands full. Among the many they try to save are two fifteen-year-olds: Mary Anne Clark, a newcomer from Hampshire, and Maria Scoggins, a stay maker. Both are seduced, ruined 'and turned upon the streets'. There they are each discovered – hospitalised – placed in asylums.

Another girl, described in an institutional report of 1849, arrives in London, aged seventeen, and makes the mistake of trusting two women she meets:

> Next morning she awoke and found her clothes and money gone; and soon after an old man was introduced to her, who violated her. Others were introduced, until she was overtaken by disease, and ... died in Bartholomew's Hospital. This incident gave rise to the formation of 'The London Society for the Protection of Young Females'.[18]

On 10 February 1859, Arthur Munby is walking in St James's Park – the salubrious West End of Emily Lewis's story – when he spies a man, whom he takes to be a 'foreigner', 'talking to [a] respectable looking girl, trying to seduce her to some brothel – exit without success. She a servant, aged 18, just run away from her place by reason of ill-treatment: didn't know London – didn't know what to do.' He tries to help her – roping in a policeman to avoid the obvious suspicion – and offers to put her up in a coffee house. He gets her name, Louisa Flatman, but nothing else; she never takes up his offer, and he fears the worse. 'So much for her' is his pessimistic conclusion.[19]

Hundreds of these cases, more or less salacious, are published in the reports of various well-meaning societies. They know what they are doing – it's compelling material, and whether readers are titillated or shocked (or more probably both), it might help increase donations and awareness. The cases enter the Victorian zeitgeist, and – since even the illiterate poor can be well informed, and have control over the shape of the stories they tell – they form the stuff from which tales like Emily Lewis's are concocted.[20] She presents herself as a complex sort of victim, trading on her youth and looks to make her purported plight – in the parlance of the day – more 'interesting'. It's a bold tactic, predicated on the idea that she will be pitied, rather than blamed, for her seduction.

William Greg, the influential mid-century author of *The Great Sin of Great Cities*, summed up the attitude of many when he conjectured that 'it is in many, probably in most instances, a brutal desire on the one side only, and a reluctant and loathing submission' on the other, and went on to sympathise even with regular prostitutes.[21] It was an attitude built on a thoroughly warped understanding of sexuality – one that couldn't or didn't care to take seriously the concept of female desire – but it might just have worked for Emily, and may be why the witnesses who best remembered her were men. It was men who responded most sympathetically to this sort of outrage, especially if it cast them in the role of the gallant, the saviour.

The decades following Emily's case see London's streetwalkers pestered nightly by well-off, well-meaning gentlemen, offering their services rather than seeking the girls'. Men like Lieutenant John Blackmore, RN, and his friend Edward Thomas, who go hunting after dark on their 'moonlight missions' – so much more romantic-sounding than gaslight – to save the fallen, preach the word, and get them into homes and hostels. It is all doubtless nobly motivated, but it is hard to read their accounts without noticing how the girls they focus on are invariably 'interesting', 'dressed in a superior style', 'very genteel', 'very well-dressed', 'of very prepossessing appearance' – always in some way differentiated from those 'of the lowest class', who hold no attraction for these refined rescuers.

Once again, we must remember that acts of 'charity' in this period tended to come loaded with catches, with the weight of unconscious prejudice, or both. And so, inevitably, the girls' words of gratitude cast their saviours in an excellent light, while those who do come away with them very often die, in the best tradition of fallen heroines, as soon as they have repented their sins.

Nonetheless, some of the exchanges the men record are fascinating. Blackmore journeys to Temple Bar, where 'Some of the miserable women here also, on learning our errand, expressed astonishment that any cared for them, and could scarcely believe us sincere.' He endeavours to rescue 'a young Jewess', whose one objection is that the dress she wears is the property of the brothel keeper, and fears that she will 'be taken into custody on the charge of stealing it'. Near Charing Cross, he waxes lyrical to one girl on the subject of Jesus Christ. She replies, 'Oh, yes, I know all that, Sir; but I am really very hungry.' An associate known only as 'J La. T' (perhaps the Irish aristocrat John La Touche) addresses various girls in the Haymarket. One rips up the tract he presses upon her 'with a laugh of mockery'. A second, apparently conflicted, cries, 'Do not be my tormentor!' A third, most eloquent of all, declares, 'I never think – I am afraid to think!'[22]

~

Humility and pathos can play well as tactics. Which of us, in Arthur Munby's position, would not be cut to the heart by Caroline Randall, nineteen, encountered in Victoria Street on 4 January 1867? The streets are 'one sheet of snow, with paths trodden but not swept'; there is a 'thick brown fog'; and Caroline 'has no home' – she 'slept last night on a step in a sheltered corner; & felt "as cold as a frog", she said'. Her plight is one thing, the phrase she finds to express it quite another – and it is those well-chosen words, 'as cold as a frog', that retain their power 150 years later.[23]

Artless or calculated, Caroline Randall's words do their work, creating the connection on which sympathy and charity – the complex negotiation of deference, supplication, condescension – rely. Confronted with a potential benefactor, the girl in the streets *needs* to disarm in this way, because the transaction is far from innocuous: the passer-by feels obliged; the onus on them – however satisfying in retrospect – creates a tension that the girl, ever vulnerable, must defuse.[24]

And while this is the case for all beggars, it becomes much more fraught once sex is in the mix. Venturing out in cloaks, under gaslights, the crusading Lieutenant Blackmore and his fellow adventurers are ready to think the best of these 'genteel' women – but only so long as they live up to his ideals of fallen virtue. It is hard for a girl in the street to play this game for more than a short conversation. As soon as those you are appealing to catch a whiff of a falsehood, the strategy collapses.

Saturday, 14 November 1857: a pair of girls in their late teens, both of them mixed race, are walking the kerbside of Blackman Street. We are in Borough, Southwark: the street is wide, the glass-paned shopfronts are those of successful tradesmen – but it's also a major thoroughfare, and the girls are careful to keep their clean white dresses back from the traffic. They've come out for the evening, trusting to the new streetlights, aiming to capitalise on the crowds going home or heading out. One, the older of the two, holds aloft a placard on which they have written 'Fugitive Slaves'; the other, optimistic, carries a box.

Passers-by stop, fumble in pockets, drop coppers into the box. But their takings have scarcely amounted to a single shilling when a police constable, who has been eyeing them for some time, saunters over. It's all done very quietly, no fuss, no trouble. That same evening, they are up before the bench at Southwark, charged with begging. Mr Combe, presiding, remands them to custody, pending a full enquiry.

What follows becomes a sensation, reported in newspapers across the country. Their case proper comes up before, not Combe, but Mr Burcham, whose feelings will play no small part in their fate. The older of the girls tells their story: they are Americans, born and raised on a slave plantation in Kentucky. Their father died 'about twelve months ago'; their mother was sold to another plantation, far off, and when they too were on the point of being parted for sale, they made their escape. The underground railroad got them to Philadelphia, where 'some free coloured persons' paid their passage across the Atlantic. Arriving in Greenock, Scotland, in the spring of that year, they begged their way to London, where a married labourer named Flynn has been putting them up in a court in Bishopsgate Street, near Spitalfields – they make the rent by selling religious tracts, by which they gain 'a few pence'.

As Mr Burcham points out, it's quite the story. But Constable Hinchcliffe, who first took them in charge, reckons it stands up. Even the two Mendicity Officers, standing by, attest that the girls are not known as beggars. Burcham, either forgetful or sceptical of the money to be made by selling tracts, asks them what they do for a living if they are not beggars. They are domestic servants, the older girl replies – at least, such was their role on the plantation. 'But people objected to them in such situations in this country owing to their colour. They were, however, able to knit gloves.'

Burcham seizes on this. Why, isn't it November, and getting cold? Gloves they shall knit! Yes, your Honour – but we haven't any wool. Good point, good point... and as they seem willing to work, Burcham contributes four shillings from the poor box, to add to the one they have taken, in order to buy wool. That should set them up well. The grateful girls are on the point of leaving when a thought strikes him. As the *Daily News* puts it, he 'earnestly exhorts' them 'not to be led away by bad women' – and to 'avoid the streets of London'.

The *Morning Chronicle* fleshes out the story. Burcham, who is all 'commiseration' for their plight, is mindful that they are strangers in England. He informs them that begging is 'not allowed in this country', and they in their turn thank him 'earnestly for the assistance he had so kindly rendered them in a strange country'. Like Blackmore with his 'genteel' prostitutes, Burcham is ready to think the best of two well-behaved girls; and indeed, the *Chronicle* – which also fixates on their skin colour, reporting that they 'are called in the slave states quadroons, being half-caste' – dubs them 'very fine looking coloured girls ... well conducted, and apparently of good education'. Just the sort, in fact, whom right-thinking men of the era are itching to rescue.

And neither Burcham nor the *Morning Chronicle* is willing to leave the girls there. A week later, the paper resumes the story, now bumped up from the minor 'Police Intelligence' to its own column, under the more sensational headline, 'Fugitive Slave Girls From Kentucky'. They work up the story again from the start: the girls are now described as 'remarkably good-looking' and 'dressed very neatly in light-coloured clothing, such as is usually worn by female slaves in the Southern States of America'. There is some padding about 'an appeal to the kindness of the English people' before we get to the update.

On 23 November, they are back before Burcham in order to show him 'their small stock of knitted caps'. Burcham is happy to inform them that 'he had not only received several small sums for their use, but letters from various persons, some of whom were of high distinction, offering to take care of them and place them in comfortable situations'. But there's a catch. He has also had an anonymous letter – the contents of which are not disclosed to the court – 'which did not speak very highly of their characters'. A new round of questioning begins. Are they still in Bishopsgate?

No, says the older girl, they are now at 'the house of Mr Smith, 101, Wentworth-street, Whitechapel'. But this is not so good: Mr Edwin, the chief clerk, informs Mr Burcham that Wentworth Street is 'full of low lodging-houses' such as Crown Court.

'Do you know Crown Court, Wentworth Street?' asks Burcham.

'Yes, sir; we lodge in a house there, at the back of number 101. We have a room there, and pay half-a-crown a week for it.'

Burcham fears the worst. 'Does anyone else live with you?' Meaning, of course, a man.

'Oh, no, sir.' She sounds shocked at the suggestion.

Next comes a bout of Burcham's old forgetfulness. 'Have you a father and mother in England?' The girl is forced to remind him, 'No, sir. My parents were slaves, and one of them died about eighteen months ago.'

But Burcham has clearly heard something. 'Is there a coloured man living in the same house with you?'

'No, sir; there is a coloured man living in the same court, but he has a wife and large family.' You can almost hear the sigh – *we're not all related, you know.* Quickly, she changes the subject. 'We have knitted some caps, and sold some, and what remains of our stock you can inspect.'

A good move: Burcham loves the caps! Things go more smoothly – but something's still troubling him. 'Do you know the name of the vessel you came from America in?'

'Yes, sir. The brig *Jane.* She left Philadelphia last spring.'

More questions – but the danger seems past. The Mendicity Officer instructed to make a full enquiry has not yet reported, and Burcham is impressed with their industry. He takes another five shillings from the pot, just to tide them over – but they 'might call again' on Monday. It sounds like a polite invitation. It isn't.

Monday comes, and the *Morning Chronicle* is still reporting. It's even bothered to find out the girls' names: the older one, who does the talking, is Rose Avery, aged twenty. Her sister Minnie is eighteen; it's Minnie who actually does the knitting. But despite her best efforts, something is starting to unravel. Attention is drawn to the fact that, 'although apparently very decently brought up, they had no idea of the months, but chiefly counted from the fall and spring of the year'. And though they claim to have 'walked up to London' from Greenock, someone points out that 'they could not say the names of the towns through which they passed'.

Constable Hinchcliffe is still on their side: he's confirmed their lodgings, that they lock up like respectable people, and that the anonymous letter seems unfounded. But Hinchcliffe's superintendent, Mr Branford, has put a Sergeant Baker on the case, while the Mendicity Society are pursuing investigations via a Mr Hewitt. When the girls appear, all of these – and also Mr Ferguson, the Society's chief officer – are in attendance. So much manpower for two poor girls!

Eyeing up the assembled men, Rose, who is 'unwell from a severe cold', makes her move. They have a letter, she says, from a gentleman at Brighton: he offers to employ them both, one as nursemaid to his son, the other in his shop. She hands the letter to Burcham. But this letter is unsigned! Had they seen him?

Yes, says Rose, 'he called at their lodgings that morning, and wanted them to go to Brighton at once' – only this court summons is delaying them.

Burcham frowns and tells her that, if the man comes again, she must bring him to the court. He has the girls' interests at heart and can't see them packed off with an unknown stranger.

It's hard to argue. While, not being their guardian, he has no legal authority, he is nonetheless *the* legal authority. Rose promises to do as he says and adds that two further callers have given them alms – a total of fifteen shillings, which has gone, however, on food and clothes.

Then why, asks Burcham, are their clothes not warmer? Rose's answer is evasive – but it's all right, Burcham is thinking of the money sent in on their behalf, and hands over more to buy warm clothing – they have only to appear again next Monday. And to cap it all, a merchant from New York comes up with fully two pounds, which he gives the constable in order to buy them warm clothes and boots – which he does. Munificence indeed! Though you can't help but think they'd rather have had the money.

It's all gone swimmingly – except for the summons to reappear. The next Monday finds them once again in court at Southwark. And this time, it's the *Morning Chronicle*'s arch-rival, the Tory *Morning Post*, that sends its reporter to the court. Whereas the left-leaning *Chronicle* has championed the girls' cause in line with its wider views on both abolition and social welfare, the *Post* is quite another matter, and it is with relish that they subtitle this item of 'Police Intelligence' as 'The Fugitive Slave Impostors – Extraordinary Deception'. Yes, it's one in the eye for the *Chronicle*, its liberal readers, and that soft-touch magistrate, Mr Burcham.

It turns out that, behind the scenes, the Mendicity Society has been hard at work, and it's their influence that has prevented the majority of the funds sent in from being passed on to Rose and Minnie. And now the carefully knitted fabric of their story is meticulously torn apart. Rose is stated to be cohabiting with 'a black man' at No. 1, not 101, Crown Court. Minnie has an Irish mother in Wentworth Street, and a sick father in the Chelsea workhouse, to whom she has been passing the greater part of the funds given them; she is a Londoner born and bred. All of this Burcham finds 'very extraordinary', clinging to the notion that 'they were not impostors' – but here is a letter from Greenock, reporting that no vessel named *Jane* has docked there in eighteen months. Rose protests. After all, 'There were many vessels named *Jane*'. But Ferguson, the Society's man, steps in: they have searched the port registries. Now, Mr Burcham, the younger girl's parents are here in court, will you question them?

▲ 0.1 John Overton, *The Common Cryes of London*
(*c*.1640). © The Trustees of the British Museum.

2.1 Samuel De Wilde, *Portrait Studies*, detail of Edmund Kean
(1802). Yale Center for British Art, Paul Mellon Collection. ▼

4.1 Adelaide Neilson as Nelly Armroyd in *Lost in London* at the Adelphi Theatre (1867). © Victoria and Albert Museum, London.

5.1 John Thomas Smith,
'Joseph Johnson' (1815).

BILLY WATERS.

Pub.d Nov.r 1 1818. for T.L. Busby by Mess.rs Baldwin. & Co Paternoster Row. & at the Artists Depository. 21. Charlotte St Fitzroy Squ.e

▲ 5.2 Thomas Lord Busby, 'Billy Waters', from
his *Costume of the Lower Orders of London* (1820).

5.3 John Dempsey, 'David Love, Commonly Called the Nottingham
Poet' (1824). Collection: Tasmanian Museum and Art Gallery. ▶

Hard Metal Spoons

▲ 7.2 John Dempsey, 'Charles McGee, Crossing Sweeper, London' (*c*.1824).
Collection: Tasmanian Museum and Art Gallery.

◄ 7.1 John Thomas Smith,
'Hard Metal Spoons' (*c*.1819).

THE "BRILL," SOMERS TOWN, IN 17 0.

▲ 7.3 'The "Brill", Somers Town, in 1780', in Walter Thornbury,
Old and New London, 5 vols (1873–78), vol. 5, p. 342.

7.4 'The Dust-Heaps, Somers Town, in 1836', in
Thornbury, *Old and New London*, vol. 5, p. 372. ▼

THE DUST-HEAPS, SOMERS TOWN, IN 1836. (*See page* 368.)

Both deny it all. But Ferguson has three witnesses from the workhouse who swear that Minnie is a regular visitor. Better still, he has a letter from Minnie to her father, which Burcham now reads.

Dear Father, – I want to know how you are. Mother has been ill, and I have been in a little trouble myself; but have got over that. I'll tell you all about it when I come on Sunday. I'll send our directions.
B[esse] Richards, Crown-court, Wentworth-street.

It must hurt to be undone by such a banal letter. Minnie – or Besse, as we must reluctantly call her – claims illiteracy, but it does not convince. Still Burcham clings to hope – from injured pride? from real sympathy? – asserting that some portions of the story must still be true, that Rose has really been in America, 'but as soon as she landed she happened to meet with some wicked persons who pressed her in a league to deceive the public'. It's the great Victorian seduction narrative in a new guise. Still, 'with great pain', he acknowledges 'that their conduct was fraudulent, and that they had carried on a gross deception on the public and himself'.

The Society's parsimony now proves its worth: the substantial funds sent in but withheld can now be returned to the donors, or else 'applied to the uses of the poor-box'. But what is to be the fate of the two impostors, whose unveiling provides the regional papers with copy for days to come? Only this: 'He told the girls to leave the court, and mind they were not taken into custody for begging – if they were they would be punished severely.' Even now, he lets the girls walk free, not even demanding the return of any sums. The newspaper does not record it, but you can almost hear the hiss of the fuming Mr Ferguson.[25]

For once, a magistrate has proved himself quite likeable – more so, certainly, than the *Morning Post*, whose proto-tabloid raking through of Minnie's parentage features deeply dehumanising language: her Black father is described as having had a daughter 'by the female with him'. Burcham's great weakness, besides a trusting heart, is that shared by the *Morning Chronicle*, and the anonymous passers-by whose sympathetic donations started the whole affair. It is 1857: they and the rest of London – including, almost certainly, Rose and Minnie/Besse – have spent five years in the grip of *Uncle Tom's Cabin* – both the original novel by Harriet Beecher Stowe, imported, serialised, pirated, and its many reincarnations as cheap play and street ballad. 1850s London is steeped in the culture of American slavery – blackface minstrelsy is all the rage – and the public laps up tragic slave stories in the same deeply problematic fashion as it obsesses over the seduction of interesting maidens.

For all that many Black Londoners are born and bred in the city, many of their white fellow citizens are all too ready to assume that they must be foreigners; something that, for once, these two girls manage to exploit. They take that exoticising assumption and attempt to turn it to their benefit. Like Emily Lewis, they are attuned to the cultural zeitgeist, but their strategy is conceived on a grander scale. Given that the chief motivation seems to have been to provide for Minnie/Besse's father, Mr Richards, in his infirmity, it is hard not to salute the girls' chutzpah. But the most remarkable thing is how they got away with it, without a fine or a spell behind bars. It was not often that the Mendicity Society failed to get its girl.

~

It seems strange to talk of what is ostensibly a charity in language more appropriate to an enforcement agency. But in effect, that is exactly what the Mendicity Society *was*. Just as the well-intentioned Foundling Hospital, in many respects a force for good, could also mirror the functions of a tribunal, a prison, a tourist attraction

– just as Thomas Barnardo's tactics could include deception and coercion and just as the criminal justice system could represent the arbitrary whims of petty tyrants – so could a charity become, in effect, a private and authoritarian police force.

The Mendicity Society was the most notorious of a number of organisations, styling themselves as benevolent – and in this instance counting royalty and aristocrats among its patrons – yet primarily devoted to exposing and locking up 'sham' beggars. Its self-appointed mission was to 'stamp out' the 'social evil' of mendicity. From 1818 onwards, the Society issued tickets to subscribers, who were in turn encouraged to give these to beggars instead of money: the ticket-holder could present it at their offices in Red Lion Square and, pending an assessment, might be given a bowl of soup or be set to work, breaking rocks or picking hemp.* But the Society also employed a number of vigilante officers, armed with cudgels, who roamed the streets in search of beggars and performers whom they would then proceed to persecute. On occasion – as we have just witnessed – these officers even played detective. More usually, however, their methods were cruder: intimidation, arrest and slander.

Monday, 31 July 1843: it is evening on Montague Street, whose imposing array of grand terraced houses, part of the newly completed Bedford development, connects the wealthy merchants of Russell Square to the learned pomp of the British Museum. Jane Ward, aged eighteen, has had what passes for a good day: that is to say, she has just exhausted her little store of lavender, which she sells to prosperous passers-by who are in no need of it, but will accept a bunch as a fragrant fiction that covers the conscience-pricking reality of a charitable transaction. And even now, one or two people stop and press coins upon her, though she has nothing to give them but

---

* We will encounter this side of their system at first hand in Chapter Six.

a grateful smile. But that's enough sentimentality, for here comes Jones, one of the Mendicity Society's enforcers, his heavy hand upon her shoulder. It's a cell for her, and an appearance before Mr Combe – yes, Mr Combe, who will meet Rose Avery and Besse Richards at Southwark fourteen years from now.

Jane Ward quivers before him. Impossible to deny the charge. But the timing of it is so cruel. 'I was only trying to get a few halfpence to buy a little lavender to sell in the streets.' And she bursts into tears.

Combe turns rather hastily to question Jones instead. 'Is she known at the Mendicity Society as a beggar?'

'No, sir, not that I am aware of.'

And now Jane bursts forth again. She has *never* begged – she had *just* sold her last bunch when he approached her.

Jones is having none of this. 'I never see [sic] any lavender at all with you.'

That will do for Combe, who would rather not have this weeping female before him. Jane is sentenced to seven days in the House of Correction, and is taken away, still 'weeping bitterly'. Such are the Mendicity Society's methods: simple, but effective.

But Jane Ward is not altogether powerless in the face of institutional persecution. She is young and friendless; her lavender is picturesque. As we know well by now, these things make a difference.

What follows is a rehearsal for the Mary Ann Donovan affair, sixteen years hence, with which this book began. Even in the first, bald report of the case, the editor of *Lloyd's Illustrated Newspaper* intervenes to protest the injustice of the case – 'she was only *poor*!' – and lambasts the officers of the Mendicity Society; the piece appears under the title 'The Crime of Being Poor', and the same issue includes an opinion piece on the case that rails against the injustice for full 400 words. The *Examiner*'s account of the case carries further details, lifted in turn from *The Times*, noting that

Jane Ward is living 'with a married couple named Street'; that none of the local police had ever seen her before; that Jones himself had marked her previously in Gower Street 'without either shoes or stockings on' – but that he '*Did not see her begging.*'

A week later, *Lloyd's* publishes a letter by 'W.C.' attacking the Mendicity Society's officials. On 9 August, questions are even asked in Parliament: Richard Milnes, MP for Pontefract, lays her case before the Home Secretary himself. This gentleman, Sir James Graham, demurs elegantly for a while, prompting Sir Robert Inglis, MP for Oxford University,[26] to weigh in:

> There ought, he thought, to be a distinction made between the sturdy and insolent beggar and the almost silent sufferer, who was sometimes met with in the streets of the metropolis. The question in this case was, did or did not the individual ask for, or did she merely receive alms? He could not help thinking that when they knew the state of suffering which existed around their own splendour and comfort, they ought to feel some sympathy in such an instance as that put forward on the present occasion[.]

The point turns, however, into a fine legal distinction about the relationship between the police and private societies, and the question drops. Nothing, in fact, is actually done for Jane Ward at all, and the only result of all this hand wringing is a lengthy exculpation of the Mendicity Society's conduct, published in their report of 1844 and publicised at length in – where else? – the *Morning Post*. In justifying their conduct, the Society – and the *Post* – try to smear Ward just as the authorities will later traduce Donovan, claiming that her father has disowned her for 'pilfering', that she has 'caused trouble in the Refuge for the Destitute', and that she has been six times apprehended for vagrancy since the age of fifteen, and four times committed to prison – vague assertions that do not tally with the evidence given at her hearing. They produce a matron of the Refuge to badmouth her, and declare that she has spent her teens 'living in St Giles's, and has supported herself by selling things in the streets' – as if, in the words of *Lloyd's*, they consider poverty to be itself a crime. They place great stress on her character 'as remarkable for falsehood, indolence, and filthiness'.

In short, a powerful society, with royal patrons and major newspapers at its back, finds it necessary to demolish the character of a teenage street seller, in order to maintain its own position. Such is the power, but also the limit, of the ideal of the innocent girl. She can shine a light on injustice and undermine institutions – but only if she is content, like Jane Ward, to play the part of victim: meek, wronged, in need of championing.[27]

~

In the final analysis, even Jane Ward's exemplary character cannot withstand the arbitrary power of implacable institutions, convinced of the righteousness of their self-appointed missions. Others fare worse still.

1821: a genuine slave girl, known only as S.B., aged seventeen, has made it to London from Montego Bay. Apprehended in begging by the Mendicity Society, her fate is decided: obviously the only suitable course is to deport her – if not necessarily back where she came from, then to some suitably exotic and far-flung part of the Empire. So convinced are the officers that they are doing this in her best interests, they seem genuinely astonished and affronted that 'when a passage was at length obtained for her, and she was about to be taken on board, she absconded, and has not again been seen'.[28]

And of course, even white London girls have 'the greatest horror' of these well-intentioned institutions. One dancer-cum-prostitute accosted by John Blackmore objects, 'Yes, but if I come, may I wear my own clothes, and not an uniform? and will they cut off my hair?' Blackmore, unable in good faith to set her mind at rest, is furious with the situation:

> how great a hindrance to the work of reclamation is the harsh treatment exercised at many of the so-called penitentiaries ... is it to be wondered at, that when situations have been provided for them, and they have got free from the restraint and rigid discipline of these institutions, they have returned to their old paths of sin?[29]

Nowhere is this lack of humanity more chilling, and the limitations upon the agency of the 'good' and humble street girl more apparent, than in the application of the Contagious Diseases Acts that are passed in the late 1860s. In 1871, a report on their operation is finally published; it runs to nearly 1,000 pages. One major effect of the Acts in military areas such as Greenwich, and at the Lock Hospital for venereal disease in Harrow Road, North Kensington, is to bring about the mass inspection of working prostitutes in dedicated 'examination houses'.

The set-up is exactly what this name suggests: in impersonal conditions of debatable hygiene, girls are stripped, peered at, and cold metal instruments inserted into (mostly) their vaginas. For the report, a string of male medical professionals – Mr Lane FRCS, a senior surgeon; his assistant, Berkeley Hill FRCS; Dr Routh, an eminent physician – line up to attest that they 'cannot conceive [of] periodical examinations having any degrading effect on a woman who will prostitute herself with any man for hire'.

To them, these are fallen women, immune to shame. This is all just routine. Others – Daniel Cooper of the Rescue Society; Mr Krause of the London City Mission; his friend Captain Browne of the Royal Artillery – know better:

> A woman who had just left the examining house, shouting that she was all right, told him in very coarse language that a girl was crying there because the doctor had hurt her with too large an instrument ... the doctor – I do not know whether I should state the actual words that I heard used – had 'jib-boomed' her with too large an instrument, and was obliged to use a smaller one, and that was the occasion of her crying. I saw her afterwards, and her face confirmed that story.

> They regarded the Act as a gross violation of their liberty; they called it disgusting that they should have to go and expose their persons, and observed that when ill they could get cured under their own doctors, and did not need in broad daylight to go up 50 at a time with policemen laughing at them, to a street in Greenwich to be examined.

> At the gate, the officer in charge of the gate was singing and whistling cheerfully, and contrasted with this, was a girl of 18 with her eyes swollen with crying.

> [I]f a girl has ever been up for examination, she is marked and known to everyone as a prostitute, and has a great difficulty in getting away from the life ... Women have told the witness that the examination has been the cause of their sinful lives; one girl said she prayed as for life not to be put on the examination chair, but she had to submit or go to prison[.]

A neighbour told me that half-a-dozen boys had been in the habit of sitting on the kerb-stone [outside the examination house], the eldest not over 11, and indulging in remarks and gestures so degrading that it made her very flesh creep.[30]

Needless to say, almost everyone whose voice is heard first-hand in evidence is a man.

~

These examinations, motivated primarily by concern for the health not of the women but of the soldiers in the local barracks, epitomise the street girl's wider plight, exposed and vulnerable at all times to the blunt instruments of male scrutiny and male force – on the street as on the inspection table. Emily Lewis, Rose Avery and Besse Richards, Jane Ward – all of them attempt to assert their agency, to turn this scrutiny and these prejudices, and consequently the odds, in their favour. All of them seek to bend the received opinions of the day, usually so constrictive, to their own ends. But they all fail. And they do so because they must operate on society's terms; the role they play, however well acted, is always that of the victim, and so they end up victimised. All are still walking, submissive, into the dread building of patriarchal authority, where they cannot hope to win.

But there is another way.

~

In 1854, Sarah Tanner, aged twenty-one, is a maid-of-all-work in Oxford Street, helping keep house for a tradesman. While she – 'a lively honest rosyfaced girl, virtuous & self possessed', albeit, apparently, 'vulgar' – scrubs and dusts, lays fires, washes linen, life is passing by outside. Let's say she's cleaning a small-paned window, looking out at the bustling crowd. She lifts the dripping rag to the glass – and lowers it again, oblivious to the pooling, soap-sudded water. She's had enough.

Regent Street, one evening, a year or two later. Sarah Tanner now walks in the midst of that crowd, 'arrayed in gorgeous apparel'. Seeing a face she knows, she smiles – she smiles a lot these days. But it's no customer – just queer old Arthur Munby, one of those who'd looked at her, talked to her even, back when she was a respectable servant. The man, perhaps, whose hungry gaze had been her inspiration.

Taking in her splendour, his eyebrows raise. 'How is this?' he says.

It's quite simple, she explains. 'Of her own accord and without being seduced', she has become a professional prostitute. And though in law, as a streetwalker, she is a 'common prostitute' (which is important, as it's the pimps and bawds who are held legally culpable, and as long as she keeps the peace the police will leave her alone), she is in truth anything but 'common' – she reads books, and takes 'lessons in writing and other accomplishments, in order to fit herself to be a companion of gentlemen'. Munby is impressed – if her 'fine hazel eyes, remarkably large and bright' are assets, so too are her deportment and learning. She keeps her room and her person spotless, she thinks 'she might get on' – and Munby, though a technically chaste husband, insists on standing her a drink.

She keeps at it for some years, dressing well 'but not gaudily', keeping her looks and temper, cultivating friends, 'getting on nicely'. On Saturday, 30 July 1859, she bumps into Munby again, he dressed for the opera, she more soberly attired than before. She is not alone, but walks with a female companion; businesslike, she offers Munby her hand to shake. 'How is this?' he says – again.

'Well, I've left the streets & settled down,' she says.

'Married?'

'Oh no! But I'd been on the streets three years, and saved up – I told you I should get on, you know – and so I thought I'd leave, and I've taken a coffeehouse with my earnings – the Hampshire Coffeehouse, over Waterloo Bridge.'

Munby laughs, and she frowns at him. 'Quite true … I manage it all myself, & I can give you chops & tea – & anything you like: you must come and see me.'

'That I will,' he says – and he does, next Thursday. Sarah, 'cooking chops on a gridiron', is too busy working to talk, but asks him to come again. Perhaps he does. It's a cosy, welcoming, respectable coffee house after all, 'just over the Bridge'. He could do worse.[31]

Take out the voluntary prostitution, and Tanner's is an exemplary Victorian narrative: the 'poor but honest' girl made good through self-improvement and hard work. She makes a solid investment and contributes to the legitimate economy; she is at all times decorous, discreet, troubling to no one. To a modern sensibility, it is almost a parable of neo-liberalism. But in his reflections, Munby italicises the word '*voluntary*' – and well he might, for this is the crux of the whole matter. To respectable Victorian society, few things are as subversive as the idea that a *decent* girl or woman might *choose* a life of prostitution – might 'prefer to walk the street in silk and satins, to have a short life and a merry one, rather than slave and drudge, and end her days after all in a workhouse'.[32] And even here, in the 1857 phrasing of J. Ewing Ritchie, there is the reassuring assumption that this life will be *short*. How much more troubling still, were the girl to survive – even to flourish.

It is not as if Victorian girls were choosing prostitution from a wide array of available careers, passing up the chance to become a Harley Street physician, an Oxford don, Home Secretary. For most of those *with* a choice, it was between this, begging, selling other wares, or as in Sarah Tanner's case, domestic service. But it could nevertheless represent a positive option, rather than being the sorry consequence of seduction or desperation. As Judith Walkowitz puts it:

> Prostitutes were masters of improvisation: they adopted a range of strategies to survive, including physical mobility and migration from countryside to the city, shifting employment between a series of menial jobs, and supplementing their income by charity, begging, and petty crime.[33]

It is far from the 'easy life' that moralists decried, but as well as danger and hardship, prostitution could bring with it economic independence – from parents or a male partner – without the ostracism or social isolation that, buying in to the attitudes of polite society, we might expect. In fact, London's prostitutes formed what might reasonably be called a sisterhood.

1853: William Greg is told a story that he passes on to readers because, in the end, it fits the conventional narrative – the girl, having sinned, dies. But that's not the point:

> A poor girl who, after a few years spent in infamy and wretchedness, was rapidly sinking into a decline, had still no means of livelihood but in the continued practice of her calling. But, with a mixture of kindness and of conscience which may well surprise us under such circumstances, her companions in degradation resolved among themselves that, as they said, 'at least she should not be compelled to die in sin,' and contributed out of their own poor and sad earnings a sufficient sum to enable her to pass her remaining weeks in comfort and repentance.[34]

If this girl had recovered, Greg would probably not have printed the anecdote – but the fact remains that he is describing an organised support network, of a sort that could even be integrated within the wider, 'respectable' community.[35] From 1868, here is Thomas Wright, another censorious writer letting on more than he means to:

> There can be no doubt, either, as to the profession of the two showy-dressing young ladies at number 4, who lie a-bed so late a-mornings, and come home in cabs so late at night, accompanied by gentlemen mostly of the seafaring persuasion, and from whose house there frequently proceeds 'a sound of revelry by night.' There can be no doubt as to how they get their living; but the nature of their calling in no way injures them in the estimation of their neighbours, by whom, indeed, they are rather looked up to, and amongst whom they play the part of ladies Bountiful, being liberal in the bestowal of cast-off dresses and bonnets ... they give freely to all corners of the drink for which the Jacks ashore 'suffer' and the person who can and does give drink is, I need hardly say, regarded by the majority of the inhabitants of our Court as a person to be respected, despite any trifling moral blemishes there may be in her character.[36]

The writers may condemn them. But their own communities do not.

Sarah Tanner may be well behaved, but she forms part of what is effectively a counterculture that, in refusing to accept the role of degraded victim, is a constant, eloquent affront to those respectable persons they encounter in the street. At times, this takes on a literally outspoken character: the girl finding her voice and answering back.

The Strand again, early evening on 10 April 1859. Even Munby is startled when, putting off an importunate prostitute with the excuse 'but it's Sunday', she teases him, improving his vocabulary in the process with a Jewish colloquialism, 'What, are you so *froom* [orthodox] as all that?'

1843: a missionary ventures into the slums to visit 'a pair of allegedly fallen women'. Finding the door ajar, he walks straight in, 'telling the person, "I have something to say to you." Evidently surprised, she said, "This is not the conduct of a gentleman to intrude in this manner." I acknowledged it and apologised.'

Nor is it merely prostitutes who check the presumption of their self-appointed betters. 1837, and another missionary complains of 'another woman, who, on my first going into the district and speaking to her about selling oranges on a Sunday, abused me very grossly, shouting after me in the street'.

1830: Edward Pelham Brenton, a naval captain who had seen service at the capture of Martinique, now spends his time exposing fraudulent beggars in the street. He is appalled when, having reported one girl to the Mendicity Society, 'the young woman has since insulted me by gesture in the streets' – though sadly he does not disclose what the gesture in question is.

1871: reflecting on a time several decades ago, 'an Old Almsgiver' recalls:

> a tract distributor on our own district long visiting a woman whose civil way of accepting tracts had raised a hope that she prized them. One day she flew at him as follows: 'Ain't you ashamed: here have I been taking your rubbishing tracts for six months and more, and never seen the ghost of a ticket for grocery, meat, or coals. You may go to Bath with your tracts in future.'[37]

~

For a girl or woman to answer back, unabashed – to take the moral high ground, even – was a shocking blow to the social hierarchy. It was not this, however, that kept moralists and missionaries awake at night. In 1858, when Sarah Tanner is still working the streets, the phrase 'social evil', newly coined, dominates the headlines and the minds of reformers. The capital-P Problem of which Tanner forms a modest part is both moral and pseudo-scientific: the spread of venereal disease is entangled with metaphors of social contagion, the corruption of propriety. James Whitehorne, a minor social reformer and abolitionist, and his more famous colleague William Acton, the eminent (and much misguided) gynaecologist, do their research, run the figures, present their findings in landmark texts, more widely read and discussed than sociological surveys tend to be.* It turns out that, far from being cadaverous, pox-ridden wraiths, preyed upon young and young in their graves, prostitutes are 'picked women, the healthiest and best, physically speaking, of the female population' (Whitehorne's phrasing), possessed 'of youth, health, good looks, and a well-proportioned frame – qualifications usually incompatible with a feeble constitution' (Acton). Inconvenient as it may be to the sensibilities of the age, very few of them die as a result of their trade, or in childbirth (which they are good at avoiding). Far more of them prosper. They do not, however, remain prostitutes for ever. Whitehorne puts the question beautifully: 'Where do they go?' And eventually, with Acton's agreement, he answers it – though he would much rather not, for the truth of it terrifies him: 'The vast majority *marry*.'[38]

This is the way the street girl can be really subversive: by conforming to the bit of the social code she is not meant to conform to – by transgressing beyond all the bounds of decency, then returning, unrebuked and unashamed, to the fold. By undermining the sanctity of the most bourgeois of institutions, and by bearing healthy children, rather than dying in the gutter.

---

* Whitehorne's *The Social Evil Practically Considered*, and Acton's *Prostitution, Considered in its Moral, Social, and Sanitary Aspects*, were ideally titled to pique the interest of respectable but prurient Victorian readers.

The same year that Whitehorne publishes his findings, 1858, there is a famous exchange in *The Times* between two self-confessed prostitutes (though neither claim has been verified, neither has been disproved). The first, styling herself 'One More Unfortunate', adopts the pose of the meek victim, arguing the case for the quiet, respectable prostitute, whose presence in the streets might even be beneficial in so far as her shameful example serves as a warning for others. Her two letters are erudite, witty, outspoken and well reasoned: she advocates compassionate reform. In response, one gentleman offers to save her if she will get directly in touch; another, less earnest, confines himself to cheap jokes. 'One More Unfortunate' replies to both, assured and articulate, and develops her theories further. But there the subject drops – until, two weeks later, an impassioned rejoinder is published by 'Another Unfortunate', disgusted by what she characterises as the superficial, mealy-mouthed apologism of 'One More Unfortunate', dismissing her as 'a mere chance intruder in our ranks'.

It is this letter that makes waves and remains notorious to this day. 'Another Unfortunate' relates her life story: though it is not quite Sarah Tanner's, it is equally self-possessed and free of guilt. I cannot pretend to do its complexities justice here – and indeed, it says very little of the street itself; this woman has left it as soon as possible, becoming a kept and influential courtesan, acquiring along with wealth and culture a pronounced strain of xenophobia and even sanctimony. But though her argument is directed in turn against the previous correspondent, married prostitutes and foreigners, her real target throughout is 'ignorant, and often ... brutal men'. She brandishes the full might of mid-Victorian rhetoric in the face of 'You reverend Mr Philanthropist' and 'you the pious, the moral, the respectable, as you call yourselves, who stand on your smooth and pleasant side of the great gulf you have dug and keep between yourselves and the dregs'. Her logic is excoriating and her style – 'we, who are not fallen, but were always down' – invigorating.

Though her accusations, which surely cause thousands to splutter over their coffee or their port, are made within the rarefied pages of *The Times*, their spirit is Sarah Tanner's. It is that of the woman who has grown up as a girl in the street; who has felt that gaze in all its power and hypocrisy upon her body; who has looked it in the eye – and, defiant, stared it down.[39]

4

The Immigrant

While the paths of Sarah Tanner and 'One More Unfortunate' lead them away from us and off the street, there are plenty of new faces to replace them. For much of our period, London is primarily a city of immigrants, with more of its citizens born elsewhere than within the sound of its bells or the caress of its smog. Most of these newcomers are young adults. Having spent three chapters growing up on the streets of London, it is time to step back, and see it anew.

Cambridge, the early 1810s: John Brown, a promising but troubled lad in his mid-teens, has just had his indenture as a cobbler's apprentice ended by court order. Things are getting too hot for him at home, and his only tie is his 'poor old grandmother' who reluctantly agrees with his argument that he should 'pursue my own course'. He has only one thought in mind. 'London was to me the great centre of attraction, whereof I had heard much and read more'. Brown spends one final night at his grandmother's:

> The next morning at a very early hour I took my leave of her, after receiving some good counsel and an affectionate farewell. Then with bundle on shoulder, and a little money in my pocket, I started for the great Metropolis.[1]

The Immigrant

Liverpool, 1808: John O'Neill, another cobbler past the days of his apprenticeship, has already upped sticks twice. Born in Waterford to a single mother – married, but deserted by his father – O'Neill's first, counterintuitive move was upriver, to Carrick-on-Suir, before heeding the call that drew so many across the Irish Sea.

His is a strange path for a boy from County Waterford, up to Liverpool rather than down to Bristol, but it's about to get back on track. He has a crumpled letter from his estranged father, giving his address as Long Alley, Moorfields, London. And it's London that calls him now, away from his own young family and towards a man he has not seen since infancy.[2]

Guiseley, Yorkshire, any time from 1861 to 1865.* Elizabeth Ann Brown, or Bland – she calls herself Lizzie, so let's do the same – is thirteen? Sixteen? Grown up a basket maker's daughter, her father variously reported as a Spaniard or a 'gypsy', she is now in service as a 'nurse girl' to a Mrs Padgett. Though the two of them get on (far better, indeed, than Lizzie does with her own family), it's no kind of life for a girl who is just becoming aware of her 'personal charms'. As it is, these are a hindrance; the other girls, resentful of her looks, tease her, while the boys are... worse. She tells Mrs Padgett 'that she intended to be *something*; that she would not live in Guiseley all her life'.

Padgett has heard this so often that, when the decisive moment comes, she fails to recognise it:

> The unhappy girl cried bitterly ... and said she could not stay at home any longer; that she should go away and live; but I did not suppose she would leave that very night, alone and unprovided with sufficient clothing to make a journey.

---

* At least we know it's Guiseley; later, some will say that Lizzie came from Zaragoza.

125

But Padgett is mistaken.[3]

In the words of one beggar woman, recorded by a nurse in around 1817, 'I'll go to Lunnun – there's nothing like Lunnun!'[4] Brown, starting from Cambridge, prides himself on being 'a good walker', and sets off on foot. O'Neill, starting from Liverpool, improvises: walking, hitching lifts in carts and by boat; the new canals are in his favour.

Lizzie, starting from Leeds two generations later, is a young, attractive, friendless girl: to do likewise would be dangerous. So instead, she takes the train.

~

Cambridge, Yorkshire, Waterford via Liverpool – hardly the most far-flung of origins for our first immigrants, but highly typical. London was sustained, indeed engorged, by just this sort of influx: young working men from the surrounding counties, girls who would mostly go into service, and – always – Irish men, women and children, from the poorest to the wealthiest, who were so integral to the life of this world city.[5] This journey itself was no small matter, giving many their first taste of a wider, more arbitrary, more cynical world.

For some it was the Poor Laws that posed the greatest difficulty. Though rewritten in the middle of our period – 1834 – the basic principle endured: paupers not 'gainfully' employed were to be relieved only in their 'parish of origin'. This meant that when found elsewhere, such as in London, or if apprehended travelling without a licence granted by a magistrate, they were liable to be sent back whence they came. Freedom of movement was a privilege reserved for those who contributed to the flow of respectable capital.[6]

James Burn first comes to London with his father – a veteran, a drunkard, afflicted by visions – starting out from Dumfries, in southwest Scotland, in 1810:

> A journey to London in those days was no trivial matter ... After we
> crossed the Border, my father made application for a pass in Carlisle,
> which was readily granted by the magistrate, when he learned the
> object of our journey. This pass enabled us to get relief in the various
> towns and villages through which we had occasion to travel.

Nonetheless, he glosses over 'a good many vicissitudes and two
incarcerations' that will occur before they make it to the capital.
Even Brown, coming only from Cambridge, has a run-in with a
constable, who wants to turn him back.[7]

For others, it is their fellow travellers who are the problem. David
Love, a seasoned Scottish itinerant who has journeyed all over these
islands, 'thought so much of London that I would live no where else'
– but en route from Salisbury, he falls in with one John Miles, who
dupes him into paying for all the latter's travelling expenses, before
running out on him when they arrive, leaving Love with barely
thruppence, 'which was a small sum in a strange place'.[8]

Luckily for O'Neill, he travels with a reliable companion from
Liverpool; together, the two of them can be on their guard. All three
of our original fortune seekers will make it to London without mishap.

~

At approaching eleven a.m. on the third day of his journey, Brown
reaches London. Footsore and weary, he has risen at dawn, shoved
his head beneath the pump, and walked the last four hours of his
journey. Approaching from the north, there will have been few
signs of what lies ahead – the city hides over the skyline, beyond
the hill, all is fields and villages until...

> I entered the modern Babylon. The din and bustle, and the
> never-ceasing stream of vehicles of every description rattling

backwards and forwards, here completely bewildered me; whilst the crowded streets and the shops displaying an inconceivable variety of articles, struck me dumb with wonder and astonishment.[9]

Passing through the relative spaciousness of Islington and Finsbury Fields, our would-be cobbler Brown pushes on to his goal. Milton Court, off old Grub Street itself, is famed as home to many shoemakers. Squeezed between Moorfields and Smithfield, it lies just inside the City of London, in a warren of twists and turns:

Here in many different windows I saw 'Lodgings' advertised in a great variety of character; but the shops and houses all bore the appearance of squalid misery; the inhabitants too seemed of the lowest description; and drunkenness and disorder appeared to revel uncontrolled. Squalid sallow-faced beings reeled about with short pipes in their mouths, cursing and swearing in the most horrible manner; whilst their ragged vestments fluttered in the wind, exposing their naked persons at every gust. But this was nothing to the disgusting conduct and wretched appearance of the women, who kept tumbling in and out of dirty gin-shops, screaming and blaspheming, with infants in their arms half naked and in the most filthy condition. Some were so helplessly drunk, that they dropped their babies in the noisome gutter and rolled over them; being incapable of getting up until set on their legs by some of their acquaintance, and assisted to their foul dens in the most bestial state imaginable. The children were the most pitiable objects my eyes had ever beheld. Almost in a state of nudity, begrimed with filth and dirt, it was impossible to tell whether they were blacks or whites; for their hair resembled a dirty thrum mop. But I must give up attempting to describe this scene, and leave the shocking picture to be completed by imagination.[10]

Brown is writing decades later, a mid-Victorian looking back; he is influenced by the vivid scenes of Hogarth's *Gin Lane* and the rhetoric of a hundred other writers. Yes, his account is embellished, hackneyed – but what it captures is less the material reality of the street, and more the reaction of the newcomer. This is his memory – over-saturated, hyperbolic, alienated and disgusted – and not the memory of a pampered aristocrat, remember, but of an apprentice cobbler with a murky reputation. He is playing up to his Victorian reading public, but the raw emotion of the experience seems real. His shock, his resort to the racialised, colonialist language of the age, testify to a young man marked for ever by his first encounter with the London street. To him, it is a hellscape.

First impressions matter; they have the power to overwhelm. Here is James Burn, the beggar boy from Dumfries, grown up a sailor and now, after years away, finding himself in the city anew:

I soon found out a mystery which has been solved by thousands before me; namely, that London was far too large for me. I was fairly lost in a wilderness of human beings; I was a mere atom in a huge mountain of humanity! and as it were an unclaimed particle of animation – a thing that belonged to nobody.

Like Brown, he recoils. It is too much to bear:

The first houseless night in London passed away, and still I strayed about like a ghost without a home. When the morning was breaking I was wandering along the dull hazy streets ... The second night came, and I shivered along the long, cold, dreary streets. I passed men who were reeling along after having left their senses and their money in the taverns. I saw scores of females who had graduated down to the lowest depths of human misery; and young men, haggard, and prematurely old, creeping along the streets like shadows in genteel rags ... On the morning of the third day, I made up my mind to leave London.[11]

David Love, deserted, disillusioned, feels the same:

[B]ehold me in London for the first time, unknown by any person, a stranger to the place, and so bewildered I did not know where to go; after wandering into many streets, I came to the outskirts, and took lodgings in the Borough. Early next morning I left London.[12]

It is not just the size of the place. This is a London that will seize hold of your loneliness and tear at it. Its streets are gripped by – in the Irish academic Nicholas Daly's phrase – 'the frenzy of the legible'.

This is a period of new and vastly cheaper printing methods, and the spread of literacy; new fonts, colours and techniques abound. Suddenly, there are signs everywhere, posters, bills, boards: an overload of text that crawls across every vertical surface; a surfeit, especially intimidating for those migrants, English or otherwise, to whom all these words are in fact illegible – but no less bewildering, perhaps more so, if you can read them. At the same time, the people around you are developing their own insider codes: the so-called 'flash' language that develops into genuine Cockney rhyming slang by the mid-nineteenth century (yes, 'apples and pears', and 'Barnet Fair' for 'hair' – but 'plate of meat' for 'street', not 'feet'), and along with it, the 'back-slang' of young clerks and costermongers rejoicing in their generation's newfound (and still rather shaky) literacy.

As one commentator observes, 'By the time a coster has spelt an ordinary word of two or three syllables in the proper way, and then spelt it backwards, it has become a tangled knot that no etymologist could unravel.' A *cart* finds itself switched with the *trac* it might travel upon, and all fear the *wen ecilop*. All of which is enough to twist out of kilter the deluge of semi-articulate sound, the newspaper vendors, the street sellers, the singing, squabbling tangle that will eventually become coherent, familiar, and fall into patterns – but only if the migrant can stick it out.[13]

Mid-century, and Joseph Manton Smith – a young married man – has come alone to London. Back home in Northampton, all his friends and family – old and new – have tried to stop him; have told him 'what a dreadful place London was, also what a wild and foolish scheme I was entering upon'. But to him the city sounds 'a perfect Paradise. I thought if I could only get there it would rain gold or something else, so go I must at all risks'. Alone from the moment of his decision – 'no one saw me off at the station' – he heads from the terminus to the centre:

> As I was wending my way along the streets, I overheard some rude person say, 'He's from the country.' ... I think it was my straw hat that seemed to take the fancy of them all, for I noticed it caused even the cabbies to smile, and the many remarks I overheard about it before I had been long in London made me quite aware of the absurdity of my personal appearance.

For the rustic above all, London is a hard place to come to.[14]

Yet here is Theodore Fontane, the German novelist, newly come to London in 1852. He will take your intimidation, your disorientation, your crisis of self. And he will match it with humanity:

He who passes St. Giles's then, takes a bright picture away with him. Out of the filthy houses and hovels in which the children have cowered freezing throughout the winter all have emerged today to bask and enjoy themselves once more in the sun. The children have taken their one pitiful toy, a homemade shuttlecock, into the street with them and while, wherever we look, everything is teeming with hundreds of these pale children grown old before their time with their bright, dark eyes, their shuttlecocks fly up and down in the air, gleaming like a swarm of pigeons on whose white wings the sunlight falls. Loud laughter, hearty and carefree as children laugh, accompanies the merry game and you pass all the gaiety with the newly-strengthened conviction that God sows the seeds of happiness everywhere and that every spot has its spring and its roses – even the dens of St. Giles's.

It is all a question of perspective. When David Love, defeated, returns to Gosport, his printer Mr Steed laughs. '"David," said he, "you had better have staid here, I hope you will go no more to London".' But Love is affronted:

> I told him the people in London had done me no harm, that I
> still longed to be there, and that if my wife had been with me,
> I would not have been here to have been laughed at by you all.

All he needs in London is some company. He will go again; he will do well there.[15]

~

Returning to Brown in the 1810s: in the throes of all this newness, he keeps enough composure to concentrate on his task. He takes refuge from the throng in a quieter side street, where:

> my eye fell upon a card in the window of a small shop, whereon
> was written in an excellent schoolboy's hand, 'Lodgings for single
> men.' I made a scrutinizing survey of the shop and its contents;
> everything appeared arranged in the most exact order ... After a
> little hesitation I entered the shop.

Though a newcomer, he is no fool, and if he is friendless, he is at least free of complications. As a young man, unencumbered, with a few shillings in his pocket, this is his first step: he can take a room, putting down a half-crown to cover his first week's rent. Hopefully, by next week, he'll have found work enough to *keep* paying it.

Brown displays more sense than most. He heads to the centre of his trade; his prospective landlady recognises him, by his 'bundle and apron', as a shoemaker; he sizes up the lodging house first, noting its meticulous arrangement, the presence of playing children, the fact that the family are in mourning for the late husband – all suggestive of a homely, stable atmosphere. He finds himself sharing a room with another cobbler, notices the latter has a small bookshelf, and immediately finds common ground in discussion of Robert Bloomfield, the labourer-poet. Within minutes, they are 'talking like old friends, for there was something in the expression of this man's face that made me feel quite at home'. In another wise move, he shares his first meal with this roommate, who proceeds to show him the sights, a just reward for his friendly advances. Day one, and all is going well.[16]

20 September 1808, and O'Neill and his companion also arrive in London. O'Neill, remember, has a quest: he is seeking his father. He is remarkably single-minded in his pursuit – and perhaps this is helpful; it shields him from the shock of the new:

> I passed along Piccadilly, regardless of the objects around me,
> merely enquiring my way to Long Alley, Moorfields, the address

given in the last letter that was sent home by my father, and it was astounding news, when told that we had nearly four miles to travel eastward before we reached that locality; but, fatigued and foot sore as we were, we resolved to reach it before we rested.

This destination – in fact nearer two and a half miles off – lies just the other side of the square from Brown's lodgings a few years later. But approaching from the west, it involves a trek right through the heart of London, including St Giles's, an arduous journey indeed for travellers who have already come far that day, thinking that London will be like Liverpool or Dublin – that once you arrive, you're more or less there. En route, they nearly fall prey to a notorious crimp – a man looking to entrap the gullible and lure them into the army or navy. An 'old Irishman', overhearing, saves them, and offers to guide them as far as Long Alley – already, their accents and dress have marked them twice, first as easy targets, then as fellow countrymen. London is vast, it contains everything – even Ireland.

Still, things are touch and go. There is no sign of O'Neill's father in Long Alley, and night is drawing in:

> We found it as difficult to procure a lodging, our beaten-down condition being against us, and only for the untiring kindness of our old fellow countryman, who was a native of Clonmel, we might have passed the night in the open air, or become the inmates of a watch-house.

Again, their status as newly arrived Irishmen polarises opinion among those they meet. But if some doors are barred, others open. O'Neill is no nearer his goal. But he has, at least, a bed, and they hunker down in Saffron Hill.[17]

Lizzie arrives at King's Cross 'late in the day in a friendless condition'. If she has spent the hours crammed inside the carriage thinking out her next steps, it does not translate into a clear plan of action. She has no contacts; her accent marks her out only as different; a single girl faces difficulties a single man does not. Whether thirteen or sixteen, she is more or less a child, and though she has worked, she has known only domesticity. She finds a smog-filled, gaslit city, far larger and fuller than that which so overwhelmed Brown some fifty years before. The multitude sweeps past her, while any whose eyes linger and whose tread slows is not to be trusted – this much, smarting from the insinuations of her fellow servants in Guiseley, she knows well enough.

And so, she wanders. South and west, drawn perhaps instinctively further into the city, but also towards the illusory safety of respectable surroundings – the pointed bricks of Bloomsbury, the porticoed and stuccoed terraces of the West End. But if these streets, genteel and monied, are broader and more peaceful than those further east, they offer far fewer prospects to a homeless girl.

At last, she finds herself on Oxford Street, amid the sudden rush, swept on west until Marble Arch looms, pale, solemn, at her left. She passes through the portal to a freer, quieter world, its broad swathes of twilit grass the closest this city comes to the wide expanses of her native Yorkshire. The buildings cease to press her in; instead, these trees feel safe. Like many before and after, she spends her first night in London among the elms of Hyde Park.[18]

~

Thanks to Brown's decisive actions on his first day, the following morning starts well: he washes, and descends to a boiling kettle and a laid table. Better still, his roommate takes him out in search of work. Cobblers' shops spill out on to the street, there is no need even to knock. Brown soon finds a man sitting at the cutting-board and asks boldly if he has need of 'a man's man'. This shoemaker – older, seasoned – looks Brown up and down. What does he see? A stripling; a yokel? 'Thee means a man's *boy*, don't thee, friend?' he says.

Brown is devastated. 'I can never forget the feeling of shame and helplessness that came over me; the quiet satire of the quaker completely overwhelmed me, and I bowed my head in sorrow.' Still, the man *is* a Quaker – as his archaic term of address suggests – and charity, mingled perhaps with guilt for his jest, moves him to give Brown a try. The youth is given a pair of boy's ankle boots 'to prove my skill upon'. Rejoicing, he returns to his friend and his lodgings. Time to set to work.

O'Neill rises in Saffron Hill. Groggy but determined, he resumes his search. This is a squalid part of town, the shabby no-man's-land between the City and Gray's Inn. At least people speak to him:

> At last I asked a man who said, with a good-humoured smile on his countenance, if the person I was enquiring after was an Irishman, 'If so,' he continued, 'your surest way to find him would be to go to St. Giles's, for,' said he, 'they all hang together like a swarm of bees.'[19]

So it's back west to St Giles's, in search of a cobbler, who in turn directs them to 'Paddy Brian, and there is not an Irish shoemaker in London but he is acquainted with [them]'. They track down Brian 'at Adam Patrick's, Horse and Groom, King Street' – that is, a good stretch south-west, in the salubrious environs of St James's Square, a stone's throw from the palace itself – but still solidly part of the Irish community. So much for the St Giles's ghetto. Brian, a rather forbidding figure, is eventually won over by O'Neill's earnestness. The two travellers are given gin and beer, and enquiries are set in train. The search continues.

Hyde Park in the foggy dew. Blinking, Lizzie is stirred into wakefulness by – a tender hand? A booted foot? The precise manner goes unrecorded, but she hastens to her feet, damp and shivering, before this strange man – tall, moustached, looming – a policeman. She sighs. Unlike many girls we have met, for her this comes as a relief, if anything. Better this figure of authority than the alternative. She is pretty and artless; her modest but unfashionable clothing and her broad Guiseley accent bear witness to the truth that gushes forth.

We know by now how much it flatters a man to play the gallant. So he takes her – not to the station, or the workhouse – but to his own home, where his wife proves equally friendly to this guileless country girl. This is less surprising than you might think: they have children of their own, and a practised domestic used to looking after infants is just what they are looking for. It is not, of course, what Lizzie is looking for. But her long hours in the street and her longer night in the park have taught her the value of a roof and a hearth. First things first: her clothes and her accent may have saved her, but they mark her out as gauche, provincial. They'll have to go.[20]

A funny thing, how one's cloth cuts both ways. Joseph Manton Smith felt the shame of his Northamptonshire straw hat. But William Read, an itinerant crossing sweeper addressing the Mendicity Committee in 1845, is of the opinion that it's worth the embarrassment:

The best dress for a beggar to wear in the streets of London was a smock-frock; it excited more compassion; though they might perhaps have been in London two or three years ... The best and most successful garb for a man to assume was that of a country labourer. Such a man might get five or six shillings a day.[21]

~

Day three, and disaster for Brown. Beset by 'indescribable fear and doubt' over the quality of his work, his apprehensions are realised when he returns to the Quaker. 'Spoiled' is the verdict – all bets are off – and his roommate can spare no more time in assisting him. Brown must walk the streets again:

> taking care to avoid all the shops where the work appeared evidently above the reach of my ability. I traversed the meanest streets that I could find: and, after many unsuccessful attempts, applied at a shabby-looking shop on Saffron Hill.

Again, his path intersects with O'Neill's – little wonder, given their shared trade. Here he meets a woman who looks like 'an Egyptian mummy … [with a] satanic stare', and fears that 'I might be pulled in and chopped into sausage-meat, or made into penny pies, for I had heard tales of the kind since my arrival in this bewildering town':

> When I looked around, and considered my lonely position in the world, my spirits sunk; I felt incompetent to struggle with the difficulties that surrounded me. The world seemed all dark, and I appeared to myself as if not belonging to the common brotherhood of mankind; there was no one on whom I had a right to call for help, and my deficiencies stared me in the face at every step I took.[22]

Brown will survive. Despite further setbacks he is eventually taken on and works solidly for a year until a strike forces him onto the street, and he leaves London 'on tramp'. His strong start and confidence are not backed up by connections or talent; in the end, he will return to Cambridge and prosper. By the time London reduces him to the level of the street, he has seen enough to know he will do better elsewhere.

O'Neill is off again: Brian's enquiries have turned up a lead in Rag Fair, so it's back east to Spitalfields, passing Moorfields on the way – he has done nothing but tread and re-tread west and east in this cock-and-bull chase. But here at last is an old friend, come to London before him. The friend tells O'Neill to follow him:

> After traversing through a labyrinth of dark, muddy lanes and alleys, he at length stopped at a cobbler's stall, and enquired for a person of the name of Landers, who I afterwards found to be John Landeragan, my father's first cousin and my own Godfather.

Family at last! They share a warm embrace, and better still, Landeragan knows where O'Neill's father is. They track him down to The Cock in Jury Street (i.e. Jewry Street), Aldgate – south for once, towards the Tower itself. Only – what an anti-climax – 'The meeting of me and my father was friendly on his part, but there was none of that warm feeling which shows the heart is interested.' Both men stay at The Cock overnight, but O'Neill awakes to find his father already gone, with 'no mention when he would return. This seemed to me to be an odd way of receiving a son after a separation of above thirty years, and, though thunderstruck and down-hearted, I made no remark.'

O'Neill is at his lowest ebb. Down to his last half-crown, he breaks into it in order to purchase a loaf of bread, only to be accused of passing counterfeit coins – the baker, perhaps, harbours the common prejudice against Irishmen. O'Neill's journey might end here in tragedy – only for the moral of the tale to kick in, in his favour. The landlady of The Cock vouches for him, and he is set free. Retiring 'to the cheerless garret, almost broken hearted', he is immediately interrupted by men he met the night before, with offers of work. A more accomplished shoemaker by far than Brown, he finds himself in demand. '[W]ith a full bag of work, and 5s. 6d. the price of my pair in my pocket, I now had no more fear on my mind of being able to do in London.' It turns out that it's not about the destination, but about the friends you make along the way.[23] O'Neill becomes a Londoner for life.

As for Lizzie... well, she is not 'Lizzie' for long. That night is the only one she will pass in the streets: before long she is an actress, styling herself as Lilian Adelaide Bland, then using her probable father's surname of Lizon or Lessont, before settling on Lilian Adelaide Neilson as the stage name that will be blazoned across England and America (see Image 4.1). By the 1870s, she commands a salary of £700 a week; by her early death in Paris, 1880, she leaves £25,000 in her will to endow a theatrical charity. A short life, but a great one – thanks in no small part to an unnamed policeman and his wife, and the honest ring of a Guiseley accent in the still morning air of Hyde Park.[24]

~

A stutter, a success, and stardom – none of our three immigrants stays on the street. But we, who remain there, do not need long to find ourselves among other newcomers. On every corner, at every stall, we can see, hear, taste, smell the contributions of a hundred cultures. Spanish oranges, Indian tom-toms, the *fantoccini* street theatres...

In the decades between the 1801 and 1851 censuses (which can hardly hope to capture the ebb and flow of the street), the Mendicity Society keeps an annual tally of its beggars' origins – those it persecutes, and those it relieves. This begins in 1803 with Matthew Martin's amateur enquiry, finding – from a total of 5,096 cases – that under half hail from London parishes, and fully a third are Irish. From 1818 (by which date the Irish have overtaken native Londoners) to 1868, the Society records French, Germans, Russians, Austrians, Prussians, Spaniards, Portuguese, Italians, Dutch, Swedes, Africans,

'Asiatics', Americans (all these by 1819), Danes, Gibraltarians, Bohemians, Greeks, Maltese, Egyptians and Channel Islanders by 1823, when, feeling the need for greater specificity, it begins to count West Indians, Sardinians, Genoese, Algerines, Swiss, Canadians, Sandwich Islanders, South Africans, those 'Born at Sea', South Americans, East Indians, St Helenians, Poles, Arabs, New South Welsh, Norwegians, those from the Isle of Man and Van Diemen's Land, Corfiots, Turks, Tartars, Chinese, Nova Scotians, Ceylonese, Hungarians and New Zealanders. By 1867, the Italians have beaten the Irish to second place.

The report tallies how many of its non-Europeans are 'Blacks' (117 of 143 in 1819; 58 in both 1820 and 1821), and from which Caribbean islands its West Indians hail. While Central America and India proper are especially perplexing omissions (are they hidden among (South) Americans and 'Asiatics', and if so, why?), and while we must presume that Belgium, so close at hand, clearly has no beggars, this is otherwise a remarkable collage of the nineteenth-century world, as captured on the London street.[25] At the same time, this is the century that invents nationalism, that gives a pseudo-scientific veneer to racism, to xenophobia, to every kind of prejudice. What sort of London are these people coming to – and what sort of London are they making?

The paths they take are harder than the train from Leeds, the road from Cambridge. April 1865: Giuseppe Bassini, still to our eyes a child, is taken from his widowed mother in – where? No one tells us; the usual story is the hills around Parma, or the groves of Sicily, somewhere poor but romantic-sounding, at any rate – and shepherded all the way to Saffron Hill (which is, by now, synonymous with Italians) by one Lorenzo Segadelli. He survives the journey, which is more than can be said for some of his young compatriots. Maria Antonia Tartaglia, aged ten, and Carlo Macera, aged eleven, take the same route, begging and dancing their way through France; both die of pneumonia five days after arriving in London, undone by fatigue, starvation – and, perhaps, the shock to the Mediterranean system of the Victorian London climate.

Bassini, however, survives, and is billeted at No. 11 with Antonio Viasani, a sort of Fagin figure, who lends him guinea pigs and a monkey in order that he might perform and beg in the streets. Bassini spends his days charming strangers with this animal pantomime, and his nights huddled up with Viasani's other boys, all Italian, all entirely at this man's mercy. Eventually, he and Viasani are apprehended. Wary, his loyalties torn, and struggling with a language he has had just months to master, Bassini sticks to the prepared story that he is sixteen, and therefore of age, not Viasani's victim. The eight judges look at this little scrap of boy and marvel. He can be no more than twelve. Viasani is convicted as a *padrone*, one who oversees an organised group of child beggars. The best Bassini can hope for is repatriation.[26]

His fate is not recorded, but his story is one among hundreds, perhaps thousands, of Italian children brought to London. The Mendicity Society begins to take note in 1821, when 'A.J.', seventeen, is:

> apprehended with two dogs and a drum. This was one of those unfortunate beings[:] the property of individuals who compel them to bring a certain sum home every night, under pain of being sent to bed with empty stomachs. In order to deprive the master of this boy's services, the Magistrates committed him for a month, when the Society obtained a passport and sent him off.[27]

That is, A.J. is considered a victim, but nonetheless imprisoned, before being – for better or worse – deported.

All this continues until late in the century, a significant phenomenon masterfully documented in John Zucchi's *The Little Slaves of the Harp*.[28] Respectable London obsesses over the plight of these Italian children, who are pitied, objectified, exoticised, perhaps more than any others – but it redoubles its prejudice against grown Italians, who are vilified as dark-skinned nuisances, sexually promiscuous, who tyrannise these children.

~

Consistently, four ethnic groups above all others come in for sustained racial discrimination, especially in encounters between the street poor and those above them: London's Irish, Italian, Jewish and Black communities. 1803: Jane Taylor, a moralising poet, publishes her *New Cries of London*, a picturesque compendium of street characters built on the usual desire to categorise, contain, stereotype – but in this instance, aimed at young children. Full of a righteous desire to spread toleration, she pens the section 'Any Old Clothes?', which takes as its subject the archetypal Jewish second-hand clothes dealer; her sister Ann provides an illustration of a hook-nosed pedlar being hissed at by a cat. Here is Jane's open-hearted counsel:

> It is the custom in London for Jews to go about crying old clothes ... Some foolish children delight in making sport of them, only because they are Jews; but it is a very cruel and idle practice ... Some Jews, indeed, are very wicked and dishonest; but then we should pity, not laugh at them: we should especially pity them for being so unhappy as to refuse and disbelieve that wise and good religion, from which every good action proceeds. Let us remember too, that, if it had pleased God, we might have been born among those poor people; and that now, if he were to leave us to our own wicked inclinations, we should be just as bad [as] any of them.[29]

Jane Taylor, incidentally, also wrote 'Twinkle, Twinkle, Little Star'. Make of that what you will.

For good measure, here is Ellen Ranyard, much fêted for her missionary work and tireless efforts among London's slums, on the subject of the Jewish street poor:

> Could *we* endure to be their neighbours? An oppressive, fusty smell assails us as we pass along by the old-clothes shops ... At the doors we encounter the cunning eye of the debased and degraded son of Israel, looking out for customers.

Such are the voices of London's self-appointed do-gooders.[30]

For sheer extremity of racial discrimination, it is hard to look beyond the Afro-Caribbean experience, as typified by the plight of 'S.G.', aged thirty-two, taken up by the Mendicity Society for begging in the street, in order to supplement the pittance he makes by mending shoes. He has scraped by at this occupation from 1823 to 1831, before which time he spent four years as a drummer in the 1st Regiment of Foot Guards, theoretically the most prestigious infantry regiment in the British Army. A good career, you might think, and a safe one – for while the regiment was involved in suppressing disturbances in both the capital and Ireland during these years, it wasn't quite on the level of receiving the charge of the Imperial Guard at Waterloo.

But in 1823, S.G. was discharged from the regiment, for the towering offence of 'not being of a sufficiently black complexion'. Some new officer, especially taken with the military fashion for employing the darkest-skinned musicians available, had found S.G.'s skin tone underwhelming, so S.G. found himself thrown out on the streets. And what does the Mendicity Society do with this military veteran, who has served his country for four years, and lived in London for twelve? In their words, he 'is now enabled to go on board an Indiaman, the *Marquess of Huntley*'. So it's deportation for him too, destination: unknown. Though S.G. originally hailed from the West Indies, the Indiamen generally sailed to the East.[31]

Remembering the determination of the Mendicity Society to expose the Avery-Richards girls as impostors, we should not be surprised that beggars and street performers of colour come in for especially harsh and relentless persecution. Their attitude is not uniformly hostile. In 1819, 'J.P. a young man of colour, native of Barbadoes' [*sic*] is brought to their offices. He 'declared he had slept in the streets for several nights, and been without food; that he had been a cook on board a Frigate, and was discharged about two years ago. He had supported himself by begging, parishes having uniformly refused to grant him relief, in consequence of his being a foreigner.' The word 'foreigner' may sound like it is doing some heavy lifting here, but it reflects the situation – for as we know, the Poor Law stipulates that parishes are mandated to provide only for their those who are born within their bounds. Moved by his plight, the Society secures him a place in a workhouse: not a fate relished by many, but – by their own standards – an act of genuine charity.[32]

Yet such compassion is rare. The next year, 1820, and 'J.F. aged 22, a native of St Domingo', is 'apprehended' in Park Lane. It is unclear what he is doing wrong – besides presuming to enter such a salubrious district – and unusually, the Society does not charge him with a specific misdemeanour in their report. Nonetheless the officers attack, four on one. J.F. resists the assault:

> during which, the constables were compelled to use their staves, in consequence of five other blacks attempting a rescue; but failing, they all decamped excepting the prisoner, who was handcuffed to the iron railing until a coach was procured. He

however, escaped, but was stopped by a Soldier, and eventually lodged in St George's Watch-house.

Imprisoned for three months, and twice flogged, 'he became so very insolent, that they [the Society] were obliged to discharge him, since which time they have not seen or heard of him' – which must come as a relief to poor J.F., so relentlessly and violently persecuted for no discernible reason. It is unclear from which part of the island of Hispaniola, then referred to by the British as St Domingo, J.F. originated – free Haiti, or the Spanish-owned east, which will declare independence a year after this incident. Either way, the London forces of order are clearly exercised beyond all proportion by J.F.'s wholly justified desire to maintain his liberty.[33]

As you will recall from the example of the Avery-Richards sisters in the previous chapter, 1852 is the year that *Uncle Tom's Cabin* first rocks London. 'J.G., a native of Africa' – whatever *that* means – is among the first to respond to this event on the street. Like them, he stands on the pavement edge, dressed in white, immaculate. Like them, he carries a placard – in fact, a sandwich board, 'which gave an account of his having been a slave, but had run away from his master to avoid his cruelty, and to save his life – that he had been flogged, kicked, and beaten'. The story he tells to passers-by, detailing his escape from America, is harrowing in the extreme:

[H]is master had inflicted several wounds on his arms with a knife, and was in the habit of putting hot chains on his legs, and linking other slaves to him while at work. That they had to work very hard, and had very little given them to eat – that they dared not complain for fear of being ill-used, and told they were lazy, and have their hands and legs tied together, and their flesh cut.

Unsurprisingly, his demonstration leads 'a large number of benevolent persons to assemble round and pity him for his past trials; even the worthy Magistrate before whom he was taken, on hearing his tale of woe, sympathised, and with a gentle admonition discharged him'. Just as unsurprisingly, the Mendicity Society investigates, eventually exposing him as 'an imposter, in the hands of parties who had dressed him for the occasion, knowing the sympathy that had been excited in the work alluded to [*Uncle Tom's Cabin*], on behalf of slaves'. Armed with this knowledge and incensed that he is making good money by this means, they get him committed to prison as a vagrant. Tough justice, they might maintain. Except that they produce no evidence that definitively disproves his story. J.G., by contrast, can point to his 'scarred flesh'.[34]

The same year, another case arises that dwarfs even the ill-treatment suffered by J.G. – and that receives infinitely more attention across the British Isles. Like nothing else, it brings home the scale of the challenge faced by immigrants of colour. And beneath it all, it hints at something else, too, on which – with better luck – a life might just be built. It starts with a migration.[35]

In 1843 or 1844, Mahomet Abraham, a sailor from Kolkata, has his first sight of England. It is also practically his last. No sooner has his barque, the *Diana*, docked at Liverpool, than he is struck down with what he will later call 'cold in my eyes'. A combination of fever and inflammation lays him low. By the time he quits the infirmary, he is 'stone blind' in his right eye, with just 'a glimmer of light' in his left. As he puts it himself: 'I can't see anything at all. – God help me.'

Early Victorian England is not exactly awash with opportunities for a visually impaired sailor of colour. He cannot take ship again; he cannot work. As the large petition he will painstakingly hand-stitch puts it:

Being a stranger, far, far away from home, [I am] forced to trust to the kind, benevolent, and humane, who feel for the misfortunes of others.

Gold is much,
The loss of health is more;
The loss of light is such
God only can restore.
The Lord loveth a cheerful giver.

Like so many before and since, Mahomet Abraham begs his way to London – 'all through London everywhere, and I have nothing else to live upon. I must beg.' And he makes a living, proudly stating that 'ever so many people have seen me'. As Edward Webb, a Mendicity Society officer, will later testify, 'I have seen him receive money, and have no doubt that his colour and want of sight bring him a large supply.'

London is charitable to this ex-sailor. But its institutions are always hovering. In 1847 he has his first run-in with George Foster, a police constable. Three years later Foster, meeting him again, takes him into custody. 'He had then in his possession two or three shillings, which I saw him receive in Cheapside in a short time.' For the forces of law and order, the greater the sum a beggar receives, the more culpable they become. In May 1851, Abraham is charged again, and a magistrate at Marlborough Street sends him to St George's workhouse. But soon he is back on the street, accompanied by a trusted guide dog. This is his life now: he, who has sailed the world over, has only a dog and the kindness of strangers in the face of disability, accident, persecution.

September 1851 – his lowest ebb: Abraham is staying at 22 George Yard, an unloved back alley connecting Wentworth Street with Whitechapel High Street, later infamous as the site where Martha Tabram would be murdered by the Ripper. 'I went out one night to buy some victuals for my dog. It was late, and I called out to the people I heard passing, where can I get any dog's meat?' For some reason he has misjudged things, lost his bearings or his dog's rations. Though he can go hungry, his guide must not. Desperate, he makes it to the High Street, appeals to the world at large. 'At last', someone stops. Her voice is young, kind – and surprisingly refined. Introducing herself as Eliza, she leads him to a cat's meat shop near at hand. In his gratitude he asks her 'to come home and take a cup of tea with me, and I would try to make her comfortable'. He has little enough to offer, in truth, to this educated young lady – but she agrees, they take tea, and they talk.

It turns out that Eliza's past is quite as eventful as his own. The eldest daughter of respectable parents hailing from the southwest, she has been raised by her maternal grandparents 'in the first style', her own parents unaccountably offloading her to their care when she was just three months old. Aged fifteen, the sudden death of these guardians forced her back upon her parents, where 'she became an unwilling inmate'. Striking up an acquaintance with a young man met at her window, Eliza soon absconded – only to discover that this man, whom she claims she hoped to bring home to her mother, was already married. Alone in the world, she adopted the name Eliza Allen, and joined a milliner's, which soon went bankrupt. Before long – she glosses over the details – she was lying in St Luke's workhouse, Newton Abbott, Devon. Her mother tracked her down, exposed her history to the overseers, and took custody of Eliza, who was removed to St Bartholomew's Hospital, London, in order 'to get her cured of a complication of loathsome disorders'.

Abraham, we may suppose, is a broad-minded fellow: the implications of Eliza's story do not seem to dismay him. But he starts to understand how a girl like her has come to be here with him, taking tea. Eliza's story continues: escape, recapture, confinement – until 1850 when she came of age and took possession of 'a small house property in Devonshire', presumably left to her by her late grandparents. It is infinitely preferable to living, disgraced, a captive of her own parents – confined to her room because, she claims, 'I said something which was not considered proper in the presence of children.'

But renewed independence does her little good. By July of 1851 – two months before meeting Abraham – she is reduced to wandering the streets of Whitechapel, 'in the last stage of destitution, filth, and rags, singing ballads'. She is now twenty-three, she has a fine voice and a good education: others will describe her as 'small-sized' and 'pretty-faced'; 'handsome'; 'lady-looking'. She has all the makings of a successful street singer. And now she is here, taking tea with Abraham; they have talked at length – it is a quarter to eleven – she too has lost track of time, and panics. As Abraham remembers it, she says 'she was shut out' – of a workhouse? A refuge? Her father's townhouse? – 'and she did not know where to go'. And so, she stays.

Eliza and Mahomet Abraham agree to live together. They decide not to form a partnership on the street itself – each has their own method and would detract from rather than complement the other's performance. Instead, she begins 'to follow him at a little distance, and lead him over the crossings', better able than the dog to judge the speed and danger of the traffic. She runs errands; he brings in the bulk of the money. Theirs is a very private existence, and though like many of their station they share a bed, what they do or do not do in it is entirely their own business.

And it works. Before long, they move from George Yard to 7 Little Halifax Street – a few paces north and east; the same community, but a better address. The months pass. There is tragedy: his old dog dies, and the new one has to be trained.

In the spring of 1852, they decide to push their luck. Eliza writes to her family's solicitor: representing herself and Abraham as man and wife – which gives her vital legal standing – she instructs him to sell the Devonshire property. But there's a snag: her parents had previously only waived their interest in the house. Now, receiving a letter on behalf of their daughter 'Mrs Abraham' asking for their consent, they descend on Little Halifax Street. Her mother takes her aside; her father, irate, questions the house's other occupants. Yes, they have been living here as man and wife for two months, and 'most luxuriously' at that. Eliza, defiant, puts on a show for her mother. Oh yes, her Mahomet brings home fifteen shillings on a good day; rarely less than seven or eight. Yes, they are married, 'seven months since at Whitechapel Church'. Reeling, the parents leave.

But they do not desist. Her father goes to Whitechapel Church, checks the register, talks to the priest: there has been no marriage. He writes to the Mendicity Society, asking for help. They receive his letter on 28 May 1852. A week later, 5 June, they have an officer in place. Henry Major tracks the couple from their home to Bishopsgate Street – a prosperous thoroughfare which lies, crucially, within the City limits. It is twenty past eleven on a Saturday morning. Major sees Eliza fasten Abraham's petition to his breast and guide him, with his dog, to 'the Sir Paul Pindar public-house, in an attitude of supplication. As soon as she had deposited him to her satisfaction against the wall, she retired from him. I soon saw him receive a penny, and I apprehended them both.'

That fateful penny spells the end for Mahomet Abraham and Eliza. Major hauls them up before Lord Mayor William Hunter, presiding over the afternoon's session at the Mansion House. He is aghast at the sight of the couple. In the words of a watching journalist, Abraham is 'a peculiarly revolting object, his head being covered with long matted hair, and the covering upon his limbs tattered and filthy in the extreme degree' – a 'jet black blind beggarman' – a 'wretched creature', standing in 'remarkable contrast' to Eliza. Every prejudice available to the Victorian mind, racist, sexist, snobbish, is awoken by this pair. Hunter turns to Major. 'Is it possible that those two persons have been living together?'

Major chooses his words carefully. Time to lay it on thick. 'I have traced them to their very bed, and have been particularly informed of their habits.'

Informed! Yes, indeed, this trap has been carefully laid. The Society's Captain Wood is conveniently present to comment on this 'singular instance of perverted taste'. He has Eliza's father's letter with him - better yet, he has Eliza's father!

The Lord Mayor looks over the letter:

Certainly this is the most horrible piece of London romance I ever heard of, and it would be quite incredible if I had not here before me all the parties concerned. Is it possible, young woman, that you can have any respect or affection for the miserable creature at your side?

Eliza - manhandled, in the dock, before her father, before the Lord Mayor himself - looks up. 'Yes; I have both respect and affection for him. I have no idea of leaving him. We can do very well together.' And - as the journalist takes care to note - she makes a point of taking Abraham's hand in hers.

Imagine, for a moment, that the story ends there. How beautiful a gesture, an affirmation. As friends or as lovers, Eliza and Mahomet are a remarkable pair; they deserve a happy ending.

Instead, Major weighs in again:

The man has been begging about for several years, and I have no doubt is well able to keep a woman in great luxury. I am convinced that the girl has been attracted by the excellent living with which he indulges her. They have been in the habit of getting the best, and she does not deny it.

Eliza can see where this is heading and is having none of it. 'Well, I can't go home and I won't go home.'

Abraham states his case plainly, adding, 'If anyone knew how a blind man was to support himself except upon the kindness of those who were not blind, he would be much obliged to be informed in what way.' It is a fair point: there can be no accusations that he is a sturdy beggar.

If the nineteenth century gives the blind few opportunities, it also acknowledges that they have a right to charity. By rights, the two should be let go. But the Lord Mayor's blood is up, and the pair are remanded in custody. Officers enter 7 Little Halifax Street and confiscate 'a large sum of money'. Once again, the law sets itself to robbery. The couple's crimes may not be in the statute book. But they will be punished – and how.

Wednesday, 9 June: after four days in the cells, they appear again before Alderman Hooper – separately this time. Though they do not yet know it, that awful Saturday of their arrest and first hearing was their last day together. The *Morning Chronicle* has its reporter ready, though they struggle to understand Abraham's speech – or affect to. 'As might be expected the justice room and the avenues to it were crowded, although no public notice had been given of the appointed time for resuming the inquiry.' If the court has sought to play this down, it has failed: the case is already a sensation, it is in all the papers.

Abraham, still led by his dog, appears first. He is clean and neat, though the journalist talks of 'a smell'. Eliza's father is there again, along with all Abraham's old foes: Henry Major, George Foster, Edward Webb. All testify, and Abraham is grilled once more – this time, the focus is on his relations with Eliza. He insists that 'she never went begging with me. I never begged with anybody but my dog.' Poor Abraham – he still thinks this trial is about the technicalities of begging.

And now an unknown voice speaks up. This is Mr Coleman, 'of the office of the Registrar-General of Seamen'. He is telling the magistrate 'that by the 7th and 8th Victoria, cap. 112, the defendant could as a Malay be sent back to India at the expense of the owners by the Lords of the Admiralty'.

Abraham shakes his head, protests – this is the first he has heard of it, he has no desire to be deported. But the alderman speaks over him. He is to spend another week behind bars:

> ... in order to make arrangements for sending you back to your own country, which I consider is a much better way of getting rid of you than by dealing with you as we deal with other beggars. I shall communicate with the proper authorities upon the subject.

And Abraham is sent down.

He knows nothing of Eliza's subsequent hearing; of her stalwart defence. Hooper, who grills her, is as incredulous as Lord Mayor Hunter. 'And did you not wish to leave him?'

'No.'

'What! not go from a perfect stranger to you – and such a stranger?'

She repeats what she told Hunter, 'I have both respect and affection for this man.'

Hooper changes tack; rakes over the details of her past. Finishing up, he makes his threats. 'Do you know that you have been violating the law in going about with this beggar, to say nothing at all about the disgrace with which you cover yourself and your family by so dreadful a course of life?'

For the first time, Eliza sounds uncertain. 'It was, I assure your lordship, the first time I had ever been with him in the streets. I merely went to put him over the crossing. I shall not do so again, I declare to you.'

Hooper is not interested in this; he is not here to discipline a petty infringement of the vagrancy laws. Behind the scenes, things have been moving fast. 'I wish to know from you whether you are willing to go abroad?'

Perhaps Eliza mistakes his meaning. Does she understand this is not to be a joint voyage? At any rate, she is through with London – with England. What has it ever done for her? 'Most certainly I am willing to go. I wish to go abroad as soon as possible. The sooner the better.'

Hooper relaxes. 'Very well. I shall communicate with those who have it in their power and inclination to send you away from the scenes of your disgrace...'

And now, surely, she understands.

Another week passes. Eliza is summoned before a third judge – this one is David Wire, the man we'll find seven years later, now Lord Mayor himself, castigating Mary Ann Donovan. Eliza, unfazed, is 'respectably dressed, and conducted herself with propriety'. Her father informs Wire that a passage has been secured to America – though the Mendicity Society will later state her destination as Sydney, with a berth on the *Lydia* – and that she will be 'taking with her ample means to protect her from want'. Has she been paid off?

Wire checks that Eliza consents to the voyage – she does. She bows, she is humility itself. She speaks of 'the misery from which she has been rescued'. She has little choice. Is she broken? Is she playing a part? Wire too has news: he has received numerous proposals of marriage from respectable gentlemen – proposals to Eliza, you understand, not himself. One is from C.R., a German from Koblenz. It is all very strange. On Saturday 19th, late in the evening, Eliza's vessel sets sail – for America? Australia? Her fate is unknown.

Monday, 21 June: Mahomet Abraham makes his final appearance before Alderman Hooper. It is unclear whether he has been informed of Eliza's fate. Hooper, with an eye to the gallery, the assembled press, makes quite the speech, exonerating the court's own conduct – it sounds like he is protesting too much – and suggesting, curiously, that Abraham actively *wants* to be deported. 'I have been endeavouring to get you sent back to your own country, as you have expressed your wish to go there; but I find that there are difficulties that I cannot control, in the attempt to do what you wish.' Clearly, there are wheels within wheels. Or perhaps, now Eliza has been got rid of, the expense of shipping off Abraham too is simply unnecessary.

Hooper continues his prepared address. Time to scotch any suggestion that they have been heavy handed:

> You have now been in prison upwards of a fortnight, and I consider that confinement a sufficient punishment for the offence you have committed in begging. I now discharge you; but I caution you against your practice of begging. The great traffic in the City requires that our pavement should not be encumbered by those who seek relief for their necessities or for any other objects. The orders which are given are not at all intended to do injury to the poorer classes. There is no intention of doing a violence to humanity in carrying out our regulations; but we must not be infested by beggars, and I therefore caution you against ever appearing here again. You have been separated from your companion, and you are never likely to meet with her again, and I advise you to drop that sort of business altogether.

Abraham listens patiently. 'I thank you, my lord. Shall I have my dog again?'

If the brevity and simplicity of this response is meant as a rebuke to Hooper's pomposity, the latter shrugs it off. 'Yes, and you shall be sent to the union [workhouse], where you will be disposed of.' And that is, more or less, that.

On 4 July, an ostensibly humorous postscript appears in *Lloyd's Weekly London Newspaper*, a *jeu d'esprit* written in the voice of 'The Blind Black Beggarman's Dog', that wraps up the affair with a few more racist quips about boot blacking and miscegenation. This case, which has run and run in every national and regional paper for weeks, is at an end. *Lloyd's*, the *Morning Chronicle*, the *Examiner* – all the liberal and radical defenders of other, white street figures we have encountered – join in the fun, reprinting the same bigoted commentaries as the *Post* and the *Spectator*. So extreme is their racial revulsion that no mention is even made of what might be supposed a more pressing objection to the union of Eliza P. and a 'Malay' named Mahomet Abraham: that of his (decidedly ambiguous) faith.

Only the Chartist *People's Paper* speaks out in Abraham's defence:

> We cannot but express surprise and indignation at its being considered 'criminal' for a blind man, of another colour, clime, and creed, petitioning for the assistance of the philanthropic in that country which has conquered his own, and plundered its inhabitants.

A lone voice of compassion – a lone skewering of hypocrisy – and even here, there is no mention of the real issue. For years, Mahomet Abraham had carried on peacefully, enduring only minor brushes with the law. His persecution truly began when he dared link his 'greasy black paw', as the *Chronicle* put it, with the pale hand of 'pretty' Eliza. Such temerity could not go unpunished; the world of mutual support they sought to build was swiftly torn apart, and oceans placed between them.

But though respectable London was not ready for Eliza and Mahomet, it appears that the world of the street *was*. For years, it had rewarded and sustained Mahomet Abraham, and for nine months, until the Society intervened, it sanctioned their relationship. As Saree Makdisi's pioneering scholarship has made clear, London's poor did not share the fixed concepts of race and class that so obsessed the wealthy, and 'mixed' relationships, even marriages, were (relatively) common – without the anxious racial designations of 'mulatto', 'octoroon', and so on, that were used in the Caribbean and the Americas. Had Eliza not been genteel by birth, had her father not contacted the Mendicity Society, they might never have troubled either the courts or the newspapers.[36]

London's streets were by no means colour-blind, nor were they some cosmopolitan utopia where the world's peoples mingled as one. But the culture of the streets was inherently open – it recognised and welcomed difference, it sought out and celebrated that which was far-flung or novel. A street performer who played up to what made them distinctive could do very well. As James Burn, the Scottish beggar boy and sailor, put it: 'To those who have not got occasion to think upon the subject, it would be a matter of surprise to learn the amount of real charity which exists in London.' However exaggerated their claims of his takings, all parties concerned agreed that Mahomet Abraham was an unusually well remunerated beggar – because of his blindness, and because of his skin.[37]

~

This prevailing attitude, on which both beggars and street entertainers depended, was a complex one. It rewarded that which was not grey, tedious, commonplace, and it indulged in altruism towards those who were afflicted, the more conspicuously the better. For the migrant, this was double edged: a conditional acceptance based upon, rather than in spite of, difference. To be liked, pitied, applauded, rewarded – but always to remain foreign. For your outsider's identity to be neither resented nor assimilated, but rather embraced as a source of entertainment. Of course, poor London had its established and integrated communities, whether Arabic or Ashkenazi – but the *street* itself was a place for standing out, not for fitting in, and such was the bargain you made. To play up to a stereotype, to exaggerate an accent or appearance, to indulge the desire of the poor and powerless to have someone even worse off, even lower down the ladder, whom they might pity in their turn. This was far from equality. But for the dispossessed, the stateless, the fugitive, it had its advantages.

Sarah Wise has brilliantly captured the appeal of the Italian performers that brought new colour, vivacity, melody to the London street. 'All in all, Italy was providing London with a better class of vagrant', she quips.[38] This came at a terrible cost, from the grim conditions endured by those children who were effectively trafficked, to the press, police and parliamentary campaigns of discrimination that coalesced around the 1864 Street Music Act championed by MP David Bass and supported by all the great writers of the age: campaigns that demonised Italians, working the new-forged tools of racism against them.[39]

Other immigrants found themselves up against similarly hard bargains. Sometime around 1830, Peter, a Black street performer, is carrying on his act. Unbeknown to him, his audience includes the celebrated engraver and antiquarian John Thomas Smith, who will record his one-man-show – though, in a typically infantilising move, he will neglect to record Peter's surname. Smith observes in admiring but condescending style:

Blacks, when they become public characters in our streets, as they are more or less masters of humour, display their wit to the amusement of the throng, and thereby make a great deal of money. They always invent some novelty to gain the attention of the crowd.

Peter may not know of Smith – but he knows enough about his audience to pitch his act to their expectations. He conducts a dialogue, much like those of celebrated (and even blacked-up) stage performers like the late Charles Dibdin, Charles Mathews or the American Thomas Rice – a dialogue between a slave and his master:

> Master. 'Oh, Peter, you very bad boy; you no work; you lazy dog.'
> Peter. 'Oh massa, 'give me this time, Peter Peter do so no more; Peter Peter no more run away.'

Peter accompanies his own impressions on guitar; he sings; he turns contortionist, passing through hoops, 'placing his head backwards between his legs and picking up a pin with his mouth from the ground, without any assistance from hands'. He combines the patter, musicality and showmanship of his famous white contemporaries with the athletic prowess of the best street acrobats – but does so on the implicit condition that he, a free and talented man of colour, plays up to the blackface tropes of a slave-owning culture. He makes more money than his white peers. But it comes at a heavy price.[40]

Some find ways of subverting these harmful stereotypes, even while playing up to them. Smith is also familiar with Thomas McConwick, an Irish immigrant – subject, albeit to a lesser degree, to similar racial expectations derived from the theatre, since many of the racist jokes that made up blackface minstrelsy had been used for generations in on-stage impressions of Irishmen. McConwick too is a skilled performer. He 'sings many of the old Irish songs with excellent effect, but more particularly that of the "Sprig of Shillelah and Shamrock so green," dances to the tunes, and seldom fails of affording amusement'. McConwick tells Smith:

> ... when he came to London, that the English populace were taken with novelty, and that by either moving his feet, snapping his fingers, or passing a joke upon some one of the surrounding crowd, he was sure of gaining money.

To augment his routine, McConwick brandishes the famed shillelagh itself, and sports an arrangement of shamrocks in his broad-brimmed hat: he has his brand down pat. McConwick 'will sport a bull or two' in order 'to please his benefactors'. A 'bull' is a sort of joke against oneself – a conspicuous malapropism, a show of stupidity – and in incorporating them into his patter McConwick, like Peter, plays up to type, embodying the comical idiot that London audiences have come to expect.[41]

Yet Smith also records that 'when the laugh is increasing a little too much against him, [he] will, in a low tone, remind [his audience] that bulls are not confined to the lower orders of Irish'. This may seem innocuous, irrelevant even – but in a performer, it is powerfully subversive. Just when a street crowd – largely English – is at its peak of humorous condescension, the rug is pulled from under them, and they are confronted, not with a capering fool, but with a skilled, self-aware artist who – at least momentarily – turns the tables. It's important to remember that, at this time, 'John Bull' is the national caricature of an Englishman – honest and sensible, but easily duped, greedy, parochial – and the shared language of 'bulls' would help drive home the point. We are not so different, you and I. Or even: the Irishman you were laughing at a second ago is wiser and wittier, well-travelled; maybe, just maybe, the joke's on you.

This is the way in which McConwick, and even Peter, can really triumph over adversity, over their status as marked-out migrants. By virtue of their talent, their persistence, their quick wits, they can perform their own, humbler version of Lizzie's transformation: from a girl from Guiseley, sleeping rough, to Adelaide Neilson, star of the stage. Even if they never leave the street, the consummate artist can assert their identity and their worth, and make themselves part of the landscape. In the next chapter, we will learn how they do it.

5

The Pro

The street knows no guilds. Apprenticeships of sorts exist for the stabler professions – some milkmaids may learn from their mothers, and the milkmaid works out of a dairy, she has an employer. The same is true of many prostitutes, collectors of dirt, errand-boys... But London's most notable street professionals, those whose work is *of* the street, rather than merely passing through it – its sweepers, sellers, entertainers – have no masters. For the most part, they are, in their strictly professional capacity, on their own. And they often start with nothing.

Wednesday, 7 February 1838: for one street singer, his first day at work – not that he knows it yet. In the grey light of dawn, a man runs east, heading from Ray Street, Clerkenwell, to Old Ford, a distance of more than four miles. The day before, the man's young wife Jane gave birth to their first child; if it lives, they will name it Francis. The man is twenty-one years old, scrawny, just five feet tall, blind in the left eye and scarred by smallpox. He is out of work, having been dismissed from a Bible-binding factory for the dread crime of 'singing a hymn quite in a low tone while working'. And possibly for protesting when asked to desist.

At any rate, he has been destitute for some time – and now his wife, near-broken by her labour, lies ill and hungry. His one hope is the kindness of 'a rich relation', possessed, so he says, of a 'miserly, ugly heart' – but possessed also of a good deal of money, which is why he is tearing east at such a rate before sunrise. Faced with his request, his ragged breaths, the desperation in his eyes... she refuses. 'It served him right, and his fool of a wife too.'

At this lowest ebb in a life of precious few high tides, the man has an idea:

> [C]rawling back homewards down-spirited and ready to perish ...
> along Whitechapel Road, the sudden idea struck me that I would
> sing a hymn or two for bread and wife, and child – but I couldn't
> just there, known as I was all about the district.

Haven't we heard something like this before? Of someone on the brink of ruin, yet too ashamed to cry out in the streets of their own neighbourhood?

Of course we have. This desperate young father is John James Bezer.[1]

Life has not been much kinder to Bezer since last we saw him. Shoemaking has worsened his poor sight; he has scraped for and lost a series of low-paid jobs; even his marriage (on the rebound) he regards as a mistake. And now he is back where he was at seven years old, without even any buns to sell: a small, unprepossessing figure, with no resource except his own voice.

His account of what follows is a revelation. At more than 2,000 words, it is too long to reproduce, and I can only urge you to read for yourself – it is freely available online.* The omens are bad: seized with his old sense of shame, the already exhausted Bezer meanders

---

* At minorvictorianwriters.org.uk/bezer/b_autobiography.htm where it is the ninth and tenth chapters, beginning with 'Love, Marriage, and Beggary'.

as far south as Brixton, away from the busiest thoroughfares, before he can bring himself to begin. Even then, his nerve – and his voice – almost fail him, 'Here goes – "God moves" – begin again – "God moves in a" – out with it, and so I did, almost choking, "God moves in a mysterious way, His wonders to perform."'

And in that instant, Bezer's career as what we would now call a busker (the term will not be generally used for several decades yet) is begun. That first day alone, he pockets six shillings and fourpence – as much as some singers make in a week – and he lays out the odd pence on bread, cheese and beer, before heading back to the sick bed, where his wife Jane lies attended by both their mothers:

> I ran to her side, and, says she, 'where have you been to?' I whispered, 'I've got a place, my dear, got to go to-morrow, a good place, too – cheer up.' It was a lie! but a white one, and I believe it is not recorded against me in the book above. I then put the six shillings on the table, and sank into a chair exhausted. 'Why, where did you get all that money?' said both mothers at once, 'I've earned it,' said I, 'Well earned it – don't bother me.' And so I had earned it, for that was a hard day's work both for body and mind, was that same 7th day of February, 1838.

It is quite the moment. Confronted with the guilt-inducing, united front of all three women, Bezer plays the classic, frustrated, patriarchal breadwinner, and rightly feels he has done an incredible thing, an honest day's work – for all that he's too ashamed to admit exactly what it was.

Uncertain, a mere beginner, Bezer relies on luck. He takes nothing on the second day, four shillings on the third. On the fourth, Saturday, he gets 'either a few halfpence under or over 7s' – so large a sum, indeed, that he can afford to be vague about the small change. The next week is a mixed bag: 2s 9d, 1s 7d, 9s 'and odd'. But in seven working days, with no outlay of capital, he has cleared more than thirty shillings by hymn-singing – and this in the depths of a miserable winter. At that rate, and keeping the Sabbath, he would earn £65 a year at a conservative estimate: an excellent upper-working-class wage.

Inculcated with the values of Dissenting* working-class society, Bezer refuses to call what he does 'work', describing it instead as 'begging'. His conscience eats at him, especially when singing the same hymns in chapel on the middle Sunday or when he meets an old friend in the street, for 'nothing seemed so recoiling to me as that any one should know what I did for my bread'. He never comes clean to his family, and he abandons his 'eight days' cadging experience' at the first possible opportunity.

This hotly contested boundary between work and begging will define this chapter as it defined the nineteenth-century street. But, looking at the thing from the 'work' side, Bezer's swift retreat from busking was a loss to the profession. Time and again in his days on the street, he demonstrates his potential to become a true pro.

~

Bezer varies his pitch – Brixton, Clerkenwell, Islington, Holloway – as he varies his songs, 'hymn after hymn, and street after street', rather than wearing out the same audience with the same tune. Yet he has favourites on both counts that serve him well – streets in Brixton, 'God Moves in a Mysterious Way' – and he returns to these at intervals. His most successful song, a hugely popular hymn by William Cowper, he sings to the Methodist tune 'Church Street' – no plodding psalm melody, but a sophisticated, ranging air, with

---

* A catch-all term for Christian Nonconformists.

some truly memorable phrases in it.[2] As befits his repertoire and his character, he is polite, humble and honest, bestowing a 'God bless you' on generous givers, and questioning especially large donations. His vocal style is also in his favour: he sings 'loudly' with a 'good strong voice' and a 'peculiar earnest manner'. Yes, he blunders – one day, he chooses for a pitch a street already occupied by a family of beggars. The father:

> soon called me aside, and with a terrible oath said he'd kill me if I dared to oppose him. I tried to explain, but to little purpose, and we parted with the comfortable assurance from him 'that I was either jolly green or a b–y rogue, and that if I didn't know that to come and cadge in a street where another cadger was working, was not against the rule in the "Siety," he'd make me know it by jumping my guts out.'

Bezer makes his single best decision right at the start, when his first rendition bags him his first penny. 'I pocketed the affront and went and spent it in Gin! ... an invisible spirit seemed to say, *Have some gin, it will give you courage.*' An absolute beginner at risk of bottling it, he knows that a drink will steady his nerves. It pays off handsomely. If only the seven-year-old Bezer with his tray of buns had had a comparable opportunity to fortify himself, who knows how differently things might have turned out.

~

Bezer's temporary trade is a new one. For centuries, people have sung in London's streets, but only lately have they begun to do so without also offering for sale the printed words of their song. The idea that you might be paid simply for the pleasure of hearing you sing – outside of a concert hall – is novel, and no wonder he himself dismisses it as begging. Those who sell as well as sing are the true ballad singers.[3] In a world before recording, where sheet music is too expensive and unintelligible for most, this is the way people get their songs.

Just two months before Bezer's brush with the profession, one of these ballad singers is subjected to a dubious immortality in the flimsy pages of a cheap serial pamphlet, *Streetology of London*. Jack Cartar, thirty years old, is Bezer's might-have-been. Like Bezer, he has known violent masters, fleeing a shoemaker's aged twelve. Unlike Bezer, he is an orphan but, abandoned to the streets, he finds himself a surrogate father: Nick Saunders, a 'notorious street-singer'. Saunders takes Cartar under his wing – a great advantage – and raises him to the trade.[4]

As he grows to man's estate, Cartar learns how to live by his voice. These are lessons that not only singers but almost anyone working in the street needs to know. How to choose your time and place, when people are not only around but in the right mood: the West End as the theatres are about to open; thoroughfares and squares on market day; the calm, green spaces outside Greenwich Fair (for it doesn't do to venture too far inside – as the street hawker William Green puts it of Bartholomew Fair, 'There were too much bustle and noise, and unless you knew just where to pitch for it, very little could be done.')[5] How to adapt to the times – which means the seasons as well as the years: every winter, Cartar switches from murder ballads to Christmas carols, swapping out his call of catastrophe or bloodshed for 'God Rest Ye, Merry Gentlemen'. How to make the most of your surroundings, choosing a corner between streets for maximum exposure; using a portico or shopfront as a proscenium arch to frame your performance, or a large wooden door as a sounding-board.

Cartar must learn how first to create, then to maintain a crowd – which is a very different thing from the beggar's trick of forming an intimate connection with an individual. A crowd can be wooed, provoked, set against itself, and once formed, this crowd can be self-perpetuating, itself a guarantee of interest that will draw new members as fast as it loses them. He must also decide upon a distinctive look.

Take Madeleine Sinclair, for instance. Here she is on 23 July 1862, dancing a Highland fling on Oxford Street to accompaniment from an Italian organ grinder, for which purpose she is attired 'in full Highland costume; wearing a Glengarry bonnet, a scarlet jacket, a sporan and a tartan kilt & stockings, his legs bare from the knee to the calf'. His? Yes: at first Arthur Munby, who is watching, is as confused as the rest of the stolid mid-Victorian crowd. '"It's a man!" said one, confidently: "I believe it's a woman," another doubtfully replied. One man boldly exclaimed "Of course it's a man; anybody can see that!" I gave her a sixpence when she came round with her tambourine'.[6] Genius!

Once appropriately dressed, your body itself becomes an asset: you can dance, gesture, stand straight and true, play an instrument, carry a sign, juggle. And your attitude has to fit your appearance: do you restrict yourself to a humble 'thank you' and 'bless you' between your songs or cries? Do you harangue, hector, accuse – or supplicate, implore? If you back your wits, you can turn comedian, bandying jokes back and forth – and even if you lack invention, there are songs that come ready-made with scripted patter, repartee that can be learned by heart. Above all, there is your voice itself. Think about your tongue and teeth; lean back slightly and don't be afraid to open your mouth wide, even if – by the social codes of the day – this looks vulgar. The great thing is to project: you will need to be loud, as loud as Madame Catalani at the King's Theatre, if your voice is to carry in the bustling street. And cry out, or sing, not only loudly, but *high*. The tread of human and horse's feet, the rumble of cart wheels, the din of labourers and machinery – these are all low noises, and if you pitch your voice high, upon a musical note, it will cut through the hubbub like the tang of sliced apple in a bowl of gruel. If you have a falsetto: use it!

All these, and many more, are the lessons the teenage Cartar takes from the example of Nick Saunders, whose own speciality is that of virtuosic scoundrel: long matted hair, tatty clothing, drooping moustache, thin cheeks. Saunders accompanies himself on the fiddle as his 'wife' sells the printed ballads – and while Cartar lacks the talent to play a similar instrument, this at least leaves his hands free to sell his own songs.

By the time his life is sketched out in *Streetology*, just as Bezer is about to embark on his own week-long stint at Brixton, Cartar has been working the streets for fifteen years: he has become a fixture, a somebody. This sort of fame is modest, local; it doesn't lift him off the street and on to the stage. But it helps secure a place in the pecking order and repeat customers, and it guards against his being lifted off the streets more bodily by watchmen, the New Police, or the constables of the Mendicity Society. He is, in short, a professional.

~

1815: time to see a master at work. And 'see' is the word – along with 'hear', of course – because, of all the professionals working the London street, this man, Joseph Johnson, is one that people look *at*. Indeed, they are so preoccupied with what is *on* his head that no one ever tries to get inside it.

Johnson is a special case. One of those looking on, sketchbook in hand once again, is John Thomas Smith. He will talk to Johnson, sketch him, write him up for publication (see Image 5.1). A decade later, a second journalist, who has also stood among the appreciative crowd around Johnson, will elaborate on the legend. These two accounts, and a single image, will endure through two centuries, pulling in writers of histories, novels, television, scholarship. I have been drawn to these scraps myself more than once before.[7] And all because Johnson, canniest of operators, has made himself a curiosity among curiosities. Black, disabled, an ex-sailor almost certainly hailing first from the Caribbean, Johnson is celebrated above all for his extraordinary headpiece: a fully rigged, two-masted brig, towering above him, that sails upon the waves of the crowd as he ducks and bobs and weaves.

Joining the crowd around this street entertainer fresh from our apprenticeship with Nick Saunders, we will see that everything Johnson does, he does exactly right. He is, above all, a singer – very probably a sheet-selling ballad singer, definitely a busker – and though by no means blessed with a virtuoso tenor voice, he has mastered his art completely.

Johnson sings sea songs. He is an old sailor; this is London after Waterloo, the undisputed maritime capital of the world, ruler of the waves. The theatres are full of the stuff. Every songwriter of note churns out sea songs. The best and most prolific of them, Charles Dibdin the Elder, dead just a year, is synonymous with the genre. The public laps it up. Moreover, Johnson's base is Tower Hill: the open, pleasant ground in front of the Tower of London, where well-to-do bankers take a stroll, and busy workers steal a few minutes' peace; where, most importantly, his pitch overlooks the Pool of London, that stretch of the Thames immediately east of London Bridge, entirely crammed with shipping. In the words of another ballad singer active in the city at the time, it is 'a famous view of many hundred ships, that are so close together, their masts appear like a wood, for miles down the river to the sea'.[8] What else but sea songs would Johnson sing?

He varies his pitch. When not on the Hill, he works the streets around, adding busy footfall to his usual strollers. Perhaps this is where he sells sheets, rather than relying on his act alone. And once a week he ventures further, hitching a free ride on a wagon to visit the market squares of Romford, Staines and St Albans – three towns lying an ideal distance east, west and north of the centre, close enough to get there and back on a market day, far enough off to have their own distinctive buzz. In Staines, he surely takes his stand beneath the conspicuous sign of the Blue Anchor: even here, twenty miles west of the port of London, his backdrop is that of the seafarer.

This sailor's reputation is invaluable. Johnson is a man of colour in an age when Englishness is, in the eyes of many, starting to take on a racial character – the myth of the white Anglo-Saxon. But his skin is not marked out just by its hue: it is weathered, cracked, salted. He proclaims his identity with his headgear and his clothing; with every note he sings and every efficient movement he makes. First and foremost, all this says, he is a British sailor: he belongs here. But it's so much more than that.

He refers to the model vessel on his head as the *Nelson* – which might possibly refer to the *Lady Nelson*, a survey vessel launched in 1798 that, at the time, had ended up in Australia – but is more probably a fictional name invented by Johnson in order to link himself to the recent war effort.[9] How ironic and how brilliant that Johnson, a subject of empire, a dispossessed merchant sailor apparently denied a pension for his service, is able to appropriate the reflected glory of an English lord: a war hero, similarly disabled, but also a white supremacist and apologist for slavery.

This model vessel, whatever its identity, is also an advertisement of Johnson's consummate skill, of the dexterity of his hands and the depths of his knowledge. It is a stamp of authenticity at a time when

such things are valued.[10] It is also integrated into his act – for we
know precisely which songs he sings best. 'The Wooden Walls of Old
England' – a rollicking patriotic anthem, marking out the country's
sailors as its surest defence. 'The British Seaman's Praise' – a song that
not only does exactly that, to the infectious strains of a toe-tapping
dance, but has a manifesto for a chorus and a moral: in peacetime,
protect the hardy tar, 'be mindful of his merit' – do not leave him to
beg on the pier. And above all, Johnson sings 'The Storm'.[11]

'The Storm' is a hell of a song. It has nine long verses and takes
six minutes to sing. Set to a hymn-like melody of such beautiful
simplicity that Handel himself arranged it for chamber orchestra,
its lyrics constitute an epic: a first-person account of a storm at sea.
I can testify that it is a draining, cathartic thing to sing – let alone
to perform as Johnson does it. Let's watch him, via the anonymous
journalist:

> This ballad-singer not only described, he demonstrated – he
> lowered the top-gallants, then the stay-sails, and as soon as the
> time came for the breeze to freshen, Joe was seen to set the braces
> with a nimbleness and success that would have extorted praise in
> the great world of a man of war. Successively you were stunned
> with the boatswain's bawl and the cheer of the crew. Next of all
> he looked like a man possessed with a raging demon, as he darted
> from place to place in mimic fury, cutting down masts, casting
> guns overboard, and gathering all hands to the pump. Here was
> an improvement on that difficult grace of poetry, making the
> words an 'echo to the sense.' Joe acted the song – he passed you
> through all the perils of the tempest, snatched you from the
> imminent wreck ... Never shall we forget the shout of satisfaction
> with which he consigned every bitter remembrance to oblivion,
> as he fervently cried, 'She rights, she rights, boys! wear off shore.'

Besides singing with 'rude strength' and 'vocal force', Johnson's genius is in what the journalist calls 'pantomime'. Originally, this was a stage song. In the likeliest printed edition that Johnson might be selling, published by R. Harrild a few streets away at 20 Great Eastcheap, the song is headed with an illustration of a sailor amid the titular storm.[12] Rather than doing something useful – any one of the dozen actions listed in the song and in the journalist's description – this sailor makes a stock gesture of horror lifted straight from the melodramatic stage, arms flung out aghast against the fury of the waves. Johnson's 'pantomime', however, is not derived from the stage, but from real life – from 'the great world of a man of war'. With every gesture, he not only summons the storm to Tower Hill; he deepens his audience's appreciation of his authenticity, his inalienable quality of having been there himself and lived to tell the tale.

This pantomime is street theatre at its best, drawing on expertise and experience to enthral and to transport its audience. Practically, his addition of the headgear also trades on 'novelty, the grand secret of all exhibitions' (Smith's words), and simultaneously makes Johnson conspicuous, standing out above the heads of the crowd, turning those heads themselves into a living sea, recruiting the mass of Londoners into the role of supporting scenery, the waves for Johnson's *Nelson*. All of which is doubly impressive when we recall that Johnson is disabled: he is doing all of this while carrying himself on an asymmetric pair of crutches.

He doesn't stress this point – you can't help but notice them – knowing full well that to present himself as in any way needy, a 'cripple', would be to sell himself short. To the audience of the day, disability is embarrassing: most people see a wooden leg, for example, as not only pitiable but intrinsically comic; Adam Smith writes that the loss of a leg is fundamentally a 'ridiculous tragedy'. Disability is also seen as a 'defect', a falling off from the human body as God intended it. All of which is bad enough if you're Horatio Nelson: ten times more so for a veteran on the streets.

The idealised poor do not draw attention to themselves, they are humble, discreet, 'the truly deserving never present themselves to the eye at all, or at least do not "obtrude" themselves'. Worse still, a culture of suspicion is growing in these years that beggars are 'shamming', feigning injury. Johnson has not actually lost a leg, just the use of them, and cannot definitively prove his disability. By making use of asymmetric crutches and putting his body through this song-and-dance routine regardless, he is destroying his own body, placing himself under immense strain in order to maintain a mobility that, with every performance, brings closer the certainty of its own ending. Johnson, however, is astute enough to deprecate his suffering. Apparently, he tells the journalist that he is – in the only scrap of reported speech that we have of his – 'damaged in his cock-pit'. By playing down his serious injury with a witty nautical metaphor, he presents himself as a fit hero for the age: humble, insouciant, the last person to make you, the able-bodied looker on, feel uncomfortable.[13]

That's still who we are though: the onlooker, staring at the boat on Johnson's head, but no closer to being inside it. In 1815 as, for entirely different reasons, in the twenty-first century, we are almost certainly failing to understand what Joseph Johnson is really feeling. In 1815, we look at the *Nelson* and see a proud sailor, a dutiful servant of empire – sad that he's on the street, but jolly good that he loves his country which, thanks to all the assembled aspects of his rhetoric, we are impelled to admit is Britain. In the twenty-first century, we almost certainly look at the vessel on this Black man's head and see, before anything else, a slave ship. At the very time Johnson is performing, every western nation save Denmark and Britain is still sending these ships across the Atlantic; and though

Britain has begun to chase some of them down, its landowners will continue to own slaves for another eighteen years. For centuries, the spectre of this ship has been *the* symbol of this worst of all trades, the ultimate icon of empire and subjection. Today, many of us are rightly alive to this association, and might view Johnson's creation as a livid accusation, righteous anger implicit in every scrap of wood, string and canvas.

But these – both then and now – are only our assumptions. To reduce Johnson, veteran sailor, master craftsman, patriot, to the single context of slavery is to do as great a disservice to his miracle of hard-won assimilation as does a complacent belief in him as simply a loyal, seafaring subject. And both sets of assumptions miss what, for Johnson, is probably... the point? The joke, even? Which is that dancing with a huge model boat on your head is not, as Smith has it, a 'novelty', but born of Johnson's Afro-Caribbean heritage: the festive ritual known as Jonkanoo.

A custom brought to the Caribbean, especially Jamaica, by enslaved Nigerians and Congolese, Jonkanoo endures today as a form of carnival across the Caribbean. In the years around 1815, numerous colonial witnesses document it on slave plantations, capturing performances in journals and images. It involves dances, parades, elaborate costumes, masks, revels, and in this period, it allows slaves at once to celebrate their own culture and to critique that of their oppressors. One absolutely central, even titular figure is the man who dances with the model boat on his head. In 1816, Matthew Gregory 'Monk' Lewis even interviews a man, John Fuller, who has made one of these models 'with his own hands ... And indeed it was as fine as paint, pasteboard, gilt paper, and looking-glass could make it.' Johnson, of course, has been a sailor – but for all we know, he has either been born on a plantation, or visited one during his years at sea – and his particular stroke of genius is to marry these two cultures. Plenty of sailors make intricate models of the ships they served on, and a number of these display them on the streets, but none before Johnson has combined this with Jonkanoo.[14]

This secret knowledge – shared by very few Londoners in 1815 – gets us a step closer to what Johnson is actually doing. Janus-headed, he performs two cultures, white and Black, imperial and enslaved. Modern scholars of early Jonkanoo have established that it offered slaves a means of resistance, subversion, insubordination – even the cultural appropriation of traditional English iconography and rituals into their own culture.[15] Does Johnson see himself as subversive? By proudly performing, and profiting from, this secret slave culture in the heart of the imperial capital, is he laying claim to the ground he dances on, in a subtle, unspoken triumph for the underdog? Or is he saddened that he cannot explain the true roots of what he is doing? Is he somehow reconciled, content with the unique blend of influences that make up his own identity? Standing in the audience, we're all fascinated by his head – but where is that head *at*? Here in London? In Jamaica? Or, just possibly, out at sea, back there in the genuine storm that may well have cost him the use of his legs – a traumatising or even inspirational brush with death that he relives every day in song?

We can never know, and perhaps it's not our place to ask. But – and this is why we're spending so much of this chapter up on Tower Hill, immersed in Johnson's complex performance – the one thing we *can* know is that he considers himself a professional. He is an immigrant, he is ageing, but his place is here, as an unparalleled, adept entertainer. For all that he has a second hat, which he carries in his hand to catch coppers, he is expressly *not* a beggar. Smith tells us that it is precisely 'in order to elude the vigilance of the parochial beadles' that he first began his routine: neither the parish nor the Mendicity Society will take him up as a beggar while he carries on his trade – proof, if proof were needed, that he is generally seen as useful, worthwhile, a social good. Legally, this is important to Johnson; it protects him. Psychologically, it must also make a world of difference – to his sense of self-worth and purpose. Yes, he will take your spare change, and gladly. But he has undeniably earned it.

~

It therefore comes as a surprise that Joseph Johnson can only claim to be the *second* most celebrated disabled Black ex-sailor performing a song-and-dance routine on the London street in the years following Waterloo. Sometime between 1814 and 1819, somewhere in the region of Seven Dials, William 'Billy' Waters lowers his fiddle. Another officious gent is asking him questions – but this one's a painter. Waters has had his portrait done before, by no less a person than Sir David Wilkie, and he knows that a bit of patience and cooperation with an artist will reward him more handsomely than a few hours' busking. (For that matter, he's frequently featured in the cartoons of George Cruikshank, and will do so for some years more – but that's different, it doesn't pay, and besides, Cruikshank is notoriously inconsistent in the minor detail of whether Waters' wooden peg leg is his left or his right.)

The man introduces himself as Thomas Lord Busby – only it turns out he's not actually a lord, while the final image he produces of Waters in all his fiddling glory is not a patch on Wilkie's. Wilkie made him heroic; Busby can only make him ugly. With the typical exaggeration of a goggling white artist, he's squashed his nose, distorted his mouth (see Image 5.2). When John Thomas Smith caricatured Joseph Johnson's features – eyes too big, lips too fat – he at least made him look friendly. Busby has made Waters into a curiosity.

For all they have in common, Waters is a very different sort of pro to Johnson. His credentials are more clear-cut for starters. His injured leg is severed at the knee; no possibility of shamming there. He has served in the Royal Navy, not merely the merchant marine, losing his leg in a fall from the top-sail yard of the mizzenmast of HMS *Ganymede* in 1812. This much he tells Busby, the painter, and his story checks out. The *Ganymede*, a twenty-gun sixth rate captured from the French in 1809, was indeed commanded by the Sir John Purvis whom Waters names as his captain; one of Waters' two modern biographers, Tony Montague, has located his service record and the logbook that mentions his fall.

He's more of a musician than Johnson too, accomplished on the fiddle. He also seems thoroughly uninterested in working the patriotic angle: the only song we hear him sing is the faintly bawdy 'Polly, Will You Marry Me?', and he wears an oversized cocked hat covered in feathers, Napoleon-style, that seems, if anything, to be a calculated send-up of military seriousness. And in truth, he has little reason to love the British war effort, which has cost him his leg – since he is, by birth, an American. Which isn't to say that he feels alienated. Whereas Johnson seems a fairly solitary figure, haunting the Hill, riding on wagons, Waters is gregarious, known to have a wife and child – 'one fine girl, five years old', he tells Busby – and is apparently to be found at the centre of lower-class social life in the drinking dens of St Giles's.

According to the Victorian antiquarian writer Charles Hindley, Waters will have another child before his premature death in 1823; Hindley also records him as referring to his performances as 'An honest living by scraping de cat-gut!' Here once again is a self-respecting professional who has overcome adversity and injury, getting his routine and his image down to a tee.

Waters is a true street celebrity, making his way into literature and legend, portrayed upon the West End stage and Staffordshire pottery figurines. Douglas Jerrold, playwright and journalist, will remember him as a 'genius' and will write of his 'grace'. Yet his celebrity status also exposes Waters to myth making, to the fantastic inventions of writers over which he has no control. We will see the damage this does him. For now, it is enough to note that, though he rightly proclaims his 'honest living' as an entertainer, he is known to London's well-to-do as the 'King of the Beggars' – one of those tenacious urban myths that, though it glorifies him in its way, denies Waters his professional status. This unasked-for reputation undermines his performances, cutting into his takings, as passers-by, familiar with the myth of Waters' secret wealth, withhold their money from the real man before them. He can hold a crowd in the palm of his hand. But he cannot control what people think of him when he lays down his fiddle and they walk away.[16]

~

A generation after Johnson and Waters, a third Black ex-seaman faced a similar struggle to keep control of his own narrative; to assert his status as a legitimate professional. This narrative starts in June 1851 – not on the London street, but on board the barque *Madeira*, as she attempts to round Cape Horn.[17]

It's midwinter in the southern hemisphere. The *Madeira* left Glasgow in February; its crew are no strangers to cold – just, not *this* cold. Fifty-five degrees south, in near perpetual darkness, the howling gale snapping off the icicles that bead on sailors' beards. The *Madeira* is an old ship, built for warmer climes, and her timbers creak with every pitch and yaw.

It is in this terrible sea that Edward Albert, twenty-one years old, feels a throbbing in his legs. Beneath canvas trousers, his skin is paling, hardening, scabbing over. Frostbite. He tells Captain Douglas, who orders him to his hammock. Below deck the roll of the ship is worse than ever, the darkness total and the cold no less. Next evening, bellies rumbling, the ship's master and mate come calling for their cook and find him worse than ever. Glances, mutters. And then the two men seize hold of Edward Albert and carry him bodily to his kitchen. The galley is a cramped and guttering space; pans swing and knock against the walls. No, he must protest, he's in no state to work – but that's not it. They've come to cure him. The oven's lit, and such a smell – in his absence, they're roasting a fowl. One of them fetches it out, he can see it's only half-done, but still he's missing the point. The officers redouble their grip on the afflicted cook – wrestle him to the ground – and thrust his numbed feet into the open red mouth of the oven.

Several years later, and Henry Mayhew, social investigator, publisher of a myriad anonymised, elaborately rewritten interviews with street workers, pays the Albert family a call early one morning. Edward is now living with his wife and infant son in rooms off a little alley near Brunswick Square, Bloomsbury. Much has passed since that fateful night in the South Atlantic. And – here's the important thing – we don't need Mayhew to tell us about it. He's come to interview Edward Albert, not by chance, but because of a pamphlet Albert himself has published.

This little book, eight pages long, tells it all. How his feet 'burst through the intense swelling', how 'mortification ensued'. It tells of the double amputation in the Valparaíso hospital; of his captain's refusal to pay compensation, or even settle the wages of one he considered 'a dead man'; of his arduous route back to Glasgow via Portsmouth and London. It gives a paper trail, names and signatures, high authorities. Unforgettably, it tells of their arrival in Valparaíso, six weeks after that terrible night – six weeks at sea without any medical attention; how Albert was sent ashore 'on the lid of a coffin'; the stench; the trance he lay in after the operation – at which point (as Albert prints it in his book):

they all tgought me dead it is generaly understood in hospitals that whenever a patient dies his coffin is prepared so it was with me and when the mon lifted m into my coffin I came out of my trance and gave teem a start so they ran off to the doctor and told him the dead man hap come to life again when he came down mnch surprised he asked me how I felt and I replied I was very weak, he then ordered me a g ass of wine. after I had drank the wine he said I had a strong constitution and would not die in a hurry*

Albert subtitles his book after this incident: *Brief Sketch of the Life of Edward Albert or the Dead Man come to Life again*. As subtitles go, it's hard to beat.[18]

There is so much to be said of Edward Albert. Much of it he says himself: in his pamphlet and in his extensive interview with Mayhew. Much more has been said recently by Natalie Prizel, the only scholar to locate a copy of Albert's book. There is more to his story – a fraudulent grocer in Glasgow; an ingenious tea-and-coffee machine; a mixed-race wife he meets in Leeds; encounters with authority figures ranging from a port admiral to the officious local policeman who now objects to Albert working as a crossing sweeper. We should note how he proclaims himself proudly 'A Native of Kingston, Jamaica' on the cover of his book, but affirms to Mayhew that Kingston is 'an English place, sir, so I am counted as not a foreigner', and that he is a 'Protestant' who regularly attends a church near King's Cross – 'I never go in, because of my legs; but I just go inside the door'. In spite of which, many of the locals 'chaff me about my misfortune – they call me "Cripple;" some says "Uncle Tom," and some says "N[*****];" but I never takes no notice of 'em at all.' Whether this is truth or bravado, Albert is affected

---

* See below for discussion of this haphazard typography.

enough to remember and report these ableist and racist slurs, but he refuses to be cowed. He has christened his young son James Edward, in a moving acknowledgment of his heritage: 'James is after my grandfather, who was a slave.'

Outrageous fortune, a sea of troubles, he has contended with it all. And, like Johnson and Waters a generation before him, Albert confronts his pain every day. Mayhew notes that he:

> ... sweeps a crossing in a principal and central thoroughfare when the weather is cold enough to let him walk; the colder the better, he says, as it 'numbs his stumps like.' He is unable to follow this occupation in warm weather, as his legs feel 'just like corns,' and he cannot walk more than a mile a-day.

He suffers phantom limbs too:

> Oh, yes, I feel my feet still: it is just as if I had them sitting on the floor, now. I feel my toes moving, like as if I had 'em ... I had a corn on one of my toes, and I can feel it still, particularly at the change of weather.

Ruefully, he recalls better times, perhaps in Glasgow, when he was more properly equipped to manage his disability:

> I used to get about a little, with two small crutches, and I also had a little cart before that, on three wheels; it was made by a man in the hospital. I used to lash myself down in it. That was the best thing I ever had.

But none of this, in all its richness, is what marks out Edward Albert as a pro. In fact, he'd be the last person to use that label. He *had* a profession, even after his injury: in a stroke of advertising genius that will be familiar to us from previous chapters, he opened a coffeehouse in Glasgow called *Uncle Tom's Cabin* – and he still sees himself as a respectable victualler. 'I am not a common cook, either,' he declares to Mayhew. 'I am a pastrycook.' His current occupation as a crossing sweeper he dismisses as mere begging, for all that it serves a purpose and that he makes up to two shillings a day. All he wants is three pounds in capital, so he can open a coffee shop again; until then, he sees himself only as a beggar. But he does himself an injustice. Pastry chef he may be, but Edward Albert has another calling. He is a writer.

Albert's last journey from Glasgow to London was by road. En route, like other bookselling itinerants before him, he had his eight-page book reprinted more than once.[19] The copy Mayhew handles is published at Hull by William Howe.[20] Despite the fact that this printer has a woodcut of a sailing ship that would do very nicely for the cover, Howe and Albert have improvised a cover 'portrait' of Albert recycled from a racist cartoon used to sell tobacco papers, 'as is evidenced,' says Mayhew, 'by the traces of a tobacco-pipe, which has been unskilfully erased'. The copy Prizel has discovered, by contrast, is printed by R. Atkinson, 206 High Street, Sunderland – and Atkinson's edition is embellished with a glorious woodcut of a British frigate under full sail.[21]

Albert has not only somehow worked his way down England's eastern seaboard, he has negotiated with several printers, sold enough copies to necessitate reprints and taken shrewd editorial decisions about cover images and knock-out subtitles. So what if the cheap printers he uses are so strapped for typeface that they are forced to substitute letters all over the place, eschew most of the punctuation and put half the e's and a's upside down? It's still a compelling narrative, backed up by official documents reproduced on the fifth page, and rounded off with an eight-verse adaptation of the prose account that Albert may well have sung himself – though he's not going to admit to anything so degrading as ballad singing in front of Mayhew. Here is the song, its verses tidied up, but its spelling and grammar left intact:

Unto a sad and mournful tale,
Kind Christians pray attend;
For I'm unfit to labour quite
Oh may you stand my frieud.

On board the barque 'Medura,'
From Glasgow we set sail
And for some time we all enjoy'd
A sweet and pleasant gale.

As cook on board my duty done
For Captain and for crew
A faithful trusty servant
They Edward Albert knew.

Twas in Eighteen-hnndred and fity-one
We rounded off Cape Horn
And oftentimes I griev'd have been
That ever I was born,

For on a cold and bitter night
My precious limbs were lost
Oh how I prayed for morning
So piercing was thy frost,

The snrgeon came to save my life
My sufferings then were great
He brought his instruments and knife
My legs to amputate

And from that nour my sufferings
In prayer I sympathise
When horrified I hear men curse
Their precious limbs aud eyes,

I cannot labour for my bread
Give what you can afford,
And God who doth the ravens feed
Will in heaven reward

It's an absolutely classic ballad, going through all the usual moves, its consistent meter making it easy to sing to any number of well-known tunes.

Albert clearly has a gift, for all that he disclaims it. And this is the really fascinating thing about his situation. A proud professional man, much injured, much aggrieved, he hates to be reduced to what he thinks of as begging. But this begging involves the composition, publication, sale, and probably the performance, of a remarkable piece of writing. His pamphlet only exists because of ill fortune. Yet it gives Albert a voice, a vehicle for literary self-expression, that few street professionals possessed. Joseph Johnson and Billy Waters, for all their fame, sing the words of others, and have no control over how they are written up or remembered. Albert can tell his own account, and even in the more celebrated pages of Mayhew, this gets him an honour that almost none of Mayhew's thousand interviewees is accorded: he is not only named, he is *cited*.

~

Edward Albert is not, however, the only songwriter on these streets. In Chapter Four, we met wandering Scotsman David Love, who reached London only to leave immediately. In 1814, he returns, with his wife, fleeing Nottingham for fear of a new law that he thinks – erroneously – will see him sent back to Scotland. Love is now a seasoned ballad singer (see Image 5.3), but he has far more in common with Edward Albert than either man does with Johnson or Waters. Let's not be side-tracked by the fact that three of these four men are Black – this is a quirk of the available evidence, indicative only of the fascination that racial difference exerted on white nineteenth-century writers, who dwelt at such length on men of colour while recording the lives of practically no named women whatsoever. No, the closest connection between these men is that Love, like Albert, is an author.

Scorning the sale of others' words, Love's first act in London is to find himself a publisher: John Evans of Long Lane.

> The first piece I got printed was the elegy I composed on the cat, and sold them pretty well. I then composed a piece on Bartholomew fair, but I did not sell them so fast as I expected. Another I made on the cries of London, which sold well. And last, my petition, which sold best of all.[22]

Love will record this trip in his prose memoir, sold by subscription back in Nottingham and running to at least three editions (he'll also produce a memoir in verse, and excerpt the London episode for sale as a separate pamphlet; he knows how to make the most of his material). But already, in 1814, he is putting himself in his writing. The piece that sells 'best of all' is not witty commentary, but a series of lines that – let's not put too fine a point on it – do his begging for him. His 'Humble Petition of David Love' consists of nineteen rhyming couplets that hover, perhaps knowingly, between pathos and bathos:

> My coat is so bare, it is thin as a feather,
> Which makes me to shiver now in this cold weather:
> My waistcoat is slender, and no more to put on,
> I pin it together, it won't hold a button.[23]

It's an entertaining way to be asked for money, and it lets Love do so as a self-respecting entertainer.

As a ballad singer too, Love is an out-and-out pro. He bases himself at 42 Fleet Lane – a little off Fleet Street – 'so that I might have an equal distance to go round the city and suburbs, to get home in good time each evening'. He finds that, handled appropriately, 'The people in London are good natured and charitable, especially to strangers'. Scoping out the best spots for singing, he makes a careful study of the city's bridges, as providing excellent footfall with little distraction – and works out which will provide the best conditions on a wet and windy night:

> Westminster bridge is the finest, and the strongest I ever saw, and seats on both sides at the top of every arch, where people may sit dry and comfortable in a storm ... Blackfriars bridge is a very strong one, but not so many seats nor so well covered ... London bridge, where you pass to the borough, is also very strong, nothing inferior to Westminster, in seats and lamps.

But for all that he is a viable, published performer, he has no qualms about manipulating his audience's charitable inclinations. He carefully cultivates a number of benefactors, who can be counted on for a shilling, and gets one to back a new print run. Once, 'a gentleman who had seen my petition' gives him half a crown; others, moved by the same piece, send money directly to his wife and child. He concludes that London contains 'more kindness, love, and tenderness, than any place in England'. But this is false modesty. If it is indeed the case, it needs an expert to tease it out. And David Love is just the man for the job.[24]

~

By 1814 Love, who in early life was as ashamed as Bezer at becoming a ballad singer, clearly has no problem with asking for money, given that he does it in so artful a fashion. Albert, who sees himself as an upstanding chef, cannot reconcile himself to the same thing. Johnson draws a clear line between performing and begging. Josiah Basset, a hawker and self-described 'vagrant', makes the same distinction when the money runs out:

> After I had been hawking about three years, a variety of circumstances tended to diminish my stock, till I got both out of money and goods. I went to the parish officers to try to get a few shillings to set me up again, but could not obtain any from them. The prospect of once more going a begging for my bread filled me with grief and fear. I sold off my box and a few books that were in it, and bought a small stock of goods.[25]

Clearly, opinions vary. The great thing about Love and Albert's way is that, of all those working on the street, they have found a way to make their distinctive voices, not merely heard, but appreciated – valued – taken seriously. Out of every individual in this book, they are the two who most successfully tell their story as an integral part of their life and work in the street.

It is, in the end, the only way to do it. No matter how acclaimed, how respectable, how mundane your work might be, the mere fact of doing it in the public street means that, almost without exception, that work is discredited variously as suspicious, useless, scandalous, inefficient, archaic, picturesque, criminal, counter-productive, or a drain on the public purse. Even those who are organised, overseen, demonstrably essential, are tainted by association with the dirt they tread upon. The blind busker is a fraud, the flower seller is a prostitute, the ballad singer is in league with pickpockets – and all of them are in the way, they block the thoroughfare, they obstruct the dizzy flow of capital that keeps modern London's respectable traders in gold watchchains and well-staffed townhouses.[26]

A pure economist, less interested in the class politics of all this persecution, might put it down to competition. Here's John Thomas Smith again, musing over the 'itinerant Staffordshire Ware vendor', who roams the streets with crockery and ornaments. He:

> is sure to sell something in every street he enters, particularly since that ware has been brought by water to Paddington, whence he and many others, who go all over the town to dispose of their stock in baskets, are regularly supplied; and in consequence of the safety and cheapness of the passage, they are enabled to dispose of their goods at so moderate a rate that they can undersell the regular shopkeeper.[27]

No rates, no overheads, no staff – you can see why it's in the interest of the propertied tradesman to vilify his cut-price rival in the street.

But sometimes it's not about politics, or even about money. Saturday, 20 July 1861, in Grosvenor Square: Kate O'Cagnay is a milkmaid in her mid-twenties, and 'for nine long years she has walked her rounds *every* day, carrying through London streets her yoke and pails, and her 48 quarts of milk, in all weathers, rain or fair'. If anyone has earned the right to the name of respectable professional, it's her. She is tall, strong, 'weatherbeaten' – and yet. As she strides through this plushest of squares, milk cans balanced upon her yoke, one of the passing men calls out, 'Well, Kate!' She is used to such things, and makes no movement that might unsettle her cargo. Recognising – *him again* – Arthur Munby, she sighs. 'Oh, Sir!'

Munby stares at her, his eyes roving. He takes in 'the full curves of her sumptuous form', 'her large hands', 'her mouth and her large grey eyes'. Noting the lack of a wedding ring – a token that has only lately become *de rigueur* – he comes right out with, 'So you are not married, after all?'

'No Sir,' she says. She is embarrassed – who wouldn't be? – and perhaps even angry, but he sees only 'a sly shamefaced smile and a downcast look'. Even Munby is aware enough to realise how this is starting to look, out in the public street, and – realising that he 'might have compromised poor Kitty's unsullied reputation' – he deliberately turns his back on her – '(vile subterfuge!)', he thinks – in order to question her further; it is some time before he lets her go.

What kind of world is this, where an honest milkmaid is obliged to work in the streets, is obliged to answer when spoken to by a gentleman – yet who, on account of her sex, her youth and the inescapable fact of being out in the open, is simultaneously subjected to interfering personal questions and the constant scrutiny of a suspicious, moralising public. What kind of society is it that requires a woman to work in this way, and yet regards her as a loose woman if she so much as stops to talk? It would not be like this in a shop. It is because she is in – and of – the street.[28]

The real irony is that so many of these street occupations, dismissed as idle, unproductive, even licentious, require attributes far in excess of many more respectable trades. We have seen those that demand virtuosic skill, courage, invention, wit. Naturally, a certain kind of Victorian morality looks down on these qualities of show(wo)manship. But it might at least give due regard to strength, endurance, patience, stoicism.

Two years later, Munby contrives to run into Kate O'Cagnay again, and this time, he manages a proper conversation. She walks, he learns:

> from [her home near] Manchester Square to Charing Cross every day and back [three miles] besides her rounds with the milk. And what time have you to be down here at the dairy of a morning? 'At half-past five, Sir,' said my maiden, simply.

Munby is aghast. 'And you work till now – after seven o'clock? Yes. Nearly fourteen hours a day; and another hour at least spent in merely trudging to the scene of labour and from it.'

Note, these are all his words: she makes no complaint. Moreover, between 1852, 'when she came to London, till [18]58 inclusive, she never had a single holiday, Sunday or workaday'. In the six years since, she has had just two months off. All of which moves Munby's rather peculiar sort of compassion:

> Her delicacy of feature and complexion is gone; utterly marred by twelve years of rough work & weather. Weather! Why, *now*, she had on the same wet shawl and bonnet that I had seen her in two hours before. And yet she is still queenly.[29]

~

O'Cagnay's working conditions – for the sake of nine shillings a week – are far from unusual. Here is Richard Phillips, radical author and activist, on sellers of strawberries – hardly, you might think, the most onerous of professions:

They consist, for the most part, of Shropshire and Welsh girls, who walk to London at this season in droves, to perform this drudgery ... these women carry upon their heads baskets of strawberries, or raspberries, weighing from forty to fifty pounds [more than twenty kilograms], and make two turns in the day, from Isleworth to market, a distance of thirteen miles each way; three turns from Brentford, a distance of nine miles; and four turns from Hammersmith; a distance of six miles. For the most part, they find some conveyance back; but even then these industrious creatures carry loads from twenty-four to thirty miles a-day, besides walking back unladen some part of each turn! ... Their morals too are exemplary; and they often perform this labour to support aged parents, or to keep their own children from the workhouse! In keen suffering, they endure all that the imagination of a poet could desire; they live hard, they sleep on straw in hovels and barns, and they often burst an artery, or drop down dead from the effect of heat and over-exertion![30]

Perhaps Phillips's prose is only so purple because his politics are red – but his observations remain valid. Meanwhile, here is James Greenwood, social investigator, on that most vilified and scabrous of professionals, the costermonger, so widely 'libelled' as a 'class' that the term 'costermonger' itself could be defined as an insult.[31]

His breakfast is a hasty affair, despatched in these winter morning hours before daylight, at a coffee-stall at Billingsgate or Farringdon Market. When he has bought his goods and drawn them home – at nine or ten o'clock, maybe – he will refresh on 'a crust and a half-pint,' but after that the course of business knows no break until dusk, when, 'between the lights,' he snatches half-an-hour or so, and feeds as heavily as his means will allow,

ere, with recruited strength, he sallies forth again to dispose, by
naptha-light, of the remains of his yet unsold stock.[32]

Hardly the lazy, idle brute of the middle-class imagination. And even
the crossing sweeper – for all that Edward Albert saw his own post as
sweep as no more than an excuse for begging – might combine the
industry and ardour of the labourer with the nous and psychology of
the performer. Especially in the decades before carts and omnibuses
proliferated to such an extent that the trade was more or less swept away
itself. Charles Manby Smith writes of the 'channel of viscous mud, a
foot deep, through which, so late as the time when George the Third
was king, the carts and carriages had literally to plough their way'. As
late as the 1810s, the sweep must 'dig a trench in the morning, and
wall up the sides of his fosse with stiff earth, hoarded for the purpose',
this cleared and practically fortified ditch being the only way to create
a path dry and clean enough for pedestrians to cross by.

But the job takes more than physical prowess: in order to gain
decent remuneration, the sweep must cultivate 'the charitable interest
they would excite in persons accustomed to meet them regularly in
their walks'. Because of this, older sweeps, especially women:

> dread to lose a connection they have been many years in forming,
> and they will even cling to it after it has ceased to be a thorough-
> fare by the opening of a new route, unless they can discover the
> direction their patrons have taken.[33]

In fact, far from being beggars-with-brooms, crossing sweepers are
beginning to sound like an essential part of the London workforce.
In the 1840s, one rather eccentric politician recognises this fact. The
'Street-Orderly System' championed by maverick reformer Charles
Cochrane (himself rather given to showmanship) employs men

'taken from workhouses and stone-yards; or they were in such a state of destitution or distress as would have compelled them to become burdens on the poors' rate'. These 'useful and reputable members of the community', says Cochrane, demonstrate daily their capacity for hard and strenuous work. Yet still:

> These men, from their connexion with workhouses, have been, unfortunately, too generally regarded as persons who are idle, depraved, and dissolute; – who have brought themselves into a state of indigence, through improvident and reckless conduct, and who are not sufficiently trustworthy to be employed with advantage to the parish.[34]

~

Wherever you look, London life is being improved by the workers in its streets. Mayhew's pages of edited interviews, *London Labour and the London Poor*, are mostly filled, not with prostitutes, thieves, scoundrels, but with people recycling, foraging, inventing, contributing to the stuff of the city. And we needn't rely on Mayhew. Holborn, the 1820s: a woman known only as 'the barker' extracts the canines of dead dogs, which:

> she sells to bookbinders, carvers, and gilders, as burnishing-tools. At other times, she frequents Thames Street, and the adjoining lanes, inhabited by orange merchants, and picks up, from the kennels, the refuse of lemons, and rotten oranges; these she sells to the Jew distillers, who extract from them a portion of liquor, and can thus afford the means of selling, at considerably reduced prices, lemon-drops and orange-juice to the lower order of confectioners. She likewise begs vials ... these she soon turns into money, at the old iron shops[.][35]

Croydon, around 1830: 'simplers' are rooting in the swamps and ditches of what is still a semi-rural village, foraging in hedgerows. Imagine yourself in smoggy central London, prisoner of bricks and paving:

> To the exertions of these poor people the public are much in-debted, as they supply our wants every day; indeed the extensive sale of their commodities ... must at once declare them to be a most useful set of people. Among the numerous articles culled from the hedges and the springs, the following are a few in constant consumption: water-cresses, dandelions, scurvy-grass, nettles, bitter-sweet, cough-grass, feverfew, hedge mustard, Jack by the hedge, or sauce-alone.[36]

Battersea, around 1850: Ned Williams is to be found skulking around ponds with a net, working perforce in isolation because no one will come near him: the stuff he dredges up reeks to high heaven. He is skimming the scummy surface for duckweed, which – thanks to his industry – will no longer clog the waters of these city ponds but will find its way across the river to the poorest neighbourhoods on its north bank, in order to feed the ducks they keep instead of pigs or chickens – living, sometimes, under their beds, and mighty fond of this stinking weed.[37] The city must be fed.[38] And in an era before the vast majority have such luxuries as free time or a kitchen, the street is the place to get your sustenance – the street, in fact, is bursting with green-ery and fresh things, borne upon the trays of hedge scrapers and ditch divers.

Nor should we fall into the trap of only valuing that which can be counted or consumed. Here is Charles Manby Smith again, getting dewy eyed after encountering an aged seller of buttercups:

The old man knew the secrets of the human heart better than I did. He was well aware that to the industrious country-bred mechanic, caged, perhaps for life, in the stony prison of the metropolis, the simple flower which brought once more within his dark and smoky dwelling the scenes and memories of infancy, would present attractions to which a penny would be light indeed in the balance; and that he should therefore find patrons and purchasers, as long as he could meet with men who had hearts in their bosoms and a few penny-pieces in their pockets.[39]

Sentimental stuff, of course. But he's not wrong. And just as valuable is the 'disabled sailor' who haunts the boundary wall of Kew Gardens. Technically, what he does is graffiti, a form of vandalism. Or, put another way, he:

has drawn in chalk ... the whole British navy, and over each representation appears the name of the vessel, and the number of her guns. He has in this way depicted about 800 vessels, each five or six feet long, and extending, with intervening distances, above a mile and a half. As the labour of one man, the whole is an extraordinary performance; and I was told the decrepit draughtsman derives a competency from passing travellers.[40]

Whatever your opinion of the Royal Navy, it is hard to dispute the value of such work: sincere, informed, detailed, laborious, both inspiration and art exhibition for thousands of pedestrians.

1845 - or thereabouts - in Pope's Head Alley in the heart of the City, two decades before the Street Music Act (mentioned in Chapter Four) that will kick up such a storm against performers. As the many proponents of that Act would see it - among them luminaries such as Charles Babbage, Thomas Carlyle, Charles Dickens - Mr

Cohen, a blind Jewish violinist, along with his harpist son and his young daughter, are making a racket, conspiring to distract busy workers.[41] But this is how one young clerk in his late teens hears this 'hour's promenade':

> His playing was not street-playing; it was fit for a concert room. His tremolo, to too refined ears, may have been a little pronounced, and the accompaniments may have been open to the charge of vamping, but the whole performance was most effective. The violinist, while playing, moved his head from side to side, and turned up his sightless eyes to the little patch of Heaven that formed the roof of the court, as it forms the roofs of the alleys in Seville. His music took us all away from our sordid surroundings, and, for the moment, he was the twin brother of the Pied Piper of Hamelin.[42]

On all sides, men pass by whose heads are full of sums; whose offices are crammed with ledgers accounting for bewilderingly vast sums of money. But the value of this street professional's labour, totted up in terms of morale, beauty, sheer unalloyed human happiness, is surely incalculable.

~

Why, then, did street professionals continue to be looked down upon, slighted and – as we have seen time and again throughout this book – persecuted? Why is Albert told to move on by a policeman? Why is Love repeatedly arrested all over England? Why is Waters said to have had numerous run-ins with the Mendicity Society and local magistrates?

Many convincing arguments have been made, often pointing to direct economic or political interest. In an age when democracy is, for many, a dirty word, the articulacy of those in the street is clearly subversive. There are many links between such people and radical, Chartist, or even Communist movements. More broadly speaking, for the disenfranchised and dispossessed even to attempt to assert their voice in public is bad enough – how much worse when they do so with not only volume but panache? Street traders threaten to undercut established guilds; entertainers cause crowds that lead to picked pockets and jammed traffic. The ad hoc sale of foraged foodstuffs invokes the idea of what has been called a 'public commons' – and the idea that any person might take their food for free from the roadside is an affront to the developing orthodoxy of capitalist enterprise.

But it's deeper than this too; less rational, even subconscious. The good people of respectable London simply cannot see these people as professionals. It is just a step too far for the bourgeois imagination. The workers of the street move to different rhythms, they occupy a different chronology. They even work on Sundays! Such people move at ease between fixed lodgings and an itinerant life, they roam far from their parish of origin, they are at ease in surroundings that alienate their betters, and they persist in carrying out their business in a space that is being repurposed by modern men as a space meant only for business to *move through* – good God, what a category error, to see the street as habitable, as a field of expertise rather than a linear conduit! They don't vote (and jolly well shouldn't); they don't fear God (and jolly well should). How, then, are they possibly to be taken as serious professionals?[43]

Having seen for ourselves what it takes to succeed in the streets, we now know better. It is important to hold on to this knowledge in the face of the way these professionals are presented by the establishment. It is all too easy to start thinking like members of the Victorian public, confronted with this petition as reproduced in Mayhew's early articles for the *Morning Chronicle*. It comes from a man described by Mayhew as 'the poor half-witted and very persecuted harp-player, so well-known in the streets of London':

> Your humble Partitionar as been obtaining a lively hood the last 4 years by playing an harp in the streets and is desirous of doing so but from the delapedated condition of my present instrument I only produce ridicule instead of a living Trusting you will be kind enough to asist me in getting another I beg to remain your humble Partitionar, FOSTER.

It is in Foster's interests, given his audience, to present himself rhetorically as 'humble'; he knows what he's doing. It nets him two pounds and ten shillings from solicitous readers, more than enough to buy a new harp. Let's credit Foster's resourcefulness in constructing his petition, rather than casting him as a hapless supplicant. His harp should not be bought at the price of our condescension, in addition to that of his contemporaries.

~

On the evening of Wednesday, 15 May 1851, street professionals of all stamps descend upon an unnamed hall in Westminster to hold a meeting 'for the purpose of refuting the statements put forth by Mr Mayhew, in his work entitled, "London Labour and the London Poor."' Mayhew's epic series of editorialised interviews, so central to the received narrative of the London street that I have had more or less to ban it to prevent it from taking over this book, is already causing controversy on its first publication as a serial in the *Morning Chronicle*. As the chairman, Mr Taylor, opens by disclosing, Mayhew himself has been invited to attend – 'but he had not thought fit to appear'. It's probably for the best: Taylor's invective is enough to shame even so brazen a character as the formidable journalist:

> Mr Mayhew had endeavoured to wage war against one of the poorest, the lowest, and the most illiterate classes of the community. Mr Mayhew had tried to injure a class of society that never injured him; he had endeavoured to show that the street-sellers were devoid of honesty, decency, and of every virtue. He had got up his book to suit the tastes and views of the upper and middle classes, and he had selected a helpless class to be the victim of his slanders – the butt and target to be fired at by public scorn and ridicule. Mr Mayhew took care never to state anything on his own authority, but always on hearsay – a ready and safe mode of circulating falsehood and calumny. (*Cheers.*)

Mr Thoresby is the next to step up. Declaring himself to be 'one of those individuals designated by Mr Mayhew a "London patterer"', he proves it by the strength of his oratory:

> [Mayhew] called together costermongers, and said to them, 'You, my men, are the finest, the noblest set of street-sellers,' but soon afterwards represented them as savages, barbarians, and destitute of all virtues. Was that giving them a good turn? But how did Mr Mayhew get his information? The street-sellers themselves would give him none, and he was compelled to seek it from the outcasts of that class, who, to ingratiate themselves with their patron, would invent the most scandalous falsehoods and ridiculous statements. Mr Mayhew holds up the 'patterers' as cheats before the public. He says they make a long tale to sell their wares; so they do; but he (Mr Thoresby) could vouch for it

that those tales contain more truth than could be found in the pages of 'London Labour and London Poor.'

A succession of speakers add their invective. Mr Hancock, a street seller (of what, we do not know) proposes a motion against the absent Mayhew; it is carried.

When we speak of the street pro, it is of people like this: proud, confident, perceptive. As stoical as Johnson or O'Cagnay, as articulate as Love or Thoresby, as accomplished as Waters or Cohen. They are self-respecting professionals. Some of them have even taken the effort to tell us so.[44]

6

The Renegade

Everywhere in the street, there are professionals being useful. And everywhere, some among their number are failing. Down and out in London, possessed of your wits, one suit of torn clothing and precious little else, the doors begin to close. Most jobs require at least the appearance of respectability; most forms of relief, strings attached or otherwise, require a fixed address. Besides, the encounter with authority in the form of the so-called charitable institution can be a harrowing one, the sort of experience to turn a desperate person against society, rather than restore them to a place within it.

British society, especially in London, is yet to sort this out two centuries later; how much more precarious, embattled, let down, are those in an age when those in authority - the police, the courts, the parishes, the charities - lack the resources, the empathy, the inclination to understand them? By turns abandoned or persecuted by a system, less from malice than from unexamined prejudice, these people become renegades. London's outcasts, its afflicted, its petty criminals. Renegades, in that they have turned - or been turned - away from the dutiful path appointed by their betters, from a steady job and a fixed abode. Renegades, in that they suffer for it.

The early 1860s: a man known only as C.I., forty-five years old, has gained his living for many years by selling in the streets. When he has sufficient means he deals in poultry and rabbits, but for a long time past he has been compelled to deal in shrimps and other articles which do not require much capital to start with.

A widower, he has been left with seven children – but a fourteen-year-old daughter 'does her best to mind the rest' while his eldest son, who is twelve, 'has a place as errand boy, and brings home 6s. per week'. It is precarious, but it's a system. Until, in the summer heat, he contracts a fever. He comes through it, but by the time he is released from the 'Fever Hospital', his children are scattered – two with a friend, five in the workhouse – and even when he reassembles his brood, it is only to 'occupy a small room on the third floor of a house in one of the most wretched and depraved courts in the neighbourhood of Hampstead Road, at a rent of 2s. 6d. per week'.

Even so, things might recover – except that the fever has wrecked both his constitution and, worst of all, his voice, the one thing absolutely necessary to his trade of street selling. Gradually, they slide into starvation. Visited by one of those busybody investigators, Joshua Stallard, he is caught between his pride and his despair:

> If I had £1, I think I could do well with it. This morning, a brother coster-monger, who did not buy anything himself, lent me 10s. I bought 3s.-worth of shrimps, and if, with my boy's assistance, we are lucky enough to sell them all, we shall realise a profit of 2s., which is all we have to find our supper, the first meal we have had to-day. To-morrow my friend will want the money for his own use, and I must go without. We starve a day, and then, if I borrow enough to earn a few shillings, we are obliged to spend it in food, and get no forwarder.

This brutal assessment impresses Stallard, who notes that 'the truth of this story is written on the man's face, and in the misery and squalor of the whole family'. But Stallard has seen many such cases; he knows the system, and – unlike C.I. – he is able to pin down the source of the problem. Under the current Poor Law, 'the system says, inexorably, an able-bodied man shall not be relieved' – and so C.I. can only apply for assistance when ill and starving, and even then 'is relieved casually' with a few shillings, all of which keeps him on the brink of disaster. How unlike 'the enlightened philanthropy of the Jews', Stallard reflects, who see the wisdom of extending enough credit to set someone up with enough capital to make a go of things. As it is, C.I. and his family are slipping into penury. In their failure to conform to the narrow demands of an inflexible system of relief, they are becoming renegades.[1]

The worst of it is C.I.'s need to pay for his outgoings up front – the 'few shillings' he is 'obliged to spend on food', along with that far from inconsiderable two and six a week on rent for one small room. Only the self-evidently well-off can get these things on credit; no one will lend to a pauper, let alone give them an unpaid bed. When times are rough, and rent impossible to come by, the most immediate place of refuge for the night is to be found in a casual ward – the temporary shelters run by workhouses and similar institutions on the rough model of Dante's Inferno.

July 1866: a 'pauper widow' using the names Ellen Stanley, Ellen Taylor and Jane Wood is hired by Stallard to visit four of these wards incognito – he wants someone 'accustomed to dirt and rags, and hardships', who 'by a course of suffering has been prepared to endure misery of the very lowest kind without a murmur of complaint', in order to provide copy for his social journalism. Her account – though watered down by Stallard, who found it 'absolutely necessary to soften down much of the language, which was too gross for publication' – is riveting, brilliantly written, and freely available online.[2]

Newington, 13 July: she gains admittance to a bare cell. 'After a time I felt very lonely, and began to cry ... and very soon my trouble was increased by finding that the place was alive with vermin, and that scores of bugs were running about the bed.' Eventually she is joined by more experienced vagrants, who know how to combat both the bugs and the oppressive heat. A woman in her fifties, a seller of 'cottons, tapes, stay-laces, and other articles', undresses. 'When she had reduced herself to complete nudity she commenced to destroy the vermin on her body, the skin being covered with sores and dirt, such as made me ill to look upon.'

Next morning, she is told there is no washing water, and remarks that it is 'a shame that they might not wash themselves, because their hands were dirtied by the oakum, and it was impossible to sell her bits of lace without soiling them'. This is the oakum – a fibrous matter used to caulk ships, literally made from old rope – which they are forced to pick for several hours in the morning before being released: a night in a bare cell is not to be had for nothing, and in this case the labour extracted by the institution directly impinges on her ability to work in the street.

17 July, a night in Lambeth: one woman, named Shipton, is driven to distraction by the constant excoriation of her bug-ridden skin – 'Roaring with madness, she stripped herself entirely naked, retaining only her bonnet and a small shawl. The clothes she took off scarcely held together, and she tore them into rags.' The attendant who restrains her remarks that 'this is the twelfth case of tearing up' she has seen.

20 July, Whitechapel: here, the women are obliged to place all their clothing in lockers to prevent theft. 'It was fearfully hot, and there was not a breath of air.' We have all known nights like this – but rarely in such circumstances:

About twelve o'clock the closeness and heat of the room became intolerable, and every one began to feel ill and to suffer from diarrhoea ... From this time the closet was constantly occupied by one or another, and the stench became dreadful.

23 July, St George's-in-the-East (modern-day Shadwell): this one's worst of all, an 'underground cellar'. Recoiling, Stallard's brave volunteer protests, 'What a dungeon! Surely I am not to sleep here! I cannot do so. I really dare not.' Her fear is real: these places are rife with cholera. Before long, 'seized with faintness, sickness, and diarrhoea', she is forced to ask the dreaded question – 'Where is the closet?' But the question scarcely needs posing: she can locate it by the smell:

I opened the door in the corner and found it, and whilst I live I can never forget it. I thought it must be the dead-house, and that I had made a mistake; and when I lifted the seat-lid I flew back, for there was no pan, and the soil reached nearly to the top. I felt too ill to remain, for even the floor was saturated and wet with the filth which oozed up out of it. I returned to the ward and vomited, which relieved me of the pain.

Yet the night is far from over, and there is no way of leaving once you have entered:

I then got very cold, and vomiting incessantly I was forced to cover myself with the [bug-ridden] rug to preserve my life; and from that moment my torture was beyond the power of any tongue to tell. It was impossible to see anything, but I felt stung and irritated until I tore my flesh till it bled in every part of my body.

She survives – but will not visit another such place for even the noblest of causes.

Those she meets, however, cannot be so discriminating. One such is Sally, or 'Cranky Sal', whose path she crosses first on 17 July at Lambeth. Sal, thirty-seven and 'stoutish', takes the newcomer's part, defending her against the suspicions of the other women. Later in the night, she shares her story.

Having roamed the countryside with a friend known as 'Navvy Nell', sleeping in haystacks, cadging change and bits of work, she and Nell have made it to London, where the latter, more successful in her ventures, is 'now well togged up' – so much so that she has abandoned Sal. Sal is now a regular of the casual wards, particularly fond of the beds at Richmond and the food at Marylebone, where she knows the nurse, and can use 'her reputation for crankiness to get into the imbecile ward'. Emboldened by their shared confidences, Sal thinks she has found herself a new partner, and suggests the next morning 'that I should go to Wimbledon with her', where there is an army camp. Alarmed, the investigator tries and fails to shake her off – 'but in Lambeth Walk she complained of thirst, and I offered her a pint of porter, which she drank with great gusto, whilst I gave her the slip and returned home'.

Yet, to her 'astonishment', after her night of hell in St George's she finds that Sal has been one of her 'fellow-sufferers'. Her crankiness is to the fore – starting a row with another inmate, she is confronted by a woman of around sixty who 'struck her a most violent blow in the face … the savage manner of her blow not only frightened Sally but all the rest'. Rising above it, however, Sal once again befriends the author – to whom she says, '"I think I have seen you before;" but I pretended not to know her'. Changing the subject, the investigator asks about her black eye, '"How did you get that?"'

The Renegade

'She replied, "because I would not let a man do as he liked with me;" upon which all the rest set up a loud laugh.' But Sal has her dignity and her honour, and defends herself against their insinuations. Later, she once again confides in the writer:

'I met a man on Saturday night in the New Cut, and he asked me if I would have a pennyworth of whelks. He seemed decently dressed, and I told him I didn't mind.'

'What time was that, Sally?' said I; and she replied, 'It was getting late. He then asked me if I would have a pie, so I said I didn't mind, and I had a twopenny pie, for I thought I might as well have a twopenny one as a penny one. Then we strolled along, and stopping at a doorway he offered me a shilling. He said that would get a lodging for the night, and by this time we reached St George's in the Borough, and he asked me if I was going to take his money, and I said "Oh no! I don't do business like that," and he gave me a violent blow. I screamed out, and he ran away. I began to cry, and a policeman came up, to whom I complained; but he only laughed at me and said that the man must have a strong stomach to fancy such as me.'

Everyone, it seems, treats Sal badly. Yet, she protests:

'I do not really do anything really bad. You know what I mean; I beg and pick up what I can, and go about anywhere for a bit of food or a night's lodging. Sometimes I make do on what they give me at these places here; sometimes I get a few pence given me.'

While the pie-buying sex-pest probably did her the greatest injury, the blows she feels the most are those of personal betrayal – and none more so than from the woman she met the week before:

'... who gave me a piece of bread-and-meat and three-quarters of a pint of beer. I thought she was going to be kind to me and be my pal, but whilst I was eating and drinking she ran away, just as the other did. I am very badly off now.'

The author is not insensible – she writes 'Poor Sally! I am convinced she is not vicious, and is to be greatly pitied.' Yet she fails to reflect on the fact that she herself, listening with such sympathy, is in fact this worst and latest Judas.[3]

A couple of years later a youth, aged around eighteen, is out of work. He pawns his watch and his clothes, he goes on tramp, in the vain hope of some casual employment on the road. Finally, he and two friends try to enlist; the friends are taken, but he is rejected for being 'half an inch too short. I had just enough for a night's lodging, and next day had to start begging.' He stalks Covent Garden, helps to shift manure 'for a few coppers', scavenges the detritus of the market, and sleeps 'in casual wards. The filthiest one was near Grosvenor Square.'

But this boy isn't just anyone. He's the nose-bleeding, self-starting, bowing-and-scraping, wheeler-dealing, father-confronting Charles Humphreys, last seen in Chapter Two. And, always with an eye to the commercial, he soon realises that, thanks to the obligatory labour:

In all casual wards they always turned you out not before eleven in the morning, and the time for earning a few coppers round the markets was gone, so as a rule I slept anywhere. Brick-fields, old carts turned up, buildings in the course of erection...

He knows a place in Great Windmill Street where you can get water, soap, a comb – all essential if you want to look like an employable person – and is not above washing his shirt 'in the canal near Kensal Green gas works'. Yet even the plucky Humphreys has his limits:

I did on one occasion lay in the green Park one afternoon dirty, and it did seem hard lines for a young fellow trying to do the right and yet to be as I was just then.

A little water did run out of my head, and I made a noise I suppose and a bobby came to me and asked me what was the matter. I told him I felt a bit downhearted; that was all. Got up and walked away.[4]

When you're on a downward spiral, sleeping rough or in a hellhole, it is easy to lose all hope. Humphreys may come through his wobble; he may not. But he and Sal, and all the others, are on the edge. One false step, one slip, one hesitation, and the life of the renegade beckons.

~

Friday, 16 February 1838: we return to John James Bezer on the ninth day of his career as a busker. As we have seen, in many ways Bezer is ill-fitted to a life on the edge: even now, aged twenty-two, he remains so innocent that he has never heard of the Mendicity Society. Walking up High Holborn, he meets a man. Specifically, the man is a living, shouting advertisement: 'Give no money to beggars, – food, work, and clothing, are given away to them by applying to the Mendicity Society, Red Lion Square.' Learning on further enquiry that, if he wants help, he will need to obtain one of the Society's tickets, he hastens to the profitable begging ground of Russell Square, where he gets a ticket 'of the third person I asked'. Proceeding to Red Lion Square, he mounts the imposing steps of No. 13 and knocks at the door 'with joy and boldness':

'What do you want,' said the opener. 'Here's a ticket, sir,' (showing it for fear he wouldn't believe me) 'I want to see the gentlemen inside.' 'O, go round the corner; that's *your* way,' and he slammed the door in my face.

Naturally, beggars are not supposed to show their faces in the square itself. Nevertheless, they do. In 'the late severe winter' of 1829-30, as Edward Pelham Brenton remembered, 'the numbers actually relieved amounted to 27,000 and upwards, and so dense was the crowd in the neighbourhood of Red Lion Square, that the inhabitants loudly, and I think, not unjustly, complained of the nuisance'.[5] In later decades and especially during the Irish famine, this number would swell to double that of 1829, at times threatening to swallow the square whole.[6] But back to Bezer, as he passes:

> round the corner, and down some dirty steps. And then such a scene presented itself to me as never can be effaced from my memory! – a hundred – fully a hundred, of the most emaciated, desolate, yet hardened, brutal-looking creatures, were congregated together in the kitchen, the majority of them munching, like so many dogs, hunks of bread and cheese. I was told to pass on, and then another hundred daguerreotype likenesses of the first hundred met my bewildered gaze, waiting to pass a wooden bar one by one.

He spends an hour in line among this 'Devil's crowd', during which he is thoroughly disabused of his hopes by the man next to him:

> 'I tells you what, old flick, you've been deceived, it[']s all lies, – they only give you a bit of bread and cheese, and you must be up to snuff to get *that*, – not one in a hundred gets more. Clothing's all my eye. And them as gets work, it's to break stones at six bob a-week – it[']s all lies I tell you.'

And so it transpires. Bezer's interview with the board of 'six gentle-men, as people call bears that are dressed well' has to be read in full to be appreciated; it is a tour de force of Dickensian injustice. Throughout, he is confronted with disbelief, condescension, suspicion:

'Are you a beggar?'
'Yes, sir.'
'How long?'
'Eight days.'
'Only eight days, – are you sure of that?' (with a cunning infidel leer).
'Yes, sir, that is all.'
'Are you married?'
'Yes, sir.'
'Ah, I thought so. How many children have you got?'
'One, sir.'
'O, I wonder you didn't say a dozen – most beggars say a dozen. How do you beg?'
'I sing hymns, sir.'
'O, one of the pious chanters,' – with a grin at the gentlemen, who grinn'd too, at his brilliant wit.

When Bezer is indiscreet enough to admit he has not applied first to his parish, one of the board erupts in righteous fury:

'Officer, you see that fellow – you'll know him again – he goes about singing hymns; he says only eight days, – is that a truth?'
'O dear no,' said the lying scamp, 'I've known him for years!'
'Ah, now, mark him well, watch for him, and directly you catch him, lock him up, and send for me. We'll have this gentleman before a magistrate, and he shall sing hymns on the treadmill.'

Somehow, Bezer talks himself out of it; in fact, so loquacious and so indignant is he, that they are more than happy to feed him, if only it will shut him up and move him on. Yet even when he gets his 'half-a-pound of bread˙ and a piece of cheese', he is not allowed to take it back to his family, but must eat it on the spot.[7]

'I shall not,' said I.

'You must.'

'I won't.'

'Then give it back.'

'I won't do that either.'

'Then come along with me,' and I was again before the immortal six.

'Sir, he won't eat his bread and cheese.'

'O, then let him give it back.'

'He won't do that, sir.'

'You must, sir,' said the Chairman to me.

'I won't.'

'You must, I tell you, it's the rule, and you must obey it.'

'I don't care about your *rules*, I want to share it with those I love, who are as hungry as I am, and if you are a Devil with no natural feelings, I am not. Get out of the way, beadle,' and out I rushed, like one mad, through the crowd of astonished beggars, right into the street, without one stopping me.

Easy to imagine yourself in Bezer's position, wishing to feed your family, unwittingly walking into the trap of severe bureaucracy. Far harder to imagine volunteering your time to serve on the board of the Society, only to conduct yourself in such an ogreish manner. Maybe these men start out full of Christian charity and idealism – tempered,

---

* Some 227 grams; by 1847 it is 60 grams more.

of course, with the prejudices of their class and their day – and grow embittered by experience; grow, perhaps, a carapace of unfeeling to guard against the barbs of sudden sympathy. But we are not concerned with their psyches, or their souls, here. It is Bezer who concerns us, pushed over the edge by this final injustice. From this hour, he is a renegade – yet it takes him from our sight, for he is immediately enlisted by his humane landlord into the cause of politics:

> 'Ah,' says he, 'there'll be no good done in this country till the Charter becomes the law of the land.'
>
> 'The Charter?'
>
> 'Yes, I'm a Chartist – they meet tonight at Lunt's Coffee House on the Green – will you come?'
>
> 'Yes.' It was only a 'Locality' meeting, but there were about sixty people present, and as one after another got up, oh, how I sucked in all they said! 'Why should one man be a slave to another? Why should the many starve, while the few roll in luxuries? Who'll join us, and be free?'
>
> 'I will,' cried I, jumping up in the midst. 'I will, and be the most zealous among you – give me a card and let me enrol.'
>
> And so ... I became a Rebel; that is to say:– Hungry in a land of plenty, I began seriously for the first time in my life to enquire WHY, WHY – a dangerous question ... isn't it, for a poor man to ask?[8]

Honest, earnest, idealistic, it makes perfect sense that Bezer reacts as he does – which extends, of course, to penning his account, which is sounding ever more like a political pamphlet, or a secular sort of conversion narrative. But others, less upstanding and without the coincidence of timing and opportunity that leads to Bezer's awakening as an activist, can hardly be blamed if their own response to similar circumstances is a little less... principled.

Spring, 1800, outside 53 Fleet Street: James Hardy Vaux is a young man, well brought up. The son of a Holborn hatter-cum-hosier, schooled in leafy Surrey, raised in part by respectable grandparents. Though short, he is fair faced, with light brown hair neatly curled, and large grey eyes. Come up to London, he has trained as an articled clerk – chucked it in for a higher salary and more freedom at a wholesale stationer's – developed a taste for high living... you can guess the rest. Having been extended substantial credit due to his appearance and accent (unlike most of those we have met) he has racked up debts for clothes and goods, and taken to quitting temporary lodgings at dead of night to avoid settling up with landlords. Fetching up at the Blue Lion, Gray's Inn Lane, he falls in with a bad crowd. From this point on, he becomes a thorough-going renegade.[9]

There follow various travels by land and sea, in love and gambling, in and out of work – and, inevitably, through the courts and the house of correction over cases of fraud, which he escapes without a conviction, yet without much else either. All of which brings him to Fleet Street on this fine spring morning. The shopfront of No. 53* is that of Messrs Laurie and Whittle, printers – and, like many printmakers, their glass panes are a riot of colour and image. As William Hone will recollect years later:

[A]t Jemmy Whittle's there was always a change of prints in springtime. Jemmy liked, as he said, to 'give the public something alive, fresh and clever, classical and correct!' ... I remember that in springtime Jemmy Whittle and [Henry] Carrington [sic]

---

* Now long gone – though the Edwardian upper storeys of the building that stands there are well worth a crane of the neck.

Bowles in St Paul's Churchyard, used to decorate their panes with twelve prints of flowers of 'the months', engraved after Baptiste and coloured 'after nature' – a show almost, at that time, as gorgeous as 'Solomon's Temple in all its glory, all over nothing but gold and jewels', which a man exhibited to my wondering eyes for a halfpenny.[10]

If, as is likely, these flower prints come from the publisher Bowles' own collection, then this window on to Fleet Street is blooming with pasque flowers, daffodils, anemones, fritillaria, violets, crown imperials, lily of the valley, hyacinths, guelder roses, jonquils, auricula, ranunculi, tulips – a riot of gaudy yellows, purples, whites; a frothing pastoral vision amid the soot and cobbles.[11] No wonder that people stop, linger, gather, nostrils vainly twitching for the scents their eyes lead them to yearn for.

Which is where Vaux enters the scene.

Earlier this morning he has been snared by Alexander Bromley, a man he met while awaiting trial, given drink and led into pick-pocketing, assured over his protestations of ineptitude that 'we should have at least one other person with us, and that he himself [Bromley] would work, while he only required me and the third man to cover him'. As Vaux has, in his own assessment, 'no scruples of conscience to overcome', the arrangement is made. And where better to operate, than where 'a crowd of gazers' stands rapt before flowers?

Bromley immediately joined the throng, we keeping close behind him wherever he moved; at length he gave us a sign to cover, and we had scarcely taken our stations, before Bromley drew back, and pulling the skirt of my coat, left the crowd, and crossing the way, turned up a court which led into another street. We followed him close, till he entered a public house, and we were no sooner

217

in a private room, than Bromley drew from under his coat a large green pocket-book, which, it seems, he had, unobserved by me, extracted from the pocket of a gentleman by whose side he stood, when we advanced to cover him.[12]

This single, decisive action nets Vaux nearly £4 for his part standing watch – as much profit as an ordinary street performer or seller might hope to make in three months – 'but my two companions having observed some police-officers in Fleet-Street, deemed it imprudent to prolong our stay in that quarter'. Vaux can scarcely believe his luck, and for all his history of debt, he has enough of a head for figures to see that, from this side of the law, the street can be an immensely profitable place of work.

Pickpocketing, like any other occupation, requires a certain skill. Thomas Wontner – who has spent time with hundreds of them in the course of his duties advising the accused before trial at the Old Bailey – judges that 'the qualifications for a pickpocket are a light tread, a delicate sense of touch, combined with firm nerves ... they generally wear pumps, or shoes of a very light make'. Like Bromley and Vaux, they make their plans and share their spoils out of sight, never loitering, and keep their tools to an absolute minimum: a small pair of scissors, to be used only in extremis, 'to cut the pocket and all off, when they cannot abstract its contents'.[13] Above all, the good pickpocket is never rash, always scoping out an opportunity before acting. A lesson that Vaux learns beneath the walls of Newgate Prison itself:

[O]bserving a grave-looking elderly gentleman, who was walking just before me, to have a pocket-book in his outside coat-pocket, I made an attempt to ease him of it; but it being of an unusual size, and rather ponderous, it slipped from my fingers, and alarmed the gentleman; who, turning round sharply, and seeing me close behind him, clapped his hand upon my shoulder, saying very drily, 'Holloa! young man, when did you come to town?' I of course affected to be much surprised, and with a look of displeasure at his freedom, begged he would explain his meaning. The stranger, staring me full in the face, and smiling sarcastically, pointed with his finger to the opposite walls; and, in a low voice, said, 'You see that stone building, my pretty youth; mark my words, that will be your resting place very soon.'[14]

Again, Vaux is luckier than most: his gentleman's appearance, though it does not fool the older man, is probably what saves him from a much nastier scene. But if he is the wiser for the experience, Bromley is not – and it is the impetuous, disreputable Bromley who brings about Vaux's downfall.

17 August 1800, a Sunday:

[A]bout one o'clock [we] entered Cheapside, when we observed a great concourse of people assembled round the door and windows of a draper's shop. [Bromley] was scrutinizing the pockets of the spectators. I was however at some distance from him, and signified my dissent by a look; in fact, I had no sooner ascertained the object of the people's curiosity, which was an attempt made in the preceding night to break the shop open, of which the shutters bore evident marks, than I beckoned to Bromley, and made the best of my way out of the crowd ... and turned round to see if Bromley was coming.

... I saw my poor companion struggling with a man who held him at arm's length with one hand, and had in the other a silk handkerchief; at the same time calling after a person who had also left the crowd, and was proceeding the contrary way (towards St Paul's) – 'Stop, sir, come back; you're robb'd!' The person called to immediately turned back, and at the same moment the fellow who held Bromley, seeing me looking earnestly at the transaction, exclaimed, pointing at me, 'Stop him in the blue coat! that's the other.' Knowing my innocence, I did not attempt to escape; and a man now advancing to the spot where I stood, seized me by the collar, and dragged me back to the crowd.[15]

Once again – reassured by his purely coincidental innocence – Vaux trusts to his respectability to save him. It does not. Their apprehenders are officers of the law; Vaux and Bromley have three silk handkerchiefs upon them; they are committed for trial. What really rankles with Vaux – pickpocket, conman, burglar, shoplifter – is the injustice: he wouldn't mind so much if he'd been caught in the act, but to be arrested the one time he hasn't stolen anything himself is a bitter irony to stomach.

~

We are by now no strangers to the law and its arbitrary machinations. Vaux and Bromley first come up before a sympathetic Lord Mayor at the Mansion House, but the arresting officers take care to represent them as 'notorious', and the discovery of 'a small knife, and a pair of scissors' among each of their effects seals it: they are sent on to the Old Bailey.[16]

Here is reform-minded Wontner again. To him, justice seems far from blindfolded, dispassionate:

I have sometimes thought, witnessing the conduct of the judges at the Old Bailey, that they, seeing it impossible to make any impression on the hardened offender, appeared to make up for this disappointment by a system of terrorism over the more timid and less offending.

He is under no illusions: a case's outcome cannot be predicted, the whims of judge and jury being wholly irrational, and easily affected by private interference – this sort of influence being 'an everyday affair'. Above all, the whole system is fatally undermined by the volume of trials and the speed of its operations – something that goes unrecorded in the official reports. 'For several sessions I made a calculation of the average time which each trial occupied. I never found it exceed eight and a half minutes, notwithstanding many cases engage the court occasionally a whole day.' Most cases, that is, take rather less than that 510-second average:

The rapidity with which the trials are despatched throws the prisoners into the utmost confusion. Fifty or sixty of them are kept in readiness in the dock under the court, to be brought up as they may be called for. These men, seeing their fellow-prisoners return tried and found guilty in a minute or two after having been taken up, become so alarmed and nervous, in consequence of losing all prospect of having a patient trial, that ... they lose all command over themselves, and are then, to use their own language, taken up to be knocked down like bullocks, unheard. Full two-thirds of the prisoners, on their return from their trials, cannot tell of any thing which has passed in the court, not even, very frequently, whether they have been tried ... conceiving, from the celerity with which the business was performed, that he had only been up to plead, or see a fresh jury empannelled ... It was a boast at the Old Bailey, that a recent city judge could dispatch sixty or seventy trials a-day.[17]

Vaux, as usual, is better off than most: he can afford the services of Mr Alley, an energetic defence counsel who knows that this is a game of prejudice and emotion, not of hard logic. Alley does a thorough job of entangling the arresting officers in contradictions and questioning their motivation, and puts moral pressure on the plaintiff – the handkerchief's owner, William Dewell:

Q. How long might you have stopped?
A. About three minutes.
Q. How long before had you felt your handkerchief?
A. Just by the Mansion-house.
Q. Upon your solemn oath, you mean to swear you did not drop your handkerchief instead of putting it in your pocket?
A. I cannot.
Q. Do you know that these men are trying for an offence for which they must be hanged, if they are convicted?
A. I did not know that.

Both defendants call character witnesses; things are looking good. Yet the verdict comes in: guilty. Perhaps it's those scissors again. The only consolation is that the jury have devalued the handkerchief from two shillings to eleven pence – for until 1808, one shilling in value was the cut-off above which theft was 'grand larceny', punishable by death (albeit invariably commuted to a lesser sentence by the late-eighteenth century), and below which it was mere 'petty larceny' – so that Vaux still hopes to get off with 'a small fine'.

Charles Humphreys, our other renegade, is offered the same punishment when he is pulled up for causing an obstruction. Defiant, Humphreys instead opts for prison, 'just to see what it was like' – only to spend his time behind bars acting boorishly, singing through the night, disdaining the food, and eventually tiring of incarceration and sending for a friend to stump up the original fine.[18] This arbitrary justice works both ways: sometimes you can more or less shrug it off. This is what Vaux is hoping for, anyway.

30 September, the last day of the session when sentences are handed down *en masse*: clearly a decision has been taken at a higher level, and forty prisoners, Vaux and Bromley among them, are sentenced together to transportation. Seven years in Australia.[19]

~

Surviving transportation, Vaux returns to London and to his renegade habits. His narrative of further fraud, cheating and pickpocketing is a compelling and intensely stressful read, forever on the point of apprehension: narrowly escaping an irate crowd outside Drury Lane theatre; only just avoiding a sentence over a snuffbox; getting into a very tight spot between a jeweller and a pawnbroker. Eventually he is caught, tried and again transported – the fate that, according to Wontner, is the only thing dreaded by the habitual offender. Wontner is told the following story by an inmate named Lee:

> A man named Shaw, who suffered for housebreaking about two years since, awoke during the night previous to his execution, and said, 'Lee!' (speaking to the man in the cell with him,) 'I have often said, I would be rather hanged than transported; but now it comes so close as this, I begin to think otherwise.' Shortly afterwards he turned round to the same man and said, 'I was wrong in what I said just now; I am still of my former opinion: hanging is the best of the two'.[20]

It is the atmosphere more than the details of Vaux's tribulations that gets to us: his crimes are so petty, so tawdry, and his profits hard-won at the price of a life of constant vigilance. The life of a renegade remakes the streets around you: a place of opportunity, yet devoid of refuge. As with the honest street worker or beggar, every prosperous passer-by represents a chance for gain – but instead of seeking to attract their attention, the slightest notice might be fatal. It is a fugitive state of mind as much as a reality, and nineteenth-century London is a dangerous place for anyone who feels it. It even breaks Vaux in the end.

~

The worst of it is that one need not be a criminal to feel this suspicion: it is enough to be conspicuously outside of respectable society to have its gaze upon you – as we have seen time and again upon the street, sometimes for better, often for worse. It is a true *culture* of suspicion, cultivated and recycled in anecdote and literature, from Ned Ward's *London Spy* (1703) to Pierce Egan's *Life in London* (1821) to Arthur Conan Doyle's 'The Man with the Twisted Lip' (1891) – in which a wealthy gentleman finds he can make far more money disguised as a beggar than in conventional employment. The seller, beggar, performer knows from the start that half the hearts among the crowd are hardened against her or him, on account of the tall tales, by turns salacious and sententious, that their owners have heard.

1883: the posthumous life story of George Atkins Brine is published under the title *The King of the Beggars*, and trades upon the 'dodges' he apparently employed when arriving in London 'on tramp' in 1847. Soap applied to the mouth will simulate a foaming fit – this is 'the epileptic dodge'. To effect 'the rheumatic dodge', he counsels:

> The arm should be tied up above the elbow with tape, rather tightly, and with a blow pipe, such as butchers use for blowing out a calf, you blow under the skin; the hand and arm then swell out nicely, and look most pitiable. The feet, to match, require an old pair of boots cut down the middle, and the stockings should be padded with cotton wool.[21]

The Renegade

The writer James Grant, whose 1838 *Sketches in London*, itself derivative of Egan, appears to be the source of much of Atkins' advice, records therein the 'most extraordinary case' of deception he has ever encountered:

> Will it be believed that this rogue, who was an excellent swimmer, was in the habit of pretending attempts at suicide, by throwing himself into the Thames, with a view to work upon the feelings of whoever chanced to see him after being taken out of the water? He always contrived to select a part of the river near which there were a number of bye-standers, while another person, who was a party to the affair, took care to give the alarm, and call aloud for some boat in the vicinity. Whenever the fellow pretending to have attempted suicide was brought out of the water, the other, affecting to have been passing accidentally at the time, addressed the spectators, and said that the unfortunate man had been induced to make the rash attempt through the greatest distress, and that this was the fourth or fifth time he had sought to put an end to his life, and that within a very short period. Every spectator who had a heart within him, believing, as all always did, the got-up tale, put his hand into his pocket, and gave something to 'the poor unhappy man.' The collections thus made often amounted to two or three pounds. This daring expedient, however, was only convenient in the summer season; winter was much too cold for doing the thing comfortably. It will be asked, in what way, then, did this consummate rogue manage to live in winter? Why, by affecting to commit suicide by hanging himself in some public place, in the evenings! ... The catastrophe was one evening very nearly realised in all its horrors. In ascending a lamp-post, after the rope had been fairly round his neck, he slipped his foot and fell, and would actually have been hanged but for the opportune appearance of his friend, who cut him down.[22]

It's a neat story, complete with pat moral. The point is less whether any of these cases are true, than that – as another author, George Smeeton, concedes in 1822 – 'the number of impostors is very insignificant, when compared with the thousands, who, from numerous causes, are obliged to beg for subsistence'.[23] Smeeton, however, places this proviso on page 189 of a volume trading on any number of recycled impostor stories, and goes on to profit from his immensely popular *Doings of London*, made up entirely of such anecdotes – which, by 1828, has already run to ten editions.[24]

These writers do real harm to those in the street, making renegades of the merely desperate. They influence the actions of institutions as well as of individuals, and in some cases, it is hard to judge whether such a story has its origin in the Mendicity Society reports or in the compilation of a Grub Street hack.

1838: the Society's annual pamphlet, by now trading chiefly on its reputation as a source of shocking stories, prints, for the first time, what amounts to a wanted notice, set in larger, bolder font than the rest of the edition:

John Quinn, a notorious impostor. – The public are particularly cautioned against the tricks of this man, who is one of the most notorious begging impostors known to the officers of the Mendicity Society. In the day-time he is seen about the west end with a tray of cutlery for sale, having a white nightcap under his hat; in the evening, and late at night, he is frequently to be found in all parts of London and Westminster, sitting on the steps of a door, apparently in the last stage of consumption, his face whitened, a white nightcap partly drawn over his face, and his legs bandaged. He has been repeatedly apprehended and imprisoned, and on one occasion sent back to Ireland, but returned to London within six weeks, to pursue his usual avocation, which he finds very profitable. He is about 25 years of age, 5 feet 6 or 7 inches high, long visage, without whiskers. In the day-time he usually wears a black coat, at night he frequently has on a light drab great coat.[25]

It is unknown if Quinn is ever caught; almost certain, however, that any number of under-the-weather cutlery sellers come in for a hard time because of it. And woe betide the renegade who is actually caught out shamming.

1850: 'A.H.', a mere child, falls into the clutches of this charitable organisation. He is a boy with:

> ... a paper pinned on his clothes, on which was written, 'No Tongue – aged 15' ... but strong suspicions being entertained that he was an impostor, the constable who had him in custody took him to a doctor, who applied a strong acid to his mouth, when his tongue presented itself.[26]

This story, resulting in the happy conclusion of a month in prison for A.H., is presented almost as comic relief.*

~

Rumour, prejudice, unearned reputation – these have real consequences, transforming innocent bystanders into scapegoats and villains simply on account of their disreputable appearance or attitude. Thursday, 19 May 1825: on a fine early evening in late spring, Frances Vane, the Marchioness of Londonderry, twenty-five years old, a coal tycoon, and seven months pregnant with her

---

* As of 2017, merely being found in possession of acid with intent carries a four-year jail term; attempting to use it, even if unsuccessful, can result in a life sentence.

fourth child, is browsing in Piccadilly. A trip to the Egyptian Hall to take in the new exhibition, then back into her carriage for the short trot to the bookshop of Nathaniel Hale – for some reason, she prefers his shop to Hatchards.

Her books purchased, she regains the street, full by now of people drawn to the coach and its livery. There is one brief, ghastly moment as a tall man, cloaked in black, comes in front of her. Mouth open, hands beseeching. Just the sort of distressing encounter her physician would have her avoid in her condition. But then, this is what her footmen are paid for: the man is moved aside in an instant. As she mounts the steps of her 'grand equipage', she may be aware of some commotion among the throng. Then again, she may not; an heiress who has known the admiration of Tsar Alexander is past paying heed to a goggling crowd. Two knocks, *drive on*, and she sails serenely out of view.

Among the onlookers is James Grant, around thirty years old, out strolling with his wife Eleanor and their two tiny children. Even at his relatively young age, James has already had, and lost, several trades – sailor in the Royal Navy, tailor, ballad singer. The Grants are not quite renegades. They can still rent a room and he wears his own clothes, a brown jacket and dark trousers, 'not very shabby'. Yes, they have twice been up before a magistrate on vagrancy charges – once 'because an Irish gentleman gave my wife a shilling in St James's square', and once 'for singing ballads in the street' – but they were discharged on both occasions. Yes, he has applied to the Mendicity Society – but the circumstances were exceptional: someone had robbed him in St Giles's, and all he wanted was a pitchfork in order to go haymaking; what he got was sixpence and a bowl of soup.

Recently, losing his keen eyesight and therefore any chance of resuming his trade as a tailor, Grant has had the same recourse as

Humphreys, succeeding where Humphreys failed, and got himself into the West Middlesex militia. Or possibly the East Middlesex, no one's looking too closely. The point is that the militia, unlike the two regular Middlesex regiments, is at no risk of being ordered overseas, and its soldiers are rarely on duty. Which is why he finds himself, along with his wife, each carrying one of their children, in Piccadilly on this fine May evening.

There's even a respectable reason why James Grant might have a particular interest in getting close to the carriage of Lady Londonderry. Three years earlier, at North Cray, a small Kentish village just outside London, he was among the beneficiaries of a programme of good works undertaken on behalf of the local landowner, Lord Castlereagh. A colossus of European diplomacy and British politics, bloodthirsty reactionary, butcher of the Irish, Castlereagh was also – thanks to a new hereditary peerage he helped bestow upon his late father – 2nd Marquess of Londonderry. On Castlereagh's death in 1822, this title passed to his half-brother Charles, the husband of Frances Vane – and along with the title, they inherited the gratitude of James Grant. Now, seeing the familiar livery in the London street, he wants to thank her for her in-laws' sake.

This interest, so plausibly born of innocent gratitude, is not how it will be painted later, in court. Admittedly, the fact that each of the Grants bears a babe-in-arms is suggestive, given what we saw in Chapter One. Grant's excuse for being in the crowd around the carriage – that he wants to see if Lady Londonderry is in good health – is undoubtedly very laudable, but given that it is motivated by remembering when the family gave him alms before, it rather reinforces the impression that he might wish to solicit alms again. There is a new Vagrancy Act as of 1824, and though its tendency is to reform previous confusion, it is bad news for anyone looking to beg in a troublesome manner.[27]

Except, James Grant does *not* beg of Lady Londonderry. He is not the tall man in the black cloak. And yet, as that man is moved aside, and the Marchioness disappears inside the carriage, a hand descends on Eleanor Grant's shoulder. And here is a strange man's face, pressing close in front of hers; he has a grip on her and is wrestling her away; it is all she can do to cling on to her child, scarce a month old, as, helpless, she is dragged from her husband.

James sees it happening; begins to shout: 'What is that for?' And now there is a second man, big and burly, James's wife and babe between them. James starts towards the struggling knot.

'We will have you too!' snarls one of the men – and only now does James see the stout stick in his hand, one of the cudgels carried by the officers of the Mendicity Society. Before he can react, a third man is upon him, and then the one with the stick joins in. He strikes James 'over my head, face, and shoulders, and also on the arm with which I supported my [other] child, and I dropped it on the ground. The stick hit the child, and I lost all patience'. Breaking free of his other assailant, James lashes out at the man who has struck his child; his fist connects with the man's mouth, draws blood. The crowd around them seethes, but the Grants, encumbered by their infants, are no match for the three men. Enraged by the blow to their leader, all three fall upon James, belabouring him with their sticks, literally tearing the coat from his back.

Almost insensible, he succumbs, and the family are dragged bodily to St James's watch house, a few doors away. As James remembers:

> On arriving at the watch-house, I was thrust into a dark dungeon place underground, without fire or candle, and was kept there till 12 o'clock next day; Wright [the officer who had beaten him] pushed me in, and I thought he would have broken my neck down the steps.

It is not until the next afternoon that someone comes for them, and even then, James is first hauled off to a public house opposite the Marlborough Street magistrate's office, where the officers put the frighteners upon him. 'Wright told me that "if I admitted my fault before the Magistrate, nothing further would come of it;" another man also came into the room and told me "that I had better beg Mr Wright's pardon".' James Grant is unbowed, and though he admits the blow in court, he maintains that he was struck first. His wife is let off, but James is committed to prison for five weeks, as none will stand him bail. In prison, Wright pays him several calls, pressuring him into a confession; desperate, Grant pretends to give in to their demands and to write a written confession, but does no such thing; at last he is released, as the charge of vagrancy will not stick.

Eventually, the law gives up on Grant. But, though several steps short of a renegade, it is his precarious existence, his fall by degrees from a settled state, his history of want, his hungry children, that count against him. In the eyes of the officers, James and Eleanor Grant are vagrants, a public nuisance. The Society's lawyer, Mr Andrews, maintains to the jury 'that no person could doubt that [the Grants] were in Piccadilly for the purpose of obtaining charity, & there were ways of obtaining alms besides asking in plain direct terms'. In his view, the deferential act of dropping a curtsey to Lady Londonderry is itself actionable – 'it was as well known what they meant, as if they said "Please to give me a few pence"' – never mind that no one saw Eleanor Grant actually curtseying. The Society goes on to libel the Grants in their public report, asserting without evidence 'that Grant and his wife have been known to the Officers many years as common insolent Street Beggars; and coercive measures must in some instances be resorted to.'

A year later, they get a second chance: the Grants find themselves once again on the street. Gleefully, the Society reports that 'James

Grant, aged 32, with his wife and child, who have infested the town several years, were again apprehended and committed'. Such is the unremitting persecution that those perceived to be renegades can suffer.[28]

~

And yet – and yet. This is not the whole story of the Grants' persecution; it omits crucial details. There are two trials, not one, and the second – in October – is brought by the Grants, against two of the officers, Wright and Jackson, on charges of assault and false imprisonment. Jackson, pleading illness, does not appear, and continues to serve as a constable for several years. Wright, however – the clear ringleader, the one who first grabbed Eleanor Grant and who struck James and his eldest child – is convicted of assault and fined 13s 4d; he will not work for the Mendicity Society again.

Still more significantly, the original struggle does not take place in an uncaring street. Though Lady Londonderry has quit the scene, plenty of others witness, protest, attempt to intervene. A gentleman on horseback cries out against the officers, who lash out at him and call him a vagabond. When he presents his card and attempts to follow them, Wright spits at him, 'I do not care a damn who, or what you are!'

Six witnesses come forward to testify for the Grants' innocence: three doctors' assistants, a saddler and the proprietors of the bookshop itself, Nathaniel and Hercules Hale, father and son. Together, their wealth of corroborating evidence acquits James Grant of one charge, albeit not the other, and later convicts Wright on one count – albeit not the other.

It's not exactly victory; indeed, it scarcely counts as justice. Yet the London street is far from silent. From Mary Ann Donovan, the Irish comb seller answering back to the Lord Mayor, to the verses written by Love and Albert or sung by Johnson or Bezer, to the Westminster patterers passing motions against Henry Mayhew, it is full of voices, articulate and bold, both willing and able to make themselves heard. It can protect its own.

~

1815: Captain Edward Pelham Brenton RN is busy exposing fraudulent beggars in St George's Fields. One of these, James Hays, is 'a pitiable object, his legs being drawn up to his body, without any flesh on them' - yet his account of how he came by his injuries, serving under Nelson on the *Agamemnon*, Brenton 'knew in a moment to be a fabrication, and told him so'. Hays admits it, but the altercation has already drawn a crowd, and Brenton rises from his stooping position to find himself 'very profusely abused by the surrounding mob', who come to Hays' defence and rail against the government 'for allowing the brave defenders of their country "*to starve in the streets*".'[29]

Summer of the same year: as thousands are dying in the fields of Belgium, an ex-sailor is being pestered in St Paul's Churchyard. At least, he *says* he is an ex-sailor; he also says he's blind, but the jury's out on George Dyball, whom John Thomas Smith has down as a renegade who 'never was a seaman', for all his 'nankeen waistcoat and trowsers', the unmistakable uniform of a naval sailor.[30]

Dyball may be a renegade, even a scoundrel. But he is loved. For some time now, the City Marshals charged with removing vagrants have had their eye on him, and as Napoleon steals a march on the Allied armies in the mud of Flanders, the officers descend. But - unlike later, when three men gang up on Grant - they only send in one. As this officer seizes hold of Dyball, the beggar's dog starts up a frenzy of yapping; the passers-by see a slender, blind sailor in the clutches of a brute. And they pile in to defend Dyball. Two of the officer's teeth go flying with the punches, and there is blood in the churchyard as he flees the scene in fear of his life.

As Blücher and Wellington pursue Napoleon back to Paris, the brave City Marshals make their statements to the House of Commons, before the newly convened Mendicity Committee. The problem with these renegades, their spokesman says, is that:

> It is a very disagreeable office for an officer to undertake, for he
> is sure to get a crowd about him, and to be ill treated; there is
> generally a serious struggle before any of those common beggars
> can be taken into custody ... These beggars immediately make
> a resistance, by falling down and screaming; and then good-
> natured people interest themselves, and desire they will not pull
> the poor creature about[.]

Philip Holdsworth, the senior Marshal, agrees that 'the people generally join with the Mendicant, and the officers are frequently ill-used; insomuch so, that one officer, the week before last, in taking up a sailor, whose dog carries his hat, was seriously hurt'. Worse still, says Holdsworth, 'there are some who are blind and lame, who think they have a privilege, and their infirmities cause the people to side with them and defend them'.[31]

Despite appearances, the renegade is rarely alone. Nor does the sympathy of the street manifest itself only in violent confrontation. The times of quiet aid are just as eloquent.

The late 1860s: Charles Humphreys is at his lowest ebb, in and out of prison, crying in the park. Forced to beg for literally a crust of bread, he discovers that at:

> ... the third turning down Edgware Road on the left hand side
> from Marble Arch there is a square. Turning to the right about

three doors from the corner, I asked the servant if she could give me anything to eat, and she said she'd see. She brought me out a fair sized parcel wrapped in brown paper. I thanked her, and she said:

'When you're by here again, give another call, and I'll always see if I can't find you something.'

Now he has food; the energy he needs to keep going. Next, he needs to work on his appearance. In Charing Cross, he befriends a young bootblack. In exchange for help with a couple of customers, the boy cleans Humphrey's filthy footwear. He is starting to look less like a renegade. But where can he find work? 'After cleaning my boots, another man who sold papers in the streets used to let me look down the "Clerkenwell News" for nothing. On this particular occasion there was a youth wanted in Eastcheap.' Where even *is* Eastcheap? The man doesn't know. But Humphreys is standing straight again, and his boots are shining. And so he does the simplest thing in the world. He asks a policeman.

As it happens, Humphreys never makes it to Eastcheap. Halfway there, an advert catches his eye in a Holborn shop window. Brim-full of confidence, he enters; secures the job. From here, he will prosper. Thanks to the kindness the street can show, his renegade days are over.[32]

~

Sometimes, just sometimes, the street has its renegades – outside society, hounded by authority – who are nonetheless untouchable; who have found that thing, whatever it is, that gets them through. November 1834, and an unnamed writer-cum-journalist is snooping around St Giles's, looking out for curious characters who will make good copy. They're in luck – though they scarcely know it at the time.

Mr Thompson's, on Buckeridge Street, is known as a 'cadging house', a den of ill-repute – that is to say, it's a lodging house and pub in a 'bad' neighbourhood. The heart of the place is the 'men's kitchen', a room for food, drink, cards, warm from the hearth and rich with the smells of cooking, sweat and tobacco that waft about on the draught from boarded-up windows. Tonight, the place is crowded, already humming, and the journalist squeezes into a corner; nurses a drink; watches.

In comes Bill Chapman. Short, squat, with light brown hair, a rolling gait and the clothes of a costermonger. But Chapman is a ballad singer, and an able one at that.[33] A roar goes up from the company. Chapman, it seems, has a reputation to live up to.

> [He] affected a superior degree of manliness. Swaggered around the room, his hat half pulled over his brows, and slouched a little on one side; assuming the scowling look of a bully, and at times the flashy air of a gallant ... [T]o show that he was a professed admirer of the kind of Eve, [he] took hold of his mistress when he entered with one hand, and waving the other above his head, sung 'My love is like the red, red rose,' in a voice at once powerful and sweet. Then taking her upon his knee, struck up 'the light, the light guitar,' in a style so exquisitely musical and rich, as fairly to disturb the card-table, and draw from the whole company a thundering round of applause, with 'Bravo, Bill!'

The journalist cannot pull their eyes away; for some reason, Chapman fascinates them:

> He appeared to be a creature of great spirit and vivacity; dashed about, throwing himself into pugilistic attitudes, and striking out, right and left, at his cronies, in sportive play ... He fell a

236

capering, singing all the while with great animation, and beating time most elegantly with heel and toe, and giving vent to the ful[l]ness of his spirits in shouts ... and, catching hold of his wench again, thrust his hand into his bosom, - pulled out a handful of silver; swore, bravadoed, - squirted tobacco juice in the grate, and boasted[.][34]

Chapman's fine Welsh voice and bravura social performance strike the journalist as copy-worthy, and the sketch is soon with the publisher. But before the results see the light of day, something happens to Chapman that changes both the story, and his status, as a confirmed - but unrepentant - renegade.

Saturday, 31 January 1835, some two months later: perhaps at Thompson's, perhaps at another 'den', Chapman is carousing with two sisters, Ellen and Isabella Watson, the latter of whom happens to be Chapman's wife, even if their union has not exactly been sanctified at the altar. All of them have been drinking, which leads to old arguments, and, well, you know what sisters can be like. Words become blows; soon Isabella is screaming death threats at her sister, and though it's all in a night's work for the trio, you can't expect the onlookers to be so phlegmatic. Next thing they know, both Chapman and Isabella Watson are being hauled off to the station house, where they give their names. Accused of cheating, imposture and creating a disturbance (Bill), and actually charged with assault and direful threats (Isabella), they are soon up before Mr Bennett, the magistrate at Hatton Garden. Ellen Watson, for her part, has fled the scene.

It's late, Mr Bennett has had a long night, and the Watson women are notorious as 'disorderly characters'; he dismisses the case, his mind on his bed. Which is when Inspector Oakley of E Division pipes up. With somewhat misplaced zeal, the weary magistrate might feel, Oakley has been making enquiries. Chapman, it transpires, is not all he seems. As Oakley puts it in ominously dehumanising terms, 'although the thing before them was attired in man's apparel, he [Oakley] had ascertained that it was a woman'.

Bennett is surprised into attentiveness. He'd thought he'd seen it all. Peering at Chapman, he asks for his name.

'It is Mary Chapman,' comes the low reply. Not the name given at the station – but then, this is under oath, and Chapman has no choice but to revert to the name on his birth certificate.

At this point, Bennett joins Oakley in proceeding to talk as if Chapman isn't in the room with them. 'I never saw a figure more like a man, and the voice is manly,' he says, as if discussing a specimen at the Royal Society.

Oakley stands a little straighter. Perhaps he even refers to his little pocket book. 'I have known her at least ten years,' he admits, finally crossing the prepositional divide from thing to human:

> ... and she always appeared in a dress similar to the one she now wears – namely, a hat, smock-frock, trousers, or knee-breeches, and until last night I always supposed her to be a man; she is known all over England as a ballad-singer, and a crier of 'The last dying speeches'.

Both men are at a loss. The opera, the theatre, the ballads are full of disguised maidens, following their true loves to sea or wrapped up in confusing plots involving twins, shipwrecks, inheritances. But generally, those are either excuses to look at sexy girls in tight breeches, or tragic tales of maidenly heroism. They do not touch the short, rough fellow before them.

Bennett is torn. Every fibre of his being tells him, *down with this sort of thing* – and yet... 'She may be a disorderly and disreputable character,' he muses, almost to himself, 'which, in fact, her dressing as a man clearly shows; but I know of no law to punish her.'

Oakley has more in his notes; perhaps they contain grounds for a charge. 'She travels the country with the woman Isabella Watson,' he offers, and they both spare a glance for Watson, still flush from the drink and the battle, but maintaining a dignified silence. 'They are both known at every race-course and fair as ballad-singers, and considered to be man and wife.'

We can't say what imputation Oakley puts upon the phrase 'man and wife', nor in what spirit Bennett takes it. He's still trying to think of a crime. 'She may have more than one reason for dressing in that manner, and passing as the husband of the woman ... I wish it was in my power to imprison her.' What is in his mind? Nothing charitable, that's for sure – fraud, deception? Neither of them breathes a word of sex – there are reporters present, for one thing, and perhaps they simply can't or won't make the imaginative leap.

Oakley's still going on, and maybe that unspoken implication hangs in the air as he observes that when they lodged at Thompson's, 'they always passed with him as man and wife; moreover, she smokes; and when Watson gives her any offence she beats her and blackens her eyes, though Watson is much taller and apparently stronger'. Who has he been talking to, this policeman, since the arrest was made? Or has he always known these things, and thought nothing of them until tonight's revelation? In Oakley's worldview, a wife-beating husband is in the natural order of things; it is only the concealed element of Chapman's identity that renders their relations troubling to him.

Asked to speak, Chapman volunteers only that 'Isabella has lived with me as my companion for many years'. Ambiguous word, that: companion. Safe, even respectable.

'Why do you dress as a man?' says Bennett, who might perhaps have asked this question earlier.

'I own I am disguised,' says Chapman, for whom the question, though surely expected, is not a happy one. 'It was owing to the cruelty of a father-in-law [i.e. stepfather] that I was first dressed in this manner.'[35] Meaning what, exactly? Abuse, unwanted attention, trauma... but Bennett doesn't want to know. 'When a man dresses as a woman, or a woman attires herself as a man,' he moralises, 'it creates a strong suspicion that it is done for a bad purpose ... If I could punish you, I would.'

The injustice flares up in Chapman; or perhaps he is angling for sympathy. 'I should not have adopted this disguise if my [step]father had not ill-treated me.'

Finally, Isabella Watson chips in. 'The poor fellow has been with me hundreds of miles as my companion, and he never got into a scrape before.'

Bennett throws up his hands. 'It is a case that puzzles me, but I must discharge the prisoner.'

It has been a long night for everyone. But the reporter for the *Morning Chronicle* is still paying attention and gets down a final observation – to my mind, the most moving detail in this or perhaps any of our cases. Unlike the two men of the law, and maybe only inadvertently, this journalist respects Chapman's chosen pronouns. 'The prisoner, who was chewing tobacco, then bowed his head, and walked out of the office with Isabella, who exclaimed, "Never mind, my lad, if we live a hundred years we will be in this manner."'[36]

Maybe for us, too, it's getting late, and I'm growing maudlin. But I find Isabella Watson's words almost indescribably beautiful. They have in them such comfort, such defiance, such a fierceness of affection. Whatever the details of their unorthodox relationship – apparently born out of a protective stratagem, a response to persecution, an effective guard against harassment as what would otherwise appear to be two women on the road and in the street;

but surely much more than this, to judge from their words and behaviour, surely a true queer partnership between the redoubtable Isabella and her flamboyant, talented, intensely vulnerable trans husband – whatever the fine details, theirs is the life of unrepentant renegades. Against all the world's authority, father, law and Church, they have found a way to be, together. The magistrate can't get to them. They know success in their profession, and an admiring social circle. The streets are theirs. If they live a hundred years, they will be in this manner.

7

The Elder

Bow, East London, sometime in the 1810s. Somewhere in these mean streets – take that word 'mean' how you will – there is a man walking about who does not fit in. He is in his mid-forties, already balding, conspicuous for his elegant clothes, his artist's tools, the brazen quality in his eyes. Curious, how someone can look at once lost and as if they own the place. To us, it is a familiar figure: John Thomas Smith, the antiquarian and artist who has sketched Joseph Johnson and so many others, looking for new subjects. At last, his flagrant gaze lights upon a man he judges as suitably exotic to merit depiction, taking his ease in the street. This man is a 'Lascar' – a sailor from what Smith would call the Orient: Mahomet Abraham, the man so persecuted in Chapter Four, would be a good example.

Busy at his work, eyes darting up and down from the man to his page, Smith's world narrows to the point of a pencil. It takes him a while to notice that the street is suddenly crowded; by the time he does, there's a veritable 'mob' gathered around him, all of them Lascars. And now three of them are coming forward, squaring up to him. Why is he sketching their friend? It's to show the police, isn't it – a likeness they can use to identify him, pin him down, fit him up for some crime. Smith is going to bring them trouble. Well, maybe they'll bring him trouble first.

Smith swallows, his mouth suddenly dry. This experience is something new, and he's not sure how to explain without enraging them further. You see, it's complicated—

And at that moment, someone else breaks in, protesting to the most vocal of the Lascars, his hands out, placating, smiling. 'Dear heart, no, this gentleman took my picture off the other day, he only does it for his amusement; I know where he lives; he doesn't want to hurt the man.' And, miraculously, things settle down. There is a public house close by, its proprietor come to see the fun; it is intimated to Smith that a round of drinks for the Lascars might put the lid on the situation. All well at last, Smith turns to his rescuer. The man spoke true: it's William Conway, a fellow Smith has only lately taken down under the title of his street cry, 'Hard metal spoons to sell or change' (see Image 7.1). Smith remembers their conversation. Resolves, when the time comes to finalise Conway's entry in his book, to give him a grateful write-up for what he will call his 'deliverance from a mob'.

As street criers go, Conway is an absolute gent. Born in 1752, he has reached his sixties without mishap; his bearing is upright, his cape and breeches clean, his manners discreet. Long, straight nose, high brow and cheekbones. Clean cut. When Smith recovers from his fright, he will record that Conway:

... first started with or rather followed his father as an itinerant trader, forty-seven years ago. This man has walked on an average twenty-five miles a day six days in the week, never knew a day's illness, nor has he once slept out of his own bed. His shoes are made from the upper leathers of old boots, and a pair will last him six weeks. He has eleven walks, which he takes in turn, and these are all confined to the environs of London; no weather keeps him within, and he has been wet and dry three times in a day without taking the least cold.

His income is steady, his luck good, his constitution untroubled by alcohol except 'at his dinner; and it is pleasant to record, that Conway in his walks, by his great regularity, has acquired friends, several of whom employ him in small commissions'. To Smith, as to much of polite society, Conway is everything a street seller should be. Still, he troubles Smith in one respect:

> It is to be hoped that this industrious man has saved some little to support him when his sinews are unable to do their duty; for it would be extremely hard, that a man who has conducted himself with such honesty, punctuality, and rigid perseverance, should be dependent on the parish.

Conway, for all his clean living, air and exercise, is growing old.[1]

~

From our perspective in this book, old age is like a second infancy in one crucial respect: we cease to hear our street workers in their own voices. By this point, the memoirs have been written – before eyesight fails – and though there are plenty of stories left to tell, they are told via others: journalists, investigators, officials. Once again, they are spoken for.

Take Mr Wicks, referred to by James Greenwood as '*our* watercress-man', as if he were a family retainer. 1867, and seventy-seven-year-old Wicks, born back while Louis XVI was still on the throne of France, is as active and articulate as ever – but we must rely on Greenwood for his history. Wicks, who had been a jeweller, grew short-sighted by the age of fifty, an occupational hazard that soon put paid to his original trade. Descending by degrees till he lodged with a watercress man, he finally 'bought out' the latter's 'basket and business' for what seems the fairly exorbitant price of ten shillings and sixpence. Already well on in years, Wicks has had to learn a whole new life in the street, and now, sitting by Greenwood's 'kitchen fire', he is in a position to share the tricks of the trade.

[I]t is a good thing to have a pen'orth of hot coffee at the 'stall' (I shall invariably find a coffee-stall in the vicinity of a watercress market), to fortify myself for the sloppy and unenviable job of sousing my goods at the nearest pump. Then I shall have to untie my unsold stock of yesterday and mix them with the fresh ones, unless, indeed, the stale ones are very 'white,' when I shall find it more profitable to throw them away and stand the loss.

Due to his poor eyesight, Wicks has to be especially wary of stale cress among his fresh stock – less a case of getting hoodwinked, than of the natural wilting of cresses since they were 'picked down in Sussex six hours ago', so that he is 'particularly careful never to buy my cresses by gas or candle light if I can help it'.

Listening to all this, Greenwood is reminded of what he has read in Henry Mayhew's *London Labour and the London Poor*, and seeks to show off, supposing that Farringdon market is the place for cresses. Indeed no, contradicts Wicks, Hackney's far cheaper, and fresher due to the proximity of the marshes. You can't believe everything you read in books.

Mention of Hackney sets Wicks grumbling:

'I've been up at Hackney,' said Mr. Wicks, 'on an early February morning, when all the water, except the running streams in which the cresses grew, was frozen as hard as iron ... Then it ain't much use: by the time you get your cresses home they are all frozen in one lump, and you have to lay them in the fender before you can pull 'em apart and tie 'em in bunches. "Oh, dear!" says the people, "what little bunches! why, it is like eating money!" 'Pon my word, it is enough to make a man cut the business, and go into the work'us.'

Wicks knows his trade. Nor is he so polite as Conway, but rather 'a disagreeable, surly-looking old curmudgeon' – as well he might be, given the turns his life has taken. A tough man, and a shrewd one. But the workhouse, or 'work'us', is on his mind. It is no idle figure of speech. He knows his time is nigh.[2]

~

Sinews, eyes, the bitter cold – a street life takes its toll. Naturally no one is keeping a precise count, measuring the tithe that London exacts of its most vulnerable citizens. But in 1840, the penny post is introduced, and the city *does* keep track of its postmen and 'letter carriers' – the latter term being used for those who tread their four rounds per day in the open street, for it is not until 1883 that they also carry parcels. And these men, it transpires, 'wear out fast' – more than two-thirds take retirement on the grounds of health before the age of sixty. Letter carriers, like their peers in the police force, do so largely on orthopaedic grounds; those responsible for the sorting do so on account of failing eyesight and mental illness. By 1855, the post office has a dedicated medical service; by 1859, there is a special pension. The street, it is recognised, is a hard workplace.[3]

New Farringdon Street, Clerkenwell, 1861: a woman visits 'her father – an old, blind street fiddler – who was ill in bed with a fever'. His wife is still living, but has gone out to the soup kitchen, where she is 'roughly treated':

> She burst into tears as she told her daughter this, and was some time before she could be comforted. They were not beggars, not tramps, and were clean and honest ... 'He's brought up a heavy family,' said the old woman, 'and never asked nobody for anything, until the frost bit him, and now he's dropped from his eating.'[4]

From frost to fever, to loss of appetite, even with the security of wife and daughter, for whom his long decades of performing have provided, the fiddler is undone by the combination of age and weather.

In December 1816, on Piccadilly, George Ford, relatively young at fifty-three, awaits 'the coming in of the morning coaches'. With no particular profession left, he has hopes of work as a porter, or as city guide to a newcomer fresh from the country. Casual work, he thinks. But he either overestimates his strength or underestimates the risk: passengers' trunks are heavy, and December pavements are treacherous with frost. It only takes one unlucky morning, one false step, for him to fall – backwards, arms scrabbling. The trunk comes down over him, a heavy, brutish thing, with vicious hard corners. The impact is incredible. Somehow, Ford crawls home – apparently, no one thinks of aiding him, least of all the owner of the trunk – and is 'confined for some weeks'. But he never really recovers; he scalds his leg, and the blow to the chest has exacerbated the asthma that plagues him in this already sooty city. His working days done, a visitor from the Benevolent Society comes to see him weekly. Making their report, the visitor sums up his case thus: 'by age rendered unfit for hard labour'. For our street workers, fifty-three is elderly.[5]

If age brings certain risks, it does not diminish others. The Mendicity Society's officers show no respect for the venerable. 1821:

a certain 'W.J.', a Scotsman, is 'well known upon the town by his long white beard'. W.J. is a veteran of the Royal Scots, officially, the 1st (Royal) Regiment of Foot – the most venerable unit in the British Army. And he has a claim to be its oldest member, having enlisted 'soon after the rebellion' – that is, after 1745, the last great Jacobite conflict, which saw the regiment's 2nd Battalion in action, picturesque in their tricornes, white knee-breeches and red coats with broad blue facings.

In 1821, the Walter Scott craze for all things Highland is at its height, and W.J. is a splendidly romantic figure of a bygone age of derring-do – as the Society notes, 'His appearance is calculated strongly to excite the feelings of the benevolent.' But not those of the Society: they mark him down for 'an incorrigible Mendicant' and set about proving that he was discharged in 1799, aged fifty-four – knocking a quarter of a century off his stated age. Not that this necessarily contradicts his claim to have joined in the 1740s – he could easily have begun as a drummer boy.

But they are less concerned with his service record than with getting their man. 'Evidence was given in Court of the dissipated habits of this old man, and he was sentenced to one month's imprisonment.'

Three years later, they are at it again. 'T.D.', sixty-seven, prefers begging to going into the workhouse; they have him sent to prison. 'M.G.', a woman of seventy, is 'on leave' from the workhouse, also begging:

The Magistrate considered that the workhouse was the best place for a woman of her age, and that she had no right whatever to be begging in the street. As a small punishment, and to prevent a recurrence of the offence, she was committed for seven days.

Reviewing the cases, the Society warns that 'Objects of this description ought not to infest the streets'. This charity really knows how to choose its words. Objects. Infest.[6]

1840, and cruellest of all:

> E.B., a single woman upwards of 60 years of age, was apprehended by one of the Society's officers begging at a carriage door, and after a violent resistance, taken for examination before a magistrate. Although presenting an appearance of extreme distress, upon being searched the sum of 25*l*. 10*s*. 10*d*. was found upon her, doubtless the produce of a long course of vagrancy ... The magistrate committed her for a month, and directed that a portion of the money found upon her should be appropriated to her maintenance in prison.

That sum represents her life savings: a truly astonishing feat for someone in her position. Not enough to set her up – too little to invest or speculate with – but impressive, nevertheless. In another walk of life, she would be commended for it. But not only do they assume, without asking, that she has come by it solely by begging; they decide to outright steal a good portion of her worldly possessions, salt in the wound of the prison sentence. What else is she supposed to have done with her money? With no address or credentials, she cannot keep it in a bank – she must carry it on her person in the face of great and daily risk. For decades, she successfully guards it against thieves and pickpockets. Her one mistake is not to reckon with the greater threat of the law. In an instant, a magistrate can undo what has taken a long life to assemble.[7]

Every once in a while, however, justice favours the aged. Chelsea, 21 September 1827: like W.J., John Lamb is an old soldier – albeit of slightly more recent vintage, 'having served 14 years and 244 days in the 20th Light Dragoons'. He's seen something of the world: in his time, squadrons of the regiment have been sent to Sicily to fight the French, South Africa to fight the Dutch, South America to fight the Spanish, Egypt to fight the Turks – a history of slaughter and appropriation that amply picked up where the regiment's record in the 1790s, fighting freed slaves in the Caribbean, had left off.

John Lamb, however, spent 'the greater part' of his service 'upon the continent, and was engaged in the Peninsular War. He had also served in Ireland, where he was discharged from the regiment ... without any compensation'. Lamb will have been part of Sir Arthur Wellesley's (later the Duke of Wellington) first victory in Portugal, at Vimeiro in 1808, and will have returned for the advance through Spain in 1812–13. Luckily for Lamb – if unfortunately for his street reputation – he missed out on Waterloo, and was less individually 'discharged' than laid off when, in December 1818, the entire regiment was disbanded. Though a veteran, then, Lamb is relatively new to the streets in 1827; he cannot have passed more than nine years in London when, on this fateful September day, he runs into William Skinner, a man revelling in the title of Inspector of Hawkers' Licences.

Skinner's job requires no great perspicacity. Lamb has a full and lusty voice; his cry of 'brooms and brushes to sell' rings clear through the streets of Chelsea. It's the work of a moment for Skinner to bustle over and ask him to produce his licence. Lamb eyes up this officious gent. He's seen worse. I've no occasion for one, he says. I'm an old soldier, which entitles me to sell my own manufacture – here brandishing his brooms with a gesture that might be taken as proud, or threatening, he'll leave it up to the gent to decide – *without* a licence.

Skinner is unimpressed, and hauls Lamb – who knows better than to resist – before the magistrate at Bow Street. But Sir Richard

Birnie, whose session it is, is in a light-hearted mood. He raises an eyebrow in Skinner's direction. 'I suppose you next intend to take all the Bavarian girls into custody,' he quips, referencing a hit song of the day, 'Buy a Broom', sung in a cod-Bavarian accent by stage stars such as Eliza Vestris.[8] 'They cry brooms, you know, and I dare say without any licence?'

His assistant, Mr Minshull, simpers at the joke, and points out that Lamb is 'merely accused of crying brooms. The Act says that the party offending must be proved to have offered his goods for sale from door to door.'

Birnie concurs; a lawyer from the Hawker's and Pedlar's Office protests, and is overruled. Birnie is much more interested in what the sacrificial Lamb has to say, which is where the old soldier gets to trot out his service record. With justifiable resentment in his voice, Lamb concludes:

> He bethought of making brooms and selling them in the streets. He had always understood that, as an old soldier, he might do so without going to the expense of taking out a licence, the amount of which would be more than he could turn in the whole year.

As on the field at Vimeiro, the old soldier carries the day: Birnie is clearly impressed with both his record and his knowledge of the law. The journalist who reports the encounter shows themself rather less knowledgeable of the army, however, making much of how Lamb 'shouldered' his broom and 'marched off in double quick time'. As the verdict demonstrates, a war veteran is to be respected. Just don't expect a reporter to be able to tell the difference between a cavalryman, as Lamb had been, and an infantryman. One hopes that Lamb never saw the account of his own triumph, at the very moment of which he is reduced in imagery to a mere foot soldier.[9]

In John Lamb's vindication – even in W.J.'s persecution – there is a glimmer of possibility. The sense that age, if attained respectably, might just afford an advantage after all. If, as we saw so long ago at the beginning of our life's journey, the mewling infant is an asset to the street supplicant, then so too is a mantle of many years: of suffering nobly borne, of experiences weathered. For those street workers and beggars dependent on the opinion of others – which is, in the final analysis, most of them – having come through the long years of general indifference, this is something to be grasped: a little compensation for the trouble it has all taken. It means ceding something of autonomy, of self-respect, but, so long as you keep control of your own narrative, and work it in your favour...

1836, evening, in Clare Market, between Holborn and the Strand: more specifically, we are between the façade of White's the tobacconist and the indifferent entrance of the tallow chandler. Here this evening, as on every evening for twenty years, stands 'poor blind Sarah Macduffick', seventy years old:

> ... dressed in a dark stuff gown, black silk bonnet, white apron, and canvas lap-bag, in which she keeps a few bundles of matches, with some stay laces on her arm, a stick in her hand, and checked handkerchief over her neck.

She is here from dusk till ten, 'depending entirely upon the public', none of whom, frankly, are in need of her matches or stays, but any number of whom might be induced to enter into the gentle formality of transaction that protects her from official harassment. It helps that Macduffick is 'extremely ladylike', and that any person paying over the odds for something they do not need receives along with it her 'heartfelt thankfulness' – which, genuine or affected, is a rare asset of Macduffick's: it takes real strength of character and purpose to remain so unrelentingly *grateful*.

She has pulled off the rare trick too of being *conspicuously* deserving – of overcoming that cruel double standard of nineteenth-century charity that requires her to be humble and undemanding in order to be worthy, while simultaneously needing to be noticed in order to get alms. Her spot is excellent, and deliberately chosen: she doesn't live here, but a walk away in Stewart's Rents, Drury Lane; she has to be brought here and back by her daughter. But it's her age that sets the seal on her worthiness, the thing that stands out first before her blindness registers or she has the chance to display her good manners – let alone to tell her story.

It's a good story, too, truly harrowing. A local, born in Holborn 'of respectable parents, on the 1st of September, 1766', all went well until her husband died in 1791, leaving her with three young children. Undaunted, 'she took to selling fish, greens, fruit, &c. in the street', and enduring the death of two of her children – until in 1809, 'her eyes became diseased in consequence of the cold and damp she was exposed to in her business'. There followed abortive, painful operations, after which, 'having lost the sight of both her eyes, and not liking to enter a workhouse, with the assistance of some friends, she furnished a basket of odds and ends'. But it doesn't end there: for as long as the things she sold had any value at all, she was vulnerable to thieves, who 'used to rob her basket with impunity' – a fact at once cruel and providing eloquent justification for the tawdry items she now proffers, things not worth the trouble of stealing. And now these devastating accumulations of a long life, each a heavy blow, finally coalesce into something with the most threadbare of silver linings: the affecting narrative of a deserving pauper.

At which point: pause. We are not Sarah Macduffick's patrons, conversing in Clare Market. To be told her story, and her plight, we are dependent on 'Jack Rag', the pseudonymous author of a six-penny serial, *Streetology of London*, sold monthly. No dry history this – it has some of the tricks and jokes common to the genre since Egan's *Life in London*, first published sixteen years earlier – but most pertinently, it's neither out-and-out fiction nor a record for posterity but, much like even Mayhew's original material that would become *London Labour and the London Poor*, a contemporary document that not only comments upon but intervenes in its own subject matter. Which is to say that, poring over this edition of *Streetology* while knowing it is topical, you start to realise something: the author gives not only Macduffick's name, but where and when she may be found – both on the street and at home.

And as her story unfolds, it takes on the aspect, not of history, but of advertisement, of character reference, the sort of thing still put out in the twenty-first century by Save the Children, Oxfam, Unicef. 'Jack Rag' is extending Sarah Macduffick's reach – directly profiting by the sale of her story, but also drumming up more interest; people who will read her case, seek her out in person or, more diffident, send donations by post. It's very possible that author, beggar, and perhaps her daughter, have come to a mutually satisfactory arrangement. Macduffick is being represented. But it's her narrative. And hopefully – for London is astonishingly full of kind hearts – it works.[10]

This is no one-off. Turning to Charles Manby Smith's *Curiosities of London Life*, published in 1853, we learn from the preface that, as is so often the case, it is cobbled together from 'contributions to the serial literature of the day' since the late 1840s. Like 'Jack Rag', this Smith is a journalist who gives as well as takes:

> With regard to ... the 'Blind Fiddler,' whose history, recorded in his own words, will be found at page 80, I ... return my acknow-ledgements to those unknown but benevolent friends who,

instigated by the publication of his story in 'Chambers's Journal,' forwarded to me the means of ameliorating in some degree the hard conditions of his lot. It is a pleasant task to return thanks for unsolicited kindness to an unfortunate stranger[.]

And, unless we are as cynical as the worst believer in sham beggars living on roast pheasants and riding in carriages, we should probably trust Smith not to have concocted the whole thing as an audacious confidence trick.[11]

Unnamed, Smith's fiddler is a problem of the sort we have been avoiding: how far are 'his own words' just that, and how far are they Smith's? Since the book is free to read online, you too can turn to page eighty and decide for yourself; his life story is too involved to give here, and if it is indeed self-authored, it would be a shame to paraphrase a genuine street voice. Still, there are aspects of the story this instrumentalist tells Smith – at the latter's home, on a 'dismally foggy and rainy afternoon in November' 1851 – that help illuminate the life of the older street worker.* Though his own blindness came about because of an accident in childhood involving fire, the street has also taken its toll: rheumatism when carrying hampers; being 'beat about by drunken men' because 'I couldn't play the tunes they wanted'; continually wet feet because benefactors only donate their boots once they're worn out, and he cannot afford to mend them; and, symptomatic of modern London, the claim that he has been knocked down 'six or seven times' by omnibuses while negotiating the increasingly busy streets of Islington.

For all this, however, London provides. Three times a week, he travels south to the City, to the houses of his 'customers', finding

---

* Though the fiddler himself protests this, 'Everybody says I'm fifty, when I'm not forty yet. I was born in 1811, sir, in Swan Alley, not far from the Artillery Ground.'

them by aid of his stick and a careful count. There, he 'plays till I gets my penny or my bread and cheese'. These regulars net him 'about three-and-sixpence a week, besides the vittles', in addition to which he 'gits bread and cheese at a house in Clerkenwell every Tuesday, and a good pint o' tea and a poun' a'most o' bread every Friday in Little Saint Thomas Apostle'. He freely admits:

> I can't fiddle very well, cos my right arm is shrivelled up wi' the fire, and I can't draw the bow rightly level with the bridge [wi]thout I sits down; and in course I can't sit down while I am walkin' about the streets; so it aint many coppers I gits from chance customers.

He is, therefore, dependent on charity, not skill, and his fiddle – much knocked about and repaired with glue – is his version of Sarah Macduffick's matches. He receives because he is blind – but also, it seems, because he looks so much older than he is. All of which keeps him independent, which is the whole point:

> I wouldn't go back upon the parish ... I liked my liberty too well, after the confinement ... in the workhouse – and I made up my mind to get my own livin' without bein' beholden to nobody.

This love of liberty, maintained, as with almost everyone in this book (excepting young Frank Bullen in Chapter Two), throughout what are often long and difficult lives, is remarkable. It is also, in the fiddler's case, a matter of perspective: his independence is maintained by patrons, after all. But hasn't he taken care to culti-vate these patrons? He has a routine, a spirit and no little courage. Above all he, like Sarah Macduffick, has put many years into this. For those who make it this far, it pays to be a street institution.[12]

~

The Elder

At the foot of Ludgate Hill, the famous City crossroads of Fleet Street and Farringdon, stands a famous street monument. Not the John Wilkes obelisk, erected in 1775 as a form of street lighting and soon passing into legend as a memorial to Wilkes, the radical Lord Mayor and reformer. But rather, the man in front of it: Charles Mackey, sometimes written McGee or Mackay, a Black crossing sweeper.[13]

Born, according to John Thomas Smith, in 1744 – or, according to the prolific Victorian urban historian John Diprose, in 1768 – Mackey is originally Jamaican, and so in all probability began life as a slave. By the 1810s, now in his later decades, he is a fixture. An institution. So much a part of the landscape, of London lore, that he features in every image of this landmark crossing place: at least eight of which are printed at the rate of one every few years between 1809 and 1837 (see Image 7.2). He has not only anecdotes and legends, but even an entire theatrical travesty written about him (this last taking the form of a truly horrific send-up of *Othello* penned by the impresario Charles Mathews in 1833). Most recently, two eminent historians of street life, Tim Hitchcock and David Hitchcock (no relation), have each produced compelling short studies of Mackey.[14] There is no need to write a third, based as they are, of necessity, upon images and accounts that look *at*, rather than *with*, Mackey. Indeed, the only trace we have of his voice is a dialect-heavy conversation in an August 1837 issue of *Streetology*, where the author meets Mackey in passing, and discusses the difficulty of looking after his money, to which the sagacious Mackey replies (with apology for the problematic rendering):

> Dat's 'zactly my way, I neber keeps none by me, I makes a pint o' gibin all de sweepins as I gets in de course of de week to ma frien, Massa Waisman, at de carner, far keep far me, till sich time as I hab gat someting worth wile, wen I draws 'em out dare an; gets

my frien Massa Lynn, ob de Bank here, for put 'em in de Stocks,
were he grow larger ebery year like a young plantan.

Though we might doubt the accuracy of the encounter, its evidence
of Mackey's financial acumen – so unusual among streetworkers – is a
more plausible version of the legend that will spring up after his death:
that he had taken so much in tips and donations over the years that he
is able to leave £7,000 in his will to Miss Waithman, daughter of the
'Master Waithman' in the above conversation, who lives on the corner
of the crossing and provides him with regular hot meals.

While we might dismiss this urban legend, why not take seriously
the idea that Mackey does indeed develop a friendship with the
Waithmans – Robert Waithman, himself a one-time Lord Mayor,
is a byword for progressive politics in this period – and takes
advantage of the connection in order to bank, even to invest, his
weekly savings? Where unlucky E.B., with no such recourse, has
her fortune snatched by the Mendicity Society, Mackey, known also
to be a regular church-goer and possessed of a fixed address, is able
to put away small sums over the course of several decades. And it's
this long career that really stands out.

We don't see a picture of Mackey until 1809, nor read of him
until October 1815, by which date he 'has lost an eye' and his hair 'is
almost white' – John Thomas Smith backing up this assessment with a
full-length portrait of an indisputably aged man. His reputation, even
fame, and perhaps his success as a recipient of alms, is rooted in his
staying power: it is only after Mackey has become an institution,
as much a fixed part of the streetscape as the obelisk behind him
(which is after all younger than himself), that he attracts significant
attention. A young Black crossing sweeper is one thing. A grizzled
ancient who has stood there for decades is quite another. As the
London Magazine puts it as early as 1824, Mackey:

... could and should bequeath 'the fruits of experience' to mankind. With his knowledge of, and intercourse with, his fellow creatures, he would manage a brace of quartos as big as Parry's Pole Books ... The world passes on before him, and he, with his back against the obelisk, remains a calm looker on![15]

Even the fanciful legend of his fortune – a weary tale rooted in old adages of wealthy beggars – takes a different form for Mackey: it is a tale of accumulation rather than deceit, the statistically boggling accretion of year mounting upon year.[*]

In Charles Mackey, we have reached the ultimate possibility of a long life in the street: pain and suffering, an undoubted portion of abuse, and – in the written accounts as, presumably, in so many face-to-face encounters – a dead weight of condescension, both excruciatingly well-meant and outright mocking. But also appreciation, recognition, memorialisation. The possibility of monetary wealth, which is breath-taking; and the strong evidence of lasting friendship, which is enviable. Diprose, our only source who postdates Mackey's lifespan, attests that he 'died in Chapel Court, 1854, in the eighty-seventh year of his age'. By Smith's reckoning, he would have been 110. Either way, we should pay our respects.

~

Mackey's example is at once salutary and poignant: such are the possibilities, and the limits, of a life lived long in the street. We are nearing the end now, and while memoirs can go out on a relative high,

---

* Nor is it incredible by that many orders of magnitude. If we assume Mackey to have been both successful and astute, and given that his food was apparently provided by the Waithmans, it is not impossible that he may have been able to save as much as ten shillings per week. Across fifty years, this would total £1,300 without accounting for inflation, interest or investments.

a complete biography has only one possible conclusion. Spring 1851: and for once we can speak only of absences. The place is described as '– Square'. Our subject, an elderly Polish man, is unnamed. And, for the first time in ten years, he is not here. Nor will he come again. According to Charles Manby Smith, writing again in *Chambers' Journal*, 'There is none to mourn his departure, and, beyond this brief testimony, no record that he ever was.' This may seem presumptuous, coming from a relative stranger. But the circumstances of the Pole's final years lead me to fear that Smith might be right.[16]

Telling his story backwards, Smith gives us the man as most recently seen and heard 'as a solo player on the trombone'. A century before the great jazz trombonists, this is a ludicrous idea, laughable; and, for a full year, this 'forlorn performer' has been, in Smith's language, a 'butt – a walking target for the stray shafts of the vagabond wit of a gaping and jibing crowd'. Two or three times a week, the man comes to this square to play and be persecuted. Boys call out for 'Paddy Carey' and 'Rory O'More', and he tries to oblige. These tunes are fast, high, lively; his attempts – 'a deep-toned wail from the sonorous brass' – are met with derision.[17] Even Smith, who sympathises, admits he sees the funny side. Can it be worth the few pitying pennies it attracts? This is no way for an old man to live. One wonders how it came to this.

The same square a decade earlier, in 1841: Smith, on his way to work, hears 'for the first time, the exhilarating strains of a brass band'. As his is the only voice we have, and he appears here in the role of audience, we may as well stick with his description:

[T]he instruments were delicately voiced, and harmonised to a degree of perfection not too common among out-of-door practitioners. My ear, not unused to the pleasing intricacies of harmony, apprised me that a quintett was going forward, composed of two cornets-à-piston, a piccola flute, a French horn, and a trombone. The strain was new, at least to me, and of a somewhat wild and eccentric character. Upon coming up with the band, I beheld five tall, erect, and soldier[ly]-looking figures, 'bearded like the pard,' and with some remaining indications of military costume yet visible in their garb.

Smith is electrified – very much the word of the day – by the performance: the fine technique, the strange melodies built upon the scales used in central Europe, and the band themselves – five Polish comrades, long used to playing together, turning heads with the exotic look of their beards and uniforms. They are part of the 'Great Emigration', the exodus of Poles that takes place in the decades after the failed November Uprising of 1830–31. Poland, a subject kingdom torn apart by Austria, Prussia and Russia, is officially no more, its last remnant forcibly absorbed into the Russian Empire, and its émigrés stream to sympathetic foreign capitals – Paris, Istanbul, London. This band of buskers is one of political refugees, seasoned veterans of the struggle; they have known hardship. They know it still.

1843: Smith, grown accustomed to their performances, aware even of falling into step with the music as he passes, his soul stirred, notices an absence: one of the cornet players is gone. Within weeks, the other four are wearing black armbands. They are now a quartet.

And so it continues. By 1845 the horn player has died – a terrible personal loss to the remaining trio, but also a critical musical problem. Without the horn part, they are unable to perform 'their own cherished national harmonies' and are forced to learn a simpler repertoire of current hit songs. It is an awkward pivot, but they are up to the task. Soon they are 'popular favourites', far more successful than before – and, speaking cynically, each benefiting from a third share, rather than a fifth, of their takings.

Smith, for one, is delighted to hear these tunes, more usually emanating from barrel organs, fiddlers and ballad singers, so well performed, and given 'an agreeable spice of foreign accentuation'. For several years they prosper in all respects but one: they are growing old. Now 'gray and grizzled', the remaining cornet falls victim to the second cholera epidemic, and the band is reduced to extremes: piccola and trombone:

> They fell into neglect and poverty, and save among those who dwelt in the line of their regular beat, who now gave from sympathy what they had once bestowed from gratification, they met with but spare encouragement. It could not last long.

Within months, the piccola player is gone – leaving the trombonist alone.

According to Smith, 'at the decease of his last friend he forsook the light and frivolous music which circumstances had compelled them to administer to the mob, and returned to the wilder and grander themes of his country and his youth' – but no one but himself can hear the other parts of the arrangement apparently playing out in his mind. This is certainly Smith's view – who is trying, as we have done, to get inside the man's head, a rare example of a contemporary writer making the supreme imaginative effort of empathy:

> He played on with an air of abstracted dignity; and one might have thought that, instead of the jibes and jeers of the blackguard mob, he heard nothing but the rich instrumental accompaniments of his buried companions, and that memory reproduced in full force to his inner sense the complete and magnificent harmonies in all their thrilling and soul-stirring eloquence, as they rung through the same echoes in the years past and gone.

He persevered to the last in treading the same ground that was trod by his brethren: it was all that was left to him of them and of their past lives. He had indeed experienced the hardest fate of the whole five.

With no source to draw on but Smith, it is hard to see the trombonist's final months in any terms but those of contrast. Dignity and mirth, past and present. A good Christian, Smith is comforted when the trombonist, too, finally succumbs – gone, he believes, to a better place than this; gone to his friends. For those of us without faith, we are left with only absences. The anonymous square. The unnamed musician. His unmarked end.

~

It is hard to inhabit the heads of those in their final days. Here more than ever we are shut out, left guessing. Few can welcome their fates as anything other than release, and while some street-workers – like Charles Mackey – are devout, many others are lamented by missionaries for their lack of religious conviction. Yet apprehension, contemplation, philosophy are themselves luxuries, and all too often may be crowded out by loud, insistent pain. Our streetworkers die of disease, accident, perhaps above all from the breakdown of bodies too long put to the test.

Saturday, 21 December 1860, just before Christmas in a city newly addicted to it: Agnes Edgell, seventy-three, keeps an oyster stall on the corner where Charles Street meets Pitfield Street, just north of where the latter runs into Old Street, the heart of north-east London. She has done so for thirty years. It's a bitter night to be out, huddled in the chair she keeps by her stall. An abstemious woman, she's gone so far tonight as to take a little warm rum and water – not only a breach of principles, but a significant expense.

The hours pass; the cold intensifies. But she needs the custom. The two women approaching are not, however, likely to pay: one is her daughter, asking if she wants anything.

'Yes,' says Agnes Edgell, simply. 'I am very cold.' The daughter, either keen to keep her mother working or knowing how pointless it is to persuade her otherwise, goes for bread and butter. Shortly before midnight Edgell, unobserved, slumps a little further down in her chair. When her daughter returns, she is motionless, scarcely alive; a local surgeon is summoned. All that John George Blackall can do when he arrives is to pronounce her dead these past five minutes. A post-mortem reveals her undiseased, in good general health save for the congestion of her heart and lungs. Cause of death: 'exposure to the cold and inclemency of the weather'. London's winters are cold, and they claim many lives.[18]

You can, of course, blame the system. Two deaths: 1824 and 1867. The first is in St Giles's. Jack Norris, known as 'the musical shrimp man', dies aged 'nearly seventy', allegedly from starvation. After fifty years of belligerent cut-and-thrust in the world of street food, vociferously carving out a monopoly in the sale of shrimps, his body has given out. Unable to continue, he had applied for relief from the parish: the overseers of St Giles's gave him 'a trifling sum' and a pass to his 'home' parish, St Margaret's Westminster. But St Giles's is where he has lived and worked for half a century. He stays and, in a few days, dies.

The second is in Southwark: 'a man who was in the prime of life, industrious, sober, a good husband, and a kind father'. For seventeen years he has hawked vegetables in the local streets; along with his wife, a street seller of flowers and ornaments, he has made a 'comfortable' home and raised a family. They have lost nine of their twelve children, however, and now 'unfavourable' markets threaten to sink their 'precarious' business. For a year, 'in order to avoid an application for parish relief', they struggle on. In the sweating heat of June 1867, reduced to a single unsanitary room in Webber Row, the family is struck by typhoid:

> In the corner opposite the door was the single bedstead, with its coarse straw mattress, thin flock bed, and single rug, and upon it lay the man, with blackened lips and parched tongue, wandering in the low delirium of typhoid fever. He lay upon his back, unable to move, or to help himself. Side by side lay the daughter, scarcely in a better state, and across the bottom of the bed lay the infant fast asleep. It was the eleventh day of the man's illness, and the ninth of his daughter's, and yet the wife, who was the only nurse, had no change of linen, and a single sheet was all that she possessed ... For three nights she had nursed him without intermission, and almost without food ... she had pawned all she had for a little tea and bread ... In a few more days matters grew worse, the woman lost her milk for the infant, the last pawn-tickets were sold ... After eight more nights of miserable watching the man died[.]

Over the course of a three-week illness, with no one in the family able to work, the parish provides a total of eight shillings in relief, more than a quarter of which comes in the form of the single linen sheet.

The inquest held for Jack Norris throws up its hands – he 'Died by the Visitation of God'. The vegetable seller gets no inquest. Dr Joshua Stallard, the physician and reformer who visited C.I. at the start of the last chapter, attends on this man too; is helpless in the face of the disease; asks, 'Is not the death of this man fairly to be regarded as a social murder?'[19]

Half of Stallard's point is that the street poor do not complain and do not ask – they are 'ignorant' of what the state, or the Church, has the capacity to provide by the 1860s. Rightly, he concludes that the authorities should account for this and supply aid without asking. For after a long life on the street, how many are likely to look upon the authorities, from whom they have known only perse-cution and interference, as a source of practical help? After a life of fierce independence, preferring any privation to the workhouse or the institution, the final act of all these people is to exert that will once more. Time and again in this chapter, everyone's dearest wish has been *not* to die in the workhouse. Independence has often killed them. But they have not flinched. They have not given in.

For those still lucid in their final moments, their defiance is not complete: there remains the fear of interference after death. This is the age of the 'resurrection men', the practice of selling bodies to surgeons, anatomists – a practice very much dreaded by the street poor, whose bodies these might be. All their lives, those in power have appropriated their bodies. The small children used as models by artists like Dorothy Tennant. The girls and young women subjected to stares, advances, assumptions. The hard labour – stone breaking or oakum picking – to which so many taken up by the Mendicity Society, or taken in by poorhouse or casual ward, are put. The unremitting theft of their individual identity as types, characters, fodder for anecdote, etchings, antiquarian ramblings. If, even in death, they fear the appropriation of their corpses, who can blame them? There will be no great respect paid to their mortal remains.

1793: Thomas Pennant visits the churchyard of St Giles-in-the-Fields – that is, the burial ground in which so many of them, living in the streets of St Giles's, will ultimately lie:

> In the church-yard I have observed with horror a great square pit, with many rows of coffins piled one upon the other, all exposed to sight and smell. Some of the piles were incomplete, expecting the mortality of the night. I turned away disgusted at the view, and

scandalised at the want of police, which so little regards the health
of the living as to permit so many putrid corpses, tacked between
some slight boards, dispersing their effluvia over the capital.

Small wonder this churchyard is notorious over the decades as an
easy target for grave robbery, for midnight exhumation.[20] Yet it is to
just such a spot that we are, finally, bound.

~

So crowded is St Giles's Churchyard that increasingly its paupers
are 'farmed out' in death, as in birth – in this case to the 'overflow'
burial ground of Old St Pancras. By 1855, by which point thousands
of its late parishioners are being carted out northwards, St Giles's
is declared full, and burials cease. A decade later, the new railway
line cuts through Old St Pancras as well. Tens of thousands of
bodies, some of them in freshly dug graves, are unceremoniously
unearthed, jumbled up, indiscriminately reburied. Even in death,
the forces of modernity will not leave the street poor alone. Even in
death, they are in the way; chivvied; moved on.

15 August 1815: laid low for the last three months, indifferent in his final illness to both the Waterloo campaign and the
sensational trial of Eliza Fenning, Jack Stuart breathes his last.
For decades he has been a celebrated and scurrilous ballad singer.
He taught George Dyball – last seen getting the better of the City
watchmen in Chapter Six – all he knows. So striking is his face,
with its full beard, clean brow, straight nose, that he once caught
the eye of sculptor John Flaxman, who preserved him in stone
as a loose-trousered sailor; you can see him still in the chancel of
Campsall Church, Yorkshire, where he stands, arms folded, at the
left of the Yarbrough memorial.[21] His dog, named Tippo after the
redoubtable ruler of Mysore, Tipu Sultan, is almost as well known

on the streets as he is. But Jack Stuart's life has been hard and short; at his death, he is just thirty-five years old.

A few days later, Stuart's mourners bear his cheap coffin out of his house in Somers Town, heading south on Chalton Street. Stuart's lodging is a new one; at this date, the area north of what will one day be the Euston Road is still going up, clay bricks thrusting themselves up among fields. It is a strange place out here on the edge of things, tentative, the city's grip not yet established (see Images 7.3 and 7.4). Uncanny to see the little procession insist itself upon the landscape, Stuart's widow leading the dog, consoled by three blind mourners, all cloaked in black: John Fountain, John Jewis and Stuart's faithful pupil, George Dyball.

No roar of trains or traffic here in 1815. Instead, two street fiddlers, William Worthington and Joseph Symonds, set the air quivering with the 104th psalm, a suitable dirge, though hardly a tune Stuart is likely to have favoured during his lifetime. Odd to think that the only reason four of these five men's names are recorded is through their connection to this minor funeral. And perhaps they too are taken by surprise as the crowd around them grows: word has got out, and London is assembling. Are they truly sorry, or just here for the spectacle? Either way, it's probably what Stuart would have wanted. This could well be the largest audience he has ever drawn.

It's a long way to Old St Pancras, since the straightest route is still barred by ditch and hedge; they wend round three sides of a rectangle before Jack Stuart's body can be committed to the earth. It's thirsty work, especially for the pallbearers, which might explain how Stuart's wake passes into legend. One of the revellers makes it through the night 'with a pair of black eyes *only*', and goes on to regale our chronicler, John Thomas Smith, with what he wants to hear, 'dancing, drinking, swearing, and fighting'. It sounds like everyone had a rare old time except for Tippo the dog, who, fifty-seven years before Greyfriars Bobby, spends three days keeping watch at Stuart's graveside, 'refusing every sort of food', before dying himself in 'howling sorrow'.[22]

It is, in short, everything you'd expect of a ballad singer's funeral. Did it all really happen? It's not a question we can answer – we can only believe. We still have Jack Stuart's likeness, thanks to Flaxman, but only know, or trust, that it is Stuart thanks to a story written down after Stuart's death – the death that itself became his main legacy. We only know of him through his funeral; nothing of his own voice remains. Indeed, very few of our street workers manage to have the last word. In one case in particular, this commonplace injustice really rankles.

Friday, 21 March 1823: another performer, more grizzled than Jack Stuart, is on his deathbed. Against his wishes, as against those of so many in this chapter, his last days are spent, not in his own home in George Street, but in St Giles's workhouse. We last met Billy Waters at the height of his professional fame, itself reached after the loss of a leg, a nationality, a livelihood at sea; since then, his personal fortunes have sunk as his notoriety has risen.

In the 1810s, his picturesque routines saw him captured in paint and print in ways that, while sometimes satirical and often racist, can scarcely have hindered his work in the street. But in his final years, Pierce Egan's runaway hit *Life in London*, also known as *Tom and Jerry*, has stolen his identity, first as a book and then, calamitously, in a theatrical adaptation by William Thomas Moncrieff. Waters is made larger than life, the details of his real-world routine augmented with all the tropes of 'flash' fiction: he is King of the Beggars, a rogue, a ladies' man, one of those shammers whose pretended poverty masks a double life of luxury.

Life in London is bigger than Billy can ever hope to be, and in a vicious spiral worthy of fable that we saw the start of in Chapter

Five, the spectre of Waters' fictitious self feeds, vampiric, upon its original as it grows. Increasingly, his street audience have heard the story before they see him. They are not prepared to give their coppers to this notorious fellow who lives it up in secret. All the credentials he has taken such care to establish – a military veteran, disabled, with a wife and two children – are supplanted in public opinion. Nor does Waters have a hand in his portrayal: though he takes to busking outside the Adelphi Theatre in the hope of scraping back some share of his stolen identity, he is not permitted to play himself on stage. That honour goes to white actors, blacked up for the part and speaking a derisory stage dialect, the first of whom is a Mr Paulo. As Waters' takings dwindle, so does his diet, and so we find Waters in the workhouse on his deathbed, allegedly 'whispering with his ebbing breath, a mild anathema, which sounded very much like: "Cuss him, dam Tom-mee-Tom-mee Jerry!["]'

The wording – if not the sentiment – is hard to believe. But how to sift through what is said of Waters within days of his death? Unlike John James Bezer, Mary Ann Donovan, Edward Albert, he never gives his side of the story; there is no account of his own voice that we can trust, to set against what is said of him after his death. And they say a lot.

Jemmy Catnach, the leading cheap printer of Seven Dials, rushes out a commemorative sheet by the following Tuesday, priced at tuppence. Ballads, books and obituaries purport to contain his final words, his last will and testament, and dance around shared scraps of conjecture – that he pawned his fiddle in his final days; that he bore a grudge against William Bodkin, Honourable Secretary of the Mendicity Society; that he twice narrowly escaped a spell on the treadmill. Before long, it all whirls away from any semblance of the man himself, so that facetious literary accounts are talking only to one another. Amid all of which, no one thinks to record the fortunes of his widow and children, nor even to make sure of his burial place, so that we cannot be certain whether his remains fertilise the soil of St Giles's or St Pancras.

Of all Waters' eulogies, only two bear the stamp of genuine respect. The first of these comes laced with knowing irony: an epitaph from Douglas Jerrold, not written until 1840:

> Ethiopian Grimaldi!* They who saw thee not, cannot conceive the amount of grace co-existent with a wooden leg – the comedy budding from timber ... Who ever danced as he danced? Waters was a genius; his life gave warranty of it, nor did his death disprove it, for he died in a workhouse.

The second eulogy is more satisfying, since it comes from the street. The 1850s: a generation after Waters' death, Henry Mayhew is interviewing another street performer, this one an exhibitor of 'Chinese Shades' – meaning, more or less, magic lanterns. The unnamed entertainer takes Mayhew through his stock of shadow plays. Almost as an afterthought, he remarks, 'There's another piece, called "Billy Waters, the celebrated London Beggar;" and that's a great hit.'

It is something like consolation. Whatever the literary liberties taken with his memory, however cruel the circumstances of his death, Billy Waters will be remembered. On the streets of London, he is dancing still.[23]

---

* Joseph Grimaldi was the most fêted clown of the age.

Epitaph

Piccadilly, Sunday, 2 September 1810: somewhere after ten o'clock at night. The legendary showman George Wombwell's circus, his newly named 'travelling menagerie', is in town. The wagons are being packed up for the road, a commotion to shatter the late summer dusk. Of all the straw-strewn caravans, those of most appalling fascination are the rank, foetid lairs of the big cats. It's bad enough for the handlers; spare a thought for the horses, new to this work, who draw the wagons. A change in the wind, and their flaring nostrils catch the reek. A stir; a growl. A team of horses bolt. Their wagon slaloms behind, a mad career down Piccadilly, a smash-up. Chaos. In the confusion two monkeys scramble free; one, sensing danger, darts into an oyster shop. Behind it is a blur of black and gold; cries of warning. The shopkeeper sizes up the situation, and slams the door. He'd rather deal with the monkey.

A big cat is loose. And though it's late, Piccadilly is crowded at the Haymarket end. Bodies shrinking back, gazes fixed forward, the throng parts. A lone gentleman remains in the road, the animal crouching before him.

Wombwell's keepers are on the scene. 'For Heaven's sake, Sir, take care, it is a tiger!' Actually, it isn't – but 'tiger' is the familiar word that will hit home in a crisis. Burning bright.

The man does not run; does not so much as move. Disconcerted, the leopard – for a leopard it is – makes 'a most wonderful spring against the side of one of the houses, and then into the middle of the street'. The man walks on and out of our story, 'refusing to tell his name'.

The leopard too stalks off, hackles up, heading west in what the papers will call 'a majestic style'. In this hour London belongs to this leopard; you can glimpse a different wildness astir in its low shadow. Every door is slammed before it, every window battened. To the left is St James's, full of half-made houses; an open basement, gravel-lined, yaws open. A refuge, a welcome darkness. The leopard slips in.

We might leave it there, prowling round the empty dwelling. In time, the keepers come up; fix a new cage at the entrance. At four in the morning, they coax it forth, and now the night tears open. Screams serrate the darkness; a noose is thrown. The enraged leopard leaps at one of its tormentors, jaws closing high upon his left arm. After a blind struggle it is got into the cage and the man is rushed to hospital. Piccadilly straightens its collar, and tries to forget the night it was unmade.[1]

~

But something is exposed in the night's adventure, a surface torn away. The leopard is a stranger to the London street, quite unlike the beasts of burden, the performing animals, and above all the dogs, that are so intrinsic to its daily workings. But for all its unlikelihood, it is this off-kilter night in Piccadilly that stands as our vagabonds' epitaph. The leopard makes the street uncanny. In its passing presence lies a truth that rewrites the usual codes: the street can be ungoverned, unstable, a place to be free. It's a momentary rewilding that, once glimpsed, cannot be unseen. And this is the spirit of the street incarnate: not intrinsically exotic, or dangerous, or unaware. But essentially *different*, fiercely independent, and able to make that difference felt. Faced with the leopard's spots, London's great and good blanch, and call the street savage. But they are wrong. The street is its own world, and it gets on very well. Only, when they come at it with a noose and a cage, with Bible and truncheon, it bares its teeth.

From birth to death, the street poor have defied idealisation as victims or supplicants, just as they have defied attempts to make them conform, defer, or simply go away. Boys fight back. Girls stare down the patriarchal gaze. People of all ages just keep coming from the world over, not only preserving but flaunting their difference and their heritage, and profiting from it. Careers are made, propriety flaunted, and independence prized beyond life itself. If one thing unites them all, it is this love of liberty. They may be cornered, by laws, by capital, by an all-too-narrow call for 'progress'. But even when the cage is laid to the entrance, they will not go quietly.

Billy Waters dies with a curse on his lips. His fame will outlive the fiction that undid him. Isabella Watson and Bill Chapman walk out together, heads held high. *If they live a hundred years, they will be in this manner.* Joseph Johnson may dance till he drops. But in defiance of the parish beadles, he will carry the subversive spirit of the plantation to the heart of the empire. Lizzie Bland, lost and alone in a London park, will rise to her feet. In scarcely a decade, she will conquer America. Rose Avery and Besse Richards stride headlong into danger. Though ultimately unmasked, for a time they will hoodwink a magistrate and the nation's press, escaping unpunished. John James Bezer springs for his master's throat. Whatever life throws at him, he will retain this rebel spirit. Edmund Kean is bound for greatness. He will shrug off ropes and collars. Mary Ann Donovan answers back. She will pay for her temerity – but she *will* be heard. This is the fate of our vagabonds: to be misunderstood, even feared, and ever wary of the waiting cage. But in the shadow of the untamed leopard, we can see the street as they would have it - free from censure, free from constraint. It is, perhaps, no more than a fleeting moment. But in that moment, London belongs to them.

Notes

Introduction

1 The sources for the Donovan case all come from the London press. Much of this is freely available online: search for 'General News', *Trewman's Exeter Flying Post or Plymouth and Cornish Advertiser* 4851 (31 March 1859), and 'Law and Crime', *Illustrated Times* 1 (26 March and 30 April 1859): 206 and 286. The case was also reported in, among others, the *Spectator* and the *Morning Chronicle*.

2 In the 1840s and '50s Henry Mayhew, a young Bohemian journalist and playwright, aided by his brother and a few friends, conducted an enormous project of interviewing what they termed 'the London Poor'. These interviews were written up, mostly by Mayhew himself: first for a regular slot in the *Morning Chronicle*, and then in four volumes as *London Labour and the London Poor*, published at the start of the 1860s. After a brief flare of public fascination this work was forgotten, superseded by the more thrilling undercover investigations of James Greenwood and others. But since the mid-twentieth century, *London Labour and the London Poor* has become one of the defining texts of the Victorian city. Judith Flanders has declared of *London Labour and the London Poor* that 'no study of nineteenth-century working-class street life could manage without it'. To me, that sounded like a challenge. You can read his first three volumes for free online at gutenberg.org/ebooks/author/48614. In print, the most accessible complete edition is the Dover reprint of 1968, edited by John D. Rosenberg. For two much cheaper recent selections, see Rosemary O'Day and David Englander (eds), *Mayhew: London Labour & the London Poor* (Ware, 2008), and Robert Douglas-Fairhurst (ed.), *London Labour and the London Poor: A Selected Edition* (Oxford, 2010). For discussion of his work – which I have, as you can see, decided to excise from this book for fear that it would take over – see: Anne Humpherys (ed.), *Voices of the Poor: Selections from the* Morning Chronicle *'Labour and the Poor' (1849–1850) by Henry Mayhew* (1971), and *Travels into the Poor Man's Country: The Work of Henry Mayhew* (Athens, Georgia, 1977); E.P.

Thompson and Eileen Yeo, *The Unknown Mayhew* (1973); Karel Williams, *From Pauperism to Poverty* (1981), 237–77; Gertrude Himmelfarb, *The Idea of Poverty: England in the Early Industrial Age* (New York, 1983); Andrew Tolson, 'Social Surveillance and Subjectification: The Emergence of "Subculture" in the Work of Henry Mayhew' (1990, revised 1997), in Ken Gelder (ed.), *The Subcultures Reader* (2nd edition Abingdon, 2005), 175–83; Regenia Gagnier, *Subjectivities: A History of Self-Representation in Britain, 1832–1920* (Oxford, 1991); Bertrand Taithe, *The Essential Mayhew: Representing and Communicating the Poor* (1996); Bryan S. Green, 'Learning from Henry Mayhew: The Role of the Impartial Spectator in Mayhew's *London Labour and the London Poor*', *Journal of Contemporary Ethnography* 31, No.2 (2002): 99–134; Chris Louttit, 'The Novelistic Afterlife of Henry Mayhew', *Philological Quarterly* 85 (2006): 315–41; Vanessa Warne, 'Clearing the Streets: Blindness and Begging in Henry Mayhew's *London Labour and the London Poor*', in Glenn Clark, Judith Owens, and Greg T. Smith (eds), *City Limits: Perspectives on the Historical European City* (Montreal, 2010), 205–26; Karl Sabbagh (ed.), *The Wayward Genius of Henry Mayhew: Pioneering Reportage from Victorian London* (2012); an entire issue of *Journal of Victorian Culture* 19 (2014); Rob Breton, 'Portraits of the Poor in Early Nineteenth-Century Radical Journalism', *Journal of Victorian Culture* 21 (2016): 168–83; and numerous pieces by Carolyn Steedman, including her *Past Tenses: Essays on Writing, Autobiography and History* (1992), 193–202; *Strange Dislocations: Childhood and the Idea of Human Interiority, 1780–1930* (1995); and 'Mayhew: On Reading, About Writing', *Journal of Victorian Culture* 19 (2014): 550–61.

3 This form of composition recalls the moveable metal type used in the printing process itself, neatly ordered in a printer's tray or *Setzkasten*.

4 At the same time, Tudor court composers delighted in incorporating various idealised street cries into polyphonic musical pieces – Orlando Gibbons' *The Cries of London* is the best known of these – the joke seeming to rest in the contrast between the rude mechanicals in the street and the high art that was fashioned from the sounds of their labour. Both practices, visual and musical, persisted well into the nineteenth century, passing through the hands of painters like Laroon, Amigoni, Sandby, Rowlandson and composers like Blewitt, Arnold and Parry – that is to say, a bunch of talented and remarkably privileged men.

5 Though frowned upon by sanitary reformers, the keeping of pigs was highly profitable: for a negligible outlay in scraps and waste food, a family or business received first a source of warmth, and later a valuable commodity for consumption or sale in pork, pigskin, trotters and so on. Unfortunately, pigs had a tendency to run wild in the streets and cause a public nusiance – hence the need for training. For more on the pig-rearing

industry, see Thomas Almeroth-Williams, *City of Beasts: How Animals Shaped Georgian London* (Manchester, 2019), 89–93.

6 John Hollingshead, *Ragged London in 1861* (1861), 158–9.

7 See note 2, above, for a fuller discussion of this work.

8 Of all the excellent work on how historians can use this sort of life-writing, the landmark book is probably still David Vincent, *Bread, Knowledge and Freedom: A Study of Nineteenth-Century Working Class Autobiography* (1981).

9 Though I use various courtroom sources, I'm most reliant on the digitised records of the Old Bailey, via Clive Emsley, Tim Hitchcock and Robert Shoemaker's remarkable online resource. They provide a superb survey of its historical value at oldbaileyonline.org/static/Value.jsp

10 Jane Humphries, *Childhood and Child Labour in the British Industrial Revolution* (Cambridge, 2010), 372.

1 The Infant

1 Tidswell is apparently quoted in Frederick W. Hawkins, *The Life of Edmund Kean. From Published and Original Sources*, two vols (1869), Vol. 1, 4. The opening pages of this volume include much of the detail on Kean's early life and are very harsh on Mary Ann Carey. An earlier account, W.B. Procter, *The Life of Edmund Kean*, two vols (1835), disagrees with Hawkins in many particulars; it seems unlikely that these issues will ever be cleared up.

2 Thomas Barnardo, *Never Had a Home: A Very Commonplace History* (1890), 2–6.

3 Lydia Murdoch, *Imagined Orphans: Poor Families, Child Welfare, and Contested Citizenship in London* (New Brunswick, 2006), especially 1–6.

4 Anthony Highmore, *Pietas Londinensis: The History, Design, and Present State of the various Public Charities in and near London* (2nd edition, 1814), 725.

5 Lynda Nead, 'Fallen Women and Foundlings: Rethinking Victorian Sexuality', *History Workshop Journal* 82 (2016): 177–87, 183.

6 *The Twenty-First Report of the Society for Bettering the Condition and Increasing the Comforts of the Poor* (1805), 53–4.

7 Today, the Foundling Museum keeps a selection of these tokens on permanent display: see foundlingmuseum.org.uk/our-art-and-objects/foundling-collections/tokens

8 The Twenty-First Report, 55–56, and in general, Ruth McClure, *Coram's Children: The London Foundling Hospital in the Eighteenth Century* (New Haven, 1981).

9 Thomas Barnardo, *'The Seed of the Righteous,' among the Children of the Poorest* (1886), 21–2.

10 John Matthias Weylland, *Valiant for the Truth* (1899), 82–7.

11 John Brown, *A Memoir of Robert Blincoe, An Orphan Boy* (Manchester,

1832), iii–iv and 7–11.

12 Josiah Basset, *The Life of a Vagrant, or the Testimony of an Outcast to the Value and Truth of the Gospel* (3rd edition, 1850), 10–14.

13 George Godwin, *London Shadows; A Glance at the 'Homes' of the Thousands* (1854), 1.

14 All ibid., 27–8.

15 All *The Nature, Design, and Rules, of the Benevolent, or Strangers' Friend Society ... Together With an Account of some of the Cases Visited in the Year 1811* (1812), 11.

16 All Anon., *Memories of a Sister of Saint Saviour's Priory* (2nd edition, 1912), 68–72.

17 Mary Moseley gives her place of residence as Duke's-place, Chelsea, but the Duke's Place in question is definitely in Pimlico, a few paces from the Royal Mews on the south side of Buckingham Palace. The avenue mentioned later is called College Walk, a common name for what the maps have down as White Stiles – later, Royal Avenue – while Jew's Row will soon be renamed Royal Hospital Row, just as Church Lane will be renamed Old Church Street.

18 *Proceedings of the Old Bailey*, case t18171029-137.

19 Constance Flower, née de Rothschild, in Lucy Cohen, *Lady de Rothschild and her Daughters, 1821–1931* (1935), 99–100.

20 *Proceedings of the Old Bailey*, case t18241202-159.

21 *Proceedings of the Old Bailey*, case t18150111-95.

22 Henry Barnet Gascoigne, *Suggestions for the Employment of the Poor of the Metropolis* (1817), 31.

23 *Proceedings of the Old Bailey*, case t18180909-311.

24 *The Report of the Society Established in London for the Suppression of Mendicity*, Vol. 6 (1824), 30–33. Macher is also mentioned in Sarah Wise's excellent *The Italian Boy: Murder and Grave-Robbery in 1830s London* (2005), 73.

25 *Italian Children. Report of the Committee of the Charity Organisation Society Appointed to Enquire into the Employment of Italian Children for Mendicant and Immoral Purposes* (2nd edition, 1877), 3.

26 Edwin Chadwick, *Report from E. Chadwick, Esq., on London and Berkshire* [Reprinted from 'Extracts from the Information received by His Majesty's Commissioners, as to the Administration and Operation of the Poor-Laws,' 1833] (1833), 78–9.

27 Thomas Beggs, *An Inquiry into the Extent and Causes of Juvenile Depravity* (1849), 93.

28 *The Times*, 28 January 1848, also cited in Beggs, *An Inquiry*, 90 fn.

29 *Minutes of the Evidence taken before the Committee appointed by the House of Commons to inquire into the state of Mendicity and Vagrancy in the Metropolis*

and its Neighbourhoods ... to which is added, The Second Report (1816), 87, 104, 107, 110.

30 Carolyn Steedman, *Strange Dislocations: Childhood and the Idea of Human Interiority, 1780–1930* (1995), 126-7.

31 Joshua H. Stallard, *Pauperism, Charity, & Poor Laws* (1868), 25.

32 A good starting point on this subject is Deborah Wynne, 'Reading Victorian Rags: Recycling, Redemption, and Dickens's Ragged Children', *Journal of Victorian Culture* 20 (2015): 34-49.

33 For three especially thought-provoking studies among many, see James R. Kincaid, *Child-Loving: The Erotic Child and Victorian Culture* (New York, 1992); Seth Koven, *Slumming: Sexual and Social Politics in Victorian London* (Princeton, 2006); and, Nancy Rose Marshall, *City of Gold and Mud: Painting Victorian London* (New Haven, 2012).

34 As cited in Lydia Murdoch, *Imagined Orphans: Poor Families, Child Welfare, and Contested Citizenship in London* (New Brunswick, 2006), 12.

35 George Reynolds, *Dr Barnardo's Homes* (1877), 13.

36 Ibid., 7.

37 Dorothy Tennant, *London Street Arabs* (1890), 7-11.

2 The Boy

1 The relevant sections of Bezer's account are excerpted in David Vincent (ed.), *Testaments of Radicalism: Memoirs of Working Class Politicians 1790–1885* (1977), 149-62. The entire memoir and extensive editorial notes by David Shaw are also freely available at minorvictorianwriters.org.uk/bezer/ – and well worth a read.

2 The Bezers seem to be pioneers in their optimism here, since the *Oxford English Dictionary* first records the idiom 'they will sell like hot cakes' in 1839, fifteen years in the future – and in a New York publication. See oed.com/view/Entry/271623 (it is a paid resource, but every library should have access). The rather confusing street cry of 'one a penny, two a penny, hot cross buns', however, dates back to at least 1733. See Charles Hindley, *A History of the Cries of London, Ancient and Modern* (1881), 218.

3 Here, as in other parts of the account, Bezer *does* misremember – and overstate – his own age by some eighteen months.

4 Alice Dolan, 'Touching Linen: Textiles, Emotion and Bodily Intimacy in England c. 1708-1818', *Cultural and Social History* 16 (2019): 145-64, 147, which contains an excellent discussion of shame in the period. The Johnson quotation is from the 1755 edition of his *Dictionary*.

5 Mary Carpenter, *Reformatory Schools, for the Children of the Perishing and Dangerous Classes, and for Juvenile Offenders* (1851), 87.

6 James Greenwood, *In Strange Company: Being the Experiences of a Roving Correspondent* (2nd edition, 1883), 79.

7 Thomas Holcroft, *Memoirs of the Late Thomas Holcroft*, three vols (1816), Vol. 1, 35.

8 This exchange is of course set down in dialogue as Bezer remembers it decades later and should be understood to convey the spirit of the exchange rather than the precise wording.

9 Frank Bullen, *Confessions of a Tradesman* (1908). The sections relevant to this chapter are vii–49.

10 Holcroft, *Memoirs*, Vol. 1, 2, 45.

11 George Acorn, *One of the Multitude* (New York, 1912), 13, 43.

12 J. Arthur Turner (ed.), *The Life of a Chimney Boy, Written by Himself* (1901), 12–17.

13 Charles Humphreys, *The Life of Charles Humphreys (Bookseller)* (1928). 12–17.

14 All from Hawkins, *The Life of Edmund Kean*, Vol. 1, 16–25, and Procter, *The Life of Edmund Kean*, Vol. 1, 10–11, 32, 39–42. The Duncan quote is from Procter, Vol. 1, 10, original emphasis. Again, the accounts differ and are largely anecdotal, but the gist appears to be reliable even if the particulars have been embellished.

15 'Early Victorian Recollections: John Munday's Memories', in Reginald Blunt, *Red Anchor Pieces* (1928), 99–121, 111.

16 Hawkins, *The Life of Edmund Kean*, Vol. 1, 21, 37; Thomas Frost, *The Old Showmen, and the Old London Fairs* (1874), 215–6.

17 All from R.F. Snowden (ed.), *Prodigal of the Seven Seas* (1949), 1–4. Harry, or Henry Warren Kelly as he became, wrote his memoir in later life when he was – extraordinarily – now mayor of the small town of Richmond in New Zealand, and in 1942 his son sent it on to Snowden for eventual publication.

18 'Early Victorian Recollections', 111–12.

19 Greenwood, *In Strange Company*, 12.

20 I am quoting from Barnardo's earliest account of this incident as reported in *The Christian*, 1872, and cited verbatim in Gillian Wagner, *Barnardo* (1979), 30–33. See also Barnardo's better-known subsequent account, extensively rewritten and featuring an unreliable life story of Jim Jarvis, *My First Arab; or, How I Began My Life Work* (1888).

21 Thomas Barnardo, *Saved from a Crime: Incidents in the Life of a Waif and Stray* (1888), 1–15.

22 John Hollingshead, 'Street Memories', in his *Ways of Life* (1861), 90–91.

23 Greenwood, *In Strange Company*, 11.

24 Bezer in *Testaments*, 165.

25 Bullen, *Confessions*, 15–16.

26 Both ibid., 40–41.

27 Holcroft, *Memoirs*, vol. 1, 41–42.

28 Greenwood, *In Strange Company*, 15.

29 Bullen, *Confessions*, 41–42.

30 Ibid., 23.

31 Ibid., 26–7.

32 Ibid., 26.

33 William Brown, *A Narrative of the Life and Adventures of William Brown* (York, 1829), 13.

34 You can hear a recording at www.cambridge.org/ballads, where it is song 24; I discuss the song at some length in the book hosted there: Oskar Cox Jensen, *The Ballad-Singer in Georgian and Victorian London* (Cambridge, 2021).

35 All from George Speaight (ed.), *Professional & Literary Memoirs of Charles Dibdin the Younger* (1956), 109–10. Exceptionally, I have removed several commas for the sake of legibility.

36 Acorn, *One of the Multitude*, 15–18.

37 'Chronicle', *Annual Register* (1855): 61–4, and *Proceedings of the Old Bailey*, case t18550409-484. Reeves' testimony is well worth reading in full.

38 Bezer in *Testaments*, 165.

39 Cited in *Ragged School Union Magazine* 2 (1850), 42–3.

40 Beggs, *An Inquiry*, 148.

41 Edward Pelham Brenton, *Observations on the Training and Education of Children in Great Britain* (1834), xxi.

42 The case was originally reported in the *Household Narrative of Current Events*: the article is available at djo.org.uk/household-narrative-of-current-events/year-1850/page-7.html. See also John Suddaby, 'The Crossing Sweeper in Bleak House: Dickens and the Original Jo', *Dickensian* 8, No.9 (1912): 246–50; and Jo Manton, *Mary Carpenter and the Children of the Streets* (1976), 11.

43 John Garwood, *The Million-Peopled City; or, One-Half of the People of London Made Known to the Other Half* (1853), 6–7.

44 Along with another, still worse case, first reported in *The Times*, this is also detailed in Beggs, *An Inquiry*, 88–9 and 92.

45 Bullen, *Confessions*, 46–7; Brown, *A Narrative*, 6, 9; Acorn, *One of the Multitude*, 16; Blunt, *Red Anchor Pieces*, 107. Robert Southey gives a vivid account of the dancing chimney sweeps:

> Three or four boys of different ages were dancing in the street; their clothes seemed as if they had been dragged through the

chimney, as indeed had been the case, and these sooty habil-
iments were bedecked with pieces of foil, and with ribbons
of all gay colours, flying like streamers in every direction as
they whisked round. Their sooty faces were reddened with
rose-pink, and in the middle of each cheek was a patch of gold
leaf, the hair was frizzed out, and as white as powder could
make it, and they wore an old hat cocked for the occasion,
and in like manner ornamented with ribbons, and foil, and
flowers. In this array were they dancing through the streets,
clapping a wooden plate, frightening the horses by their noise,
and still more by their strange appearance, and soliciting
money from all whom they met.

Robert Southey (pseud. Manuel Alvarez Espriella), *Letters from England*,
three vols (1814), Vol. 1, 143–4.
46 Acorn, *One of the Multitude*, 35; Bullen, *Confessions*, 12–13.
47 Bullen, *Confessions*, 38, 49.
48 Acorn, *One of the Multitude*, 17; Humphreys, *The Life*, 20; 'Police',
Lloyd's Illustrated Newspaper 51 (12 November 1843): 9.
49 Hawkins, *The Life of Edmund Kean*, Vol. 1, 39.
50 Holcroft, *Memoirs*, Vol. 1, 22–5.
51 Blunt, *Red Anchor Pieces*, 113; Humphreys, *The Life*, 21.
52 Bezer in *Testaments*, 164–5.

3 The Girl
1 Derek Hudson (ed.), *Munby, Man of Two Worlds: The Life and Diaries of
Arthur J. Munby, 1828–1910* (1972), 143. For more on crossing sweepers,
see Judith Flanders, *The Victorian City: Everyday Life in Dickens' London*
(2012, new edition 2013), 49–50; a good fictionalised account is given
in Augustus Mayhew, *Paved with Gold, or, The Romance and Reality of the
London Streets* (1858, 2nd edition 1971).
2 Other jobs, similarly deceptive in the level of skill required to succeed, are
equally androgynous. One made iconic by Henry Mayhew is the selling of
watercresses, and much has been written, primarily by Carolyn Steedman,
on the eight-year-old girl he interviews in this trade – an encounter also
recycled in his brother Augustus' vivid novel *Paved with Gold*, 79.
3 Hudson, *Munby*, 143.
4 Ibid., 53.
5 All in Thomas Barnardo, *A City Waif: How I Fished for and Caught Her*
(1880), esp. 2–18.

6 The landmark work on historical working-class autobiography estimates that just ten per cent of memoirs were by women – and that most of these were written in the twentieth, rather than the nineteenth century: John Burnett, David Vincent and David Mayall (eds), *The Autobiography of the Working Class: An Annotated, Critical Bibliography*, three vols (Brighton, 1984–9), Vol. 1, xxiii. Judith Walkowitz sums up one aspect of the problem thus:

> One problem has been the paucity of historical sources that allow entry into the inner life of the prostitute. Illiterate women rarely left ego documents, while their personal statements extracted from legal testimonies were heavily mediated 'through the discourse of those doing the recording'. Legal evidence, even police notes, may include a striking description of a prostitute's milieu or a short first-person statement from the woman herself. But such evidence rarely summons up a streetwalker's complex thinking about her social world and embodied self.

'The Politics of Prostitution and Sexual Labour', *History Workshop Journal* 82 (2016): 188–98, 192.

7 Again, see especially Carolyn Steedman, 'The Watercress-Seller', in her *Past Tenses: Essays on Writing, Autobiography and History* (1992), 193–202, and also John Seed, 'Did the Subaltern Speak? Mayhew and the Coster Girl', *Journal of Victorian Culture* 19 (2014): 536–49; *The Report of the Society Established in London for the Suppression of Mendicity*, Vol. 5 (1823), 27.

8 Steedman, 'The Watercress-Seller', 195.

9 *My Secret Life*, eleven vols (1888; new edition New York, 1966). This much-discussed work is perhaps best analysed in Ian Gibson, *The Erotomaniac: The Secret Life of Henry Spencer Ashbee* (2002). Ashbee was born in 1834, and the work claims to be a retrospective written late in life, all of which suggests most of its events 'take place' in the 1850–70s. The controversial critic Steven Marcus has defended the work's contents thus, 'As simple social history, then, the facts and details of *My Secret Life* are interesting and useful' – quoted in the new edition of *My Secret Life*, Vol. 1, xvi. It should be noted, however, that Marcus reads the work as 'authentic' – a decision that will seem bizarre to anyone who has read it. I am using *My Secret Life* here above all as a crystallisation of the issues at stake in moments of encounter and transaction.

10 All ibid.: Vol. 2, 389–90; Vol. 3, 433–4; Vol. 5, 1029.

11 Steven King and Christiana Payne, 'The Dress of the Poor', *Textile History* 33 (2002): 1–8, 2.

12 *My Secret Life*, Vol. 3, 437.

13 See especially C.M. Jackson-Houlston, '"The Burial-Place of the Fashions": The Representation of the Dress of the Poor in Illustrated Serial Prose by Dickens and Hardy', *Textile History* 33 (2002): 98–111; Beverly Lemire, *The Business of Everyday Life: Gender, Practice and Social Politics in England, c. 1600–1900* (Manchester, 2005); and Vivienne Richmond, *Clothing the Poor in Nineteenth-Century England* (Cambridge, 2013).

14 Organisations were, of course, not above holding both attitudes simultaneously. In 1852, the Mendicity Society's constables 'apprehended' a sixteen-year-old Irish girl with a younger sibling whose main offence was 'dwelling particularly on her Sister's age and incapability of contributing to her own support'. Noting in passing that this younger girl 'of tender years' had previously been sexually assaulted, the Society's report nevertheless wrote the child off as 'a most abandoned character'. *The Report of the Society Established in London for the Suppression of Mendicity*, Vol. 35 (1853), 42.

15 For Walkowitz, see especially her *Prostitution and Victorian Society: Women, Class, and the State* (Cambridge, 1980); *City of Dreadful Delight: Narratives of Sexual Danger in Late-Victorian London* (Chicago, 1992); and 'The Politics of Prostitution'. The last of these is especially compelling on questions of female agency and the ways in which historians have sought to nuance and appreciate this.

16 Not the better-known blacking factory, Warren's, made famous by the honour of numbering a twelve-year-old Charles Dickens among its workers twenty years earlier.

17 *Proceedings of the Old Bailey*, case t18440701-1858. Frustratingly, it has proved impossible to trace the case or any of those involved beyond the report of the trial itself. Incidentally, the aunt and uncle, James and Elizabeth, also have the surname Lewis, but there is no suggestion that they are related to the defendant.

18 *The Nature, Design, and Rules, of the Benevolent, or Strangers' Friend Society ... Together With an Account of some of the Cases Visited in the Year 1808* (1809), 40–44; *Fourth Report of the London Society for the Protection of Young Females, and Prevention of Juvenile Prostitution* (1839), 19; cited in Michael Ryan, *Prostitution in London, with a Comparative View of that of Paris and New York* (1839), 125–7; Beggs, *An Inquiry*, 103–4.

19 Hudson, *Munby*, 21.

20 Much has been written by Tim Hitchcock and others on the agency of paupers in their self-fashioning, especially in relation to letters and petitions. See also Peter D. Jones, '"I cannot keep my place without being

deascent": Pauper Letters, Parish Clothing and Pragmatism in the South of England, 1750-1830', *Rural History* 20 (2009): 31-49.

21 William Greg, *The Great Sin of Great Cities* (1853), 2-4.

22 Blackmore, *London*, esp. 53-95; and Edward W. Thomas, *Twenty-Five Years' Labour among the Friendless and Fallen* (2nd edition, 1886), esp. 18-20. The quotations are all from Blackmore.

23 Hudson, *Munby*, 236.

24 There is an extensive scholarship on this subject. Two good introductions – one historical, one sociological – are the Introduction of Michael J. Braddick and John Walter (eds), *Negotiating Power in Early Modern Society: Order, Hierarchy and Subordination in Britain and Ireland* (Cambridge, 2001), 1-42, esp. 5; and Candace Clarke, *Misery and Company: Sympathy in Everyday Life* (Chicago, 1997).

25 The affair is briefly summarised in *The Report of the Society Established in London for the Suppression of Mendicity*, Vol. 40 (1858), 18-19. Of the many articles printed and recycled in various newspapers, the five key pieces, on which I draw here, are: 'The Police Courts', *Daily News* 3591 (18 November 1857): 7; 'Police Intelligence', *Morning Chronicle* 28364 (18 November 1857): 8; 'Fugitive Slave Girls From Kentucky', *Morning Chronicle* 28371 (26 November 1857): 3; 'The Fugitive Slaves From Kentucky', *Morning Chronicle* 28375 (1 December 1857): 6; and Police Intelligence', *Morning Post* 26191 (9 December 1857): 7.

26 Remarkably, this remained a constituency until 1950.

27 All from – in chronological order – 'Police', *Examiner* 1853 (5 August 1843): 11; 'The Crime of Being Poor' and 'Lloyd's Weekly London Newspaper', *Lloyd's Illustrated Newspaper* (6 August 1843): 7; 'Street Mendicancy.–Jane Ward', *Hansard* (HC Deb 09 August 1843, Vol. 71, cc410-2); 'The Mendicity Society', *Lloyd's Illustrated Newspaper* (13 August 1843): 3; *The Report of the Society Established in London for the Suppression of Mendicity*, Vol. 26 (1844), 16-17; 'Suppression of Mendicity', *Morning Post* (13 May 1844): 2. Note that the last two items, from 1844, give her name as Julia Ward, rather than Jane.

28 *The Report of the Society Established in London for the Suppression of Mendicity*, Vol. 4 (1822), 57.

29 Blackmore, *London*, 182-83.

30 *Report of Royal Commission upon the Administration and Operation of the Contagious Diseases Acts* (1871), Vol. 2, Minutes of Evidence. Quotations are from xl-liv and 615-48.

31 Hudson, *Munby*, 40-41. The excerpt is famous and easily accessible online. For the aside about common prostitutes, see Robert D. Storch,

'Police Control of Street Prostitution in Victorian London: A Study in the Contexts of Police Action', in David H. Bayley (ed.), *Police and Society* (1977), 49–72, 53–4 and 68; and Walkowitz, *Prostitution and Victorian Society*, 14.

32 J. Ewing Ritchie, *The Night Side of London* (1857), 24–25.

33 Walkowitz, 'The Politics of Prostitution', 192.

34 Greg, *The Great Sin*, 9.

35 As argued in Walkowitz, *Prostitution and Victorian Society*, 29–30.

36 Thomas Wright, *The Great Unwashed. By The Journeyman Engineer* (1868), 142–43.

37 Hudson, *Munby*, 30; *Eighth Report of the London City Mission* (1843), 20; *City Mission Magazine* 2 (1837), 156; Edward Pelham Brenton, *A Letter to the Committee of Management for the Suppression of Mendicity, in Red Lion Square* (1830), 14; *The Confessions of an Old Almsgiver; or, Three Cheers for the Charity Organisation Society* (1871), 22.

38 James C. Whitehorne, *The Social Evil Practically Considered* (1858), 9–14; William Acton, *Prostitution, Considered in its Moral, Social, and Sanitary Aspects* (2nd edition, 1870), 27–44.

39 Five issues of *The Times* are relevant here, of which the fourth is the most celebrated. Though it is difficult to find these in their entirety for free online, any library should have a subscription to *The Times*'s archive. See: *The Times* (4 February 1858): 12; 6 February: 10; 11 February: 10; 24 February: 12; and 25 February: 7. The fourth letter is also freely accessible at lauraagustin.com/letter-from-the-prostitute-that-didnt-want-saving-1858

4 The Immigrant

1 John Brown, *Sixty Years' Gleanings from Life's Harvest. A Genuine Autobiography* (2nd edition, New York, 1859), 29.

2 John O'Neill, 'Fifty Years' Experience of an Irish Shoemaker in London', *St. Crispin, A Weekly Journal* 1–3 (1869–70): 240. See also Liam Harte, *The Literature of the Irish in Britain: Autobiography and Memoir, 1725–2001* (Basingstoke, 2009), 15.

3 Laura C. Holloway, *Adelaide Neilson: A Souvenir* (1885), 26–28. See also M.A. De Leine, *Lilian Adelaide Neilson. A Memorial Sketch, Personal and Critical* (1881), 4–6.

4 Henry Barnet Gascoigne, *Suggestions for the Employment of the Poor of the Metropolis* (1817), 31.

5 While the stereotype is of the impoverished rural poor, recent work has emphasised the contributions of Irish migration to the arts and sciences. For two very different but complementary accounts, see Lynn Hollen Lees,

Notes

Exiles of Erin: Irish Migrants in Victorian London (Manchester, 1979), and David O'Shaughnessy (ed.), *Ireland, Enlightenment and the English Stage, 1740–1820* (Cambridge, 2019).

6 For two excellent accounts of the original system, see Audrey Eccles, *Vagrancy in Law and Practice under the Old Poor Law* (Farnham, 2012), and David Hitchcock, *Vagrancy in English Society and Culture, 1650–1750* (2016).

7 James D. Burn, Autobiography of a Beggar Boy (2nd edition, 1856) 16–18; Brown, *Sixty Years' Gleanings*, 30.

8 David Love, *The Life, Adventures, and Experience, of David Love. Written by Himself* (3rd edition, Nottingham, 1823), 67, 72–73.

9 Brown, *Sixty Years' Gleanings*, 30.

10 Ibid., 31.

11 Burn, *Autobiography*, 95, 96.

12 Love, *The Life*, 73.

13 Nicholas Daly, *The Demographic Imagination and the Nineteenth-Century City: Paris, London, New York* (Cambridge, 2015), 107; *A Dictionary of Modern Slang, Cant, and Vulgar Words* (1859), 119–45; Ritchie, *Night Side of London*, 192–93.

14 Joseph Manton Smith, *Stray Leaves from my Life Story* (1885), 19–21.

15 Theodor Fontane, *Journeys to England in Victoria's Early Days, 1844–1859*, trans. Dorothy Harrison (1939), 81; Love, *The Life*, 73. Exceptionally, I have amended the punctuation in the latter quotation for clarity.

16 Brown, *Sixty Years' Gleanings*, 31–35.

17 O'Neill, 'Fifty Years', 240.

18 Holloway, *Adelaide Neilson*, 28–29.

19 O'Neill, 'Fifty Years', 240–41. This is truth as much as prejudice: for two centuries, St Giles's was 'little Ireland' – and a region where that national character was inseparable from a reputation for vagrancy and poverty. See, for example, Lees, *Exiles of Erin*, 66, or Ellen Ranyard, *The Missing Link; or, Bible-Women in the Homes of the London Poor* (1859), 5–7.

20 Holloway, *Adelaide Neilson*, 29–30.

21 C.J. Ribton-Turner, *A History of Vagrants and Vagrancy and Beggars and Begging* (1887), 257–58.

22 Brown, *Sixty Years' Gleanings*, 36–37.

23 O'Neill, 'Fifty Years', 254–55. For a breakdown of the fluctuating price of a loaf and its central importance to the economy of the poor, see James Treble, *Urban Poverty in Britain, 1830–1914* (1979), 157–61.

24 Holloway, *Adelaide Neilson*, 31 and throughout; and J. Gilliland, 'Neilson, Adelaide [real name Elizabeth Ann Brown; known as Lizzie Ann Bland; married name Elizabeth Ann Lee] (1848–1880)', *Oxford Dictionary*

of National Biography (2004).

25 Matthew Martin, *Letter to the Right Hon. Lord Pelham, on the State of Mendicity in the Metropolis* (1803), 7–8; and the *Reports of the Society Established in London for the Suppression of Mendicity*, Vols 1–50 (1819–68).

26 *Italian Children*, esp. 18 and 33–35.

27 *The Report of the Society Established in London for the Suppression of Mendicity*, Vol. 4 (1822), 56.

28 John E. Zucchi, *The Little Slaves of the Harp : Italian child street musicians in nineteenth-century Paris, London, and New York* (Quebec, 1992).

29 Jane Taylor and Ann Taylor, *The New Cries of London, with Characteristic Engravings* (1803), 6–7.

30 Ranyard, *The Missing Link*, 2.

31 *The Report of the Society Established in London for the Suppression of Mendicity*, Vol. 14 (1832), 41–42.

32 *The Report of the Society Established in London for the Suppression of Mendicity*, vol. 2 (1820), 29–30.

33 *The Report of the Society Established in London for the Suppression of Mendicity*, Vol. 3 (1821), 27–28.

34 *The Report of the Society Established in London for the Suppression of Mendicity*, Vol. 35 (1853), 38–39.

35 In what follows, I have drawn on *The Report of the Society Established in London for the Suppression of Mendicity*, Vol. 35 (1853), 36–38, and a succession of press reports: each item was subsequently reproduced across dozens of publications. I have Tom Hughes and his blog *Victorian Calendar* to thank for the reference to the *People's Paper*. See especially: 'Extraordinary Romance', *Morning Chronicle* (7 June 1852): 7; 'Police Intelligence–Wednesday', *Morning Chronicle* (10 June 1852): 8; 'The Police Courts', *Daily News* (21 June 1852): 6; 'Law Intelligence', *Daily News* (22 June 1852): 7; 'Law and Police', *Era* (27 June 1852): 14; and 'The Blind Beggarman's Dog', *Lloyd's Illustrated Newspaper* (4 July 1852): 7.

36 Saree Makdisi, *Making England Western: Occidentalism, Race, and Imperial Culture* (Chicago, 2014), throughout and especially the preface, e.g. xviii.

37 Burn, *Autobiography*, 19.

38 Wise, *The Italian Boy*, 83–84 and 91.

39 There is an extensive literature on the subject, and the 1864 Act in particular: more than is appropriate to quote here. An accessible starting point might be James Winter, *London's Teeming Streets, 1830–1914* (1993).

40 John Thomas Smith, *The Cries of London: exhibiting several of the Itinerant Traders of Antient and Modern Times* (1839), 52. Note that Smith died in 1833; this is one of several posthumous publications, here edited by J.B.

Nichols and revised by Francis Douce.
41 Ibid., 67.

5 The Pro

1 Here and below, all details from Bezer in *Testaments*, esp. 178–83.

2 'Church Street' is now thoroughly obscure, but there is a four-part setting from the period reproduced in Martin V. Clarke, 'The *Illingworth Moor Singers' Book*: A Snapshot of Methodist Music in the Early Nineteenth Century', *Nineteenth-Century Music Review* 7 (2010): 81–103, Figure 5.

3 Concerning whom, I have no choice but to recommend my own *The Ballad-Singer* as the first port of call.

4 'Jack Rag' (ed.), *Streetology of London; or, the Metropolitan Papers of the Itinerant Club* (1837), 85–88.

5 Charles Hindley (ed.), *The Life and Adventures of a Cheap Jack. By One of the Fraternity* (1876), 126–27.

6 Hudson, *Munby*, 131.

7 Johnson's original appearances are in John Thomas Smith, *Vagabondiana; or, Anecdotes of Mendicant Wanderers through the Streets of London* (1817), 33, which reproduces a standalone etching of 1815; and in 'London Ballad Singers', *The Mirror of Literature, Amusement, and Instruction* 6 (9 July, 1825): 42. These are reworked in John Timbs, *Curiosities of London* (1855), 10–11. In fiction, Johnson has cameos in both Susanna Clarke, *Jonathan Strange & Mr Norrell* (2004), 319; and *Taboo*, created by Steven Knight, Tom Hardy, and Chips Hardy, aired on BBC One, 2017, episodes 1 and 6. The chief scholarly treatments of Johnson are probably in Kwame Dawes, 'Negotiating the Ship on the Head: Black British Fiction', *Wasafiri* 14 (1999): 18–24; Mark Stein, *Black British Literature: Novels of Transformation* (Ohio, 2004), 103–04; Peter Reed, '"There Was No Resisting John Canoe": Circum-Atlantic Transracial Performance', *Theatre History Studies* 27 (2007): 65–85; Eddie Chambers, 'Black British Artists: Celebrating Nelson's Ships', at theibtaurisblog.com/2014/07/02/black-british-artists-celebrating-nel-sons-ship; Susan Valladares, 'Afro-Creole Revelry and Rebellion on the British Stage: Jonkanoo in Obi; or, Three-Fingered Jack (1800)', *Review of English Studies*, New Series (2018): 1–21. My own contributions are two versions of one lengthy article, in 'Joseph Johnson's Hat, or, The Storm on Tower Hill', *Studies in Romanticism* 58 (2019): 545–69, and *The Ballad-Singer*, 169–89.

8 Love, *The Life*, 154.

9 This brig has a dedicated website, ladynelson.org.au, and a replica still sails today. My articles on Johnson wade pedantically through the other

possibilities before fetching up at this speculative link.

10 Oskar Cox Jensen, 'Of Ships and Spectacles: Maritime Identity in Regency London', *Nineteenth Century Theatre and Film* 46 (2019): 136-60.

11 All three may be heard via www.cambridge.org/ballads, while the Bodleian has numerous cheap print copies of their lyrics at ballads.bodleian.ox.ac.uk

12 ballads.bodleian.ox.ac.uk/view/edition/255

13 For the discussion of disability at this time, see Teresa Michals, 'Invisible Amputation and Heroic Masculinity', *Studies in Eighteenth-Century Culture* 44 (2015): 17-39, which includes the Adam Smith quotation at 20; Martha Stoddard Holmes, 'Working (with) the Rhetoric of Affliction: Autobiographical Narratives of Victorians with Physical Disabilities', in, James C. Wilson and Cynthia Lewiecki-Wilson (eds), *Embodied Rhetorics: Disability in Language and Culture* (Carbondale and Edwardsville, 2001), 27-44; and Martha Stoddard Holmes, *Fictions of Affliction: Physical Disability in Victorian Culture* (Ann Arbor, 2004).

14 For references and further discussion, see my articles mentioned above, and for the original quotation, Matthew Lewis, *Journal of a Residence Among the Negroes in the West Indies* (1845, reprinted Stroud, 2005), 33. For more on the model ships, see my 'Of Ships and Spectacles'.

15 See especially Tim Barringer, Gillian Forrester and Barbaro Martinez-Ruiz (eds), *Art and Emancipation in Jamaica: Isaac Mendes Belisario and His Worlds* (New Haven, 2007), 1, 31, 72; Elizabeth Maddock Dillon, *New World Drama: The Performative Commons in the Atlantic World, 1649-1849* (Durham and London, 2014), 203-4; Simon Gikandi, *Slavery and the Culture of Taste* (Princeton, 2011), 273; Peter Reed, *Rogue Performances: Staging the Underclasses in Early American Theatre Culture* (New York, 2009), 117-20; and Kathleen Wilson, *The Island Race: Englishness, Empire and Gender in the Eighteenth Century* (2003), 164.

16 Simplest, I think, to give only one endnote on William Waters. His two current biographers are Tony Montague and my colleague Mary Shannon. Neither of their books is complete at time of writing, but Shannon's existing article is far and away the best place to start and the most authoritative source for all the extant material on Waters: 'The Multiple Lives of Billy Waters: Dangerous Theatricality and Networked Illustrations in Nineteenth-Century Popular Culture', *Nineteenth Century Theatre and Film* 46 (2019): 161-89. This article references all the relevant works and reproduces most of the images of Waters. Of the aspects discussed in the present chapter, see especially Thomas Lord Busby, *Costume of the Lower Orders of London. Painted and Engraved from Nature* (1819, 2nd edition 1820), 1; Charles Hindley, *The True History of Tom and Jerry* (1888), 102-4; Douglas

Jerrold, 'The Ballad-Singer', in *Heads of the People: Being Portraits of the English*, two vols (1840), Vol. 2, 297. The Wilkie (attrib.) painting is at rmg.co.uk/collections/objects/rmgc-object-254220; the details of HMS *Ganymede* are at threedecks.org/index.php?display_type=show_ship&id=4420; and you can hear me singing 'Polly, Will You Marry Me?' via www.cambridge.org/ballads, under 'Recordings'.

17 What follows stems from two key sources: Mayhew, *London Labour*, Vol. 2, 490-93; and Natalie Prizel, '"The Dead Man Come To Life Again": Edward Albert and the Strategies of Black Endurance', *Victorian Literature and Culture* 45 (2017): 293-320.

18 The book itself is reproduced in its entirety in Prizel's article – a rare and brilliant decision on her part. Its original is held in the University of Washington Libraries, HV4545.A4 / b B74 Special Collections.

19 For much more on which, see my 'The *Travels* of John Magee: Tracing the geographies of Britain's itinerant print-sellers, 1789-1815', *Journal of Cultural and Social History* 11 (2014): 195-216.

20 Presumably a relative of the ballad printer John Howe based at 48 Blanket Row.

21 For Howe, see ballads.bodleian.ox.ac.uk/search/printer/Howe%2C%20J. The woodcut of the ship is used for 'The Deep, Deep Sea', on edition Harding B 11(789). Coincidentally, the other woodcut on this sheet is of a blackface minstrel – in this case playing a banjo, and clearly not the image described by Mayhew.

22 Love, *The Life*, 151.

23 Ibid., 78-79.

24 Ibid., 150-57.

25 Basset, *The Life of a Vagrant*, 60.

26 For much more on this, see my *The Ballad-Singer*, Chapter Two.

27 Smith, *Cries of London*, 61.

28 Hudson, *Munby*, 107.

29 Ibid., 178-80.

30 Richard Phillips, *A Morning's Walk from London to Kew* (1817), 226-29.

31 See oed.com/view/Entry/42335, second definition.

32 Greenwood, *In Strange Company*, 42.

33 Charles Manby Smith, Curiosities of London Life (1853), 44-46, 55-56.

34 Charles Cochrane, *How to Improve the Homes of the People!* (1849), 14.

35 George Smeeton, *Doings in London* (10th edition, 1828), 114-15.

36 Smith, *Cries of London*, 77-78.

37 Smith, *Curiosities*, 20-22.

38 For the new, definitive account, see Charlie Taverner, *Street Food: Hawkers and the History of London* (Oxford, 2022).

39 Smith, *Curiosities*, 194.

40 Phillips, *A Morning's Walk*, 379.

41 See Winter, *London's Teeming Streets*, and Cox Jensen, *The Ballad-Singer*, especially the conclusion, for further context and references.

42 John Hollingshead, *My Lifetime*, two vols (1895), Vol. 1, 63.

43 A lot of excellent work has been done on this. A great place to start is Stephen Jankiewicz, 'A Dangerous Class: The Street Sellers of Nineteenth-Century London', *Journal of Social History* 46 (2012): 391–415. For a thought-provoking parallel, see Oliver Zimmer, *Remaking the Rhythms of Life: German Communities in the Age of the Nation-State* (Oxford, 2013).

44 'Meetings: and Democratic Intelligence', *Reynolds's Newspaper* 40 (18 May 1851).

6 The Renegade

1 Joshua H. Stallard, *London Pauperism amongst Jews and Christians* (1867), 150-53.

2 Both Seth Koven and Luke Seaber vouch for the likely authenticity of her account, which is easily accessible via Google Books and other online repositories. Joshua H. Stallard, *The Female Casual and her Lodging* (1866). The quotations in this paragraph are from 3-4.

3 All ibid., 19-56.

4 Humphreys, *The Life*, 31-33.

5 Brenton, *A Letter*, 3.

6 In the winter of 1841, 630 tickets were presented on a single day; in 1847, they recorded 55,721 unregistered cases. *Reports of the Society Established in London for the Suppression of Mendicity*, Vols 24 and 30 (1842 and 1848), respectively at 11 and 21-23.

7 *The Practice of the Mendicity Society. By 'One who knows it well'* (1847), 14. The same source specifies half as much cheese as bread – 1/4 lb – and a pint, or 568 ml, of dubious soup: 'The objection of beggars is mostly made to the soup, but this article has over and over again been tested and approved by impartial persons'.

8 All from Bezer in *Testaments*, 184-87.

9 James Hardy Vaux, *Memoirs of James Hardy Vaux, a Swindler and Thief* (2nd edition, 1830; first edition 1819), 2-23. Vaux's editor at the time, a Mr Field, cautions that 'The reader must ... believe as much or little as he pleases of the following story' (vii), but his modern editor, Noel McLachlan, has cross-checked the account with all available records and concluded that Vaux's recollections are 'a true story in their broad outline and are generally reliable as to events, names, and dates ... their accuracy is, I think, really quite formidable and vindicates Vaux's boast that he possessed an exceptionally

good memory' (New edition, 1964, xxxiii). We must expect some embellishment of detail, but – as you will see later in the chapter – there are indeed other, more official sources that verify much of Vaux's account.

10 William Hone, *The Every-day Book*, three vols (1825–33), Vol. 2, 543.

11 Carington Bowles (ed.), *Bowles's Florist: Containing sixty plates of beautiful flowers, regularly disposed in their succession of blowing* (1777). A digital edition is accessible at digital.library.wisc.edu/1711.dl/7DX3RYR3UJDCN8Q. With thanks to *The Printshop Window* blog for the lead, via theprintshopwindow. wordpress.com/2020/12/04/jemmy-whittle-the-devil-st-dunstan-and-the-laughing-boy/

12 Vaux, *Memoirs*, 105–6.

13 Thomas Wontner, *Old Bailey Experience* (1833), 363.

14 Vaux, *Memoirs*, 113.

15 Ibid., 114–15.

16 Ibid., 117–18.

17 All from Wontner, *Old Bailey Experience*, respectively 11, 38, 49, 52–53, 59–60.

18 Humphreys, *The Life*, 47–48.

19 Vaux, *Memoirs*, 118–23, and *Proceedings of the Old Bailey*, case t18000917-73. Note that Vaux is recorded officially as 'James Low'; the report itself gives his name correctly, but underestimates his age by two years.

20 Wontner, *Old Bailey Experience*, 48.

21 George Atkins Brine, *The King of the Beggars: The Life and Adventures of George Atkins Brine. A True Story of Vagrant Life* (1883), 14, 19–20, 29.

22 James Grant, *Sketches in London* (1838), 34.

23 George Smeeton, *Biographia Curiosa; or, Memoirs of Remarkable Characters of the Reign of George the Third* (1822), 189.

24 George Smeeton, *Doings in London.*

25 *The Report of the Society Established in London for the Suppression of Mendicity*, Vol. 20 (1838), 41–42.

26 *The Report of the Society Established in London for the Suppression of Mendicity*, Vol. 33 (1851), 41.

27 Lionel Rose, *'Rogues and Vagabonds': Vagrant Underworld in Britain, 1815–1985* (1988), 4–12.

28 All from 'Police', *The Times* (21 May 1825): 4; 'Westminster Sessions.– Thursday', *Morning Chronicle* (21 October 1825): 4; and *The Report of the Society Established in London for the Suppression of Mendicity*, Vol. 9 (1827), 42–50.

29 Brenton, *A Letter*, 9–10.

30 Smith, *Vagabondiana*, 20, and first print (in the British Library facsimile edition).

31 All from *Minutes of the Evidence taken before the Committee*, 26–27, 37–38.

32 Humphreys, *The Life*, 32–34.

33 Etymologically speaking, this is neatly appropriate. Chapmen sold chap-books – usually cheap, unbound pamphlets, often containing songs as well as stories and riddles, which they would sing or recite in public places to aid their sale. See oed.com/view/Entry/30593, second definition.

34 *The Dens of London Exposed* (1835), 74–80.

35 The use of 'father-in-law' for 'stepfather' was common until later in the nineteenth century; see oed.com/view/Entry/68504, second definition.

36 'Police Intelligence', *Morning Chronicle* 20416 (2 February 1835): 4.

7 The Elder

1 Smith, *The Cries of London*, 63–64.

2 James Greenwood, *Unsentimental Journeys: or, Byways of the Modern Babylon* (1867), 117–21.

3 David Green, Douglas Brown, Kathleen McIlvenna, and Nicola Shelton, '"The Postman Wears Out Fast": Retiring Sick in London's Victorian Post Office', *London Journal* (2019): 1–26, esp. 1–10.

4 Hollingshead, *Ragged London*, 26.

5 *Report of the Committee of the Benevolent, or Strangers' Friend Society* 1 (1817), 25–26.

6 *The Report of the Society Established in London for the Suppression of Mendicity*, Vols 4 (1822), 29; and 7 (1825), 46.

7 *The Report of the Society Established in London for the Suppression of Mendicity*, Vol. 23 (1841), 35.

8 As discussed in – and recorded for – Chapter Four of Cox Jensen, *The Ballad-Singer*.

9 'Bow Street', *Star* (4 October 1827).

10 'Jack Rag', *Streetology*, 54–56.

11 Smith, *Curiosities*, vii–viii. The original piece was published as 'The Blind Fiddler', *Chambers's Edinburgh Journal* 16 (December 1851): 411–13.

12 Smith, *Curiosities*, 80–89.

13 Most of the relevant sources, especially the images, are comprehensively cited in the two works mentioned in the following note. But see particularly Smith, *Vagabondiana*, 24–25 and plate 11; John Diprose, *Some Account of the Parish of Saint Clement Danes (Westminster) Past and Present*, two vols (1868), Vol. 1, 164–65; Charles Mathews, *Othello, the Moor of Fleet Street* (1833, new edition Tübingen, 1993); and see in addition to these, 'Fleet-street Biography', *London Magazine* 9 (April 1824): 417–24, 417; and 'Jack Rag', *Streetology*, 31–32.

14 See respectively historyonics.blogspot.com/search/label/Charles%20
McCay and 'The Begging Places' in Charlotte Grant and Alistair Robinson
(eds), *Cultures of London: Legacies of Migration* (2022).

15 It should be noted that the *London Magazine*'s general thrust is satirical,
and its treatment of Mackey racist, in an article mocking the presumption
of a certain Joseph Brasbridge to publish his own memoir. Still, its words
contain the kernel of a real sentiment: here was a man who had seen things
in his time.

16 'The Bereaved Trombone', in *Chambers's Edinburgh Journal* 15 (1851):
331-32, and reprinted in Smith, *Curiosities*, 124-29. Of all the anecdotal
tales I encountered in my research, this is among the best written; I found it
deeply affecting, and recommend readers to the original, easily accessed via
Google Books or similar.

17 Both tunes are still well known, and recorded versions abound.

18 Excerpted and reported in a footnote in Hollingshead, *Ragged London*, 68.

19 'The Musical Shrimp Man', *The Cabinet of Curiosities: Or Wonders of the
World Displayed* (1824), 348-49; Stallard, *London Pauperism*, 80-84.

20 For a full treatment of the topic, see Ruth Richardson, *Death, Dissection
and the Destitute* (2nd edition, 2001). The quotation from Pennant is ibid., 60.

21 'London Ballad Singers', 53; *Art Journal* 7 (1868): 2-3.

22 Smith, *Vagabondiana*, 19-20.

23 See Chapter Five, note 16, for full references of Billy Waters. The Catnach
broadside, 'The Merry Will & Testament of Master Black Billy', is reproduced
and discussed in James Hepburn, *A Book of Scattered Leaves: Poetry of Poverty in
Broadside Ballads of Nineteenth-Century England*, two vols (Cranbury, 2000-1),
Vol. 2, 308-9, while a number of other pieces are compiled in Hindley, *The
True History of Tom and Jerry*, 102-8. For the Mayhew quotation, see Mayhew,
London Labour, Vol. 3, 76. I should note also that Mary Shannon, at time of
writing, has hopes of settling, among other things, the location of his burial.

Epitaph

1 'Escape of a Tiger', *Morning Post* 12354 (5 September 1810): 4; 'Presence
of Mind', *Morning Post* 12357 (8 September 1810): 3; Thomas Frost, *The
Old Showmen, and the Old London Fairs* (1874), 232-33. The *Post*'s first,
more sensational account calls the animal a Bengal tiger; its second, a
hesitant correction, gives 'tiger or leopard'; Frost, who is the authority
with access to other sources and who supplies many additional details, is
clear that it is a leopard.

Bibliography

Unless otherwise stated, the place of publication is taken to be London.

Newspapers and Periodicals
Annual Register
Art Journal
Blackwood's Edinburgh Magazine
Chambers' Edinburgh Journal
Chambers' Miscellany
City Mission Magazine
Cornhill Magazine
Daily News
Era
Examiner
Hansard
Household Narrative of Current Events
Household Words
Illustrated Times
Jottings from the Shade of the City of London
Justice of the Peace, and County, Borough, and Parish Law Recorder
Leisure Hour
Lloyd's Illustrated Newspaper
London Magazine
London Review of Books
Macmillan's Magazine
Mirror of Literature, Amusement, and Instruction
Morning Chronicle
Morning Post
Pall Mall Gazette

Quarterly Review
Ragged School Union Magazine
Reynolds's Newspaper
Spectator
St. Crispin, *A Weekly Journal devoted to the interest of boot and shoe makers*
Star
The Times
Trewman's Exeter Flying Post or Plymouth and Cornish Advertiser
War Cry and Official Gazette of the Salvation Army

Electronic Databases
19th-Century British Library Newspapers: find.galegroup.com/bncn/start. do?prodId=BNCN
Bodleian Library, Broadside Ballads Online: ballads.bodleian.ox.ac.uk
British Museum Collection Database Online: britishmuseum.org/research/ search_the_collection_database.aspx
British Periodicals: https://ezproxy.ouls.ox.ac.uk:2303/home.do
Eighteenth-Century Collections Online: gale.com/intl/primary-sources/ eighteenth-century-collections-online
The Making of the Modern World: gale.com/intl/primary-sources/the-making-of-the-modern-world
The Proceedings of the Old Bailey, 1674–1913 (POB): oldbaileyonline.org
Oxford Dictionary of National Biography (ODNB): oxforddnb.com
The Times Digital Archive: infotrac.galegroup.com/itw/infomark/0/1/1/ purl=rc6_TTDA?

Reports of Institutions
An Account of a Meat and Soup Charity, Established in the Metropolis, in the Year 1797 (1797).
An Act for Further Improving the Police in and near the Metropolis: (17th August 1839) (1839).
Annual Reports of the London City Mission (1835–45).
Annual Reports of the Ragged School Union (1847–1944).
Annual Reports of the Society Established in London for the Suppression of Mendicity (1819–68).
The Benevolent or Strangers' Friend Society, Established 1785 (1879).
Chadwick, Edwin, *Report from E. Chadwick, Esq., on London and Berkshire* (reprinted from 'Extracts from the Information received by His Majesty's Commissioners, as to the Administration and Operation of the Poor-Laws', 1833).

The First Report, Presented to the General Meeting [of the Associate Institution for Improving and Enforcing the Laws for the Protection of Women] (1846).

Fourth Report of the London Society for the Protection of Young Females, and Prevention of Juvenile Prostitution (1839).

Italian Children. Report of the Committee of the Charity Organisation Society Appointed to Enquire into the Employment of Italian Children for Mendicant and Immoral Purposes (2nd edition, 1877).

The Ladies' Royal Benevolent Society (Late Dollar) (1819).

Minutes of the Evidence taken before the Committee appointed by the House of Commons to inquire into the state of Mendicity and Vagrancy in the Metropolis and its Neighbourhoods ... to which is added, The Second Report (1816).

The Nature, Design, and Rules, of the Benevolent, or Strangers' Friend Society ... Together With an Account of some of the Cases Visited (1803–13).

New Police Report for 1817. The second report of the select committee (1817).

Report from Committee on the State of Mendicity in the Metropolis, Ordered by the House of Commons to be Printed, 11 July 1815 (1815).

Report of the Committee for Investigating the Causes of the Alarming Increase of Juvenile Delinquency in the Metropolis (1816).

Report of Royal Commission upon the Administration and Operation of the Contagious Diseases Acts (1871).

Reports of the Society for Bettering the Condition and Increasing the Comforts of the Poor (1803–5, 1811, 1815).

Report(s) of the Committee of the Benevolent, or Strangers' Friend Society (1817–46).

Life Writing

Acorn, George, *One of the Multitude* (New York, 1912).

Barrett, Rosa M., *Ellice Hopkins, a Memoir* (1907).

Basset, Josiah, *The Life of a Vagrant, or the Testimony of an Outcast to the Value and Truth of the Gospel* (3rd edition, 1850).

Blunt, Reginald, *Red Anchor Pieces* (1928).

Brine, George Atkins, *The King of the Beggars: The Life and Adventures of George Atkins Brine. A True Story of Vagrant Life* (1883).

Brown, John, *A Memoir of Robert Blincoe, An Orphan Boy* (Manchester, 1832).

Brown, John, *Sixty Years' Gleanings from Life's Harvest. A Genuine Autobiography* (2nd edition, New York, 1859).

Brown, William, *A Narrative of the Life and Adventures of William Brown* (York, 1829).

Bullen, Frank, *Confessions of a Tradesman* (1908).

Burn, James D., *Autobiography of a Beggar Boy* (2nd edition, 1856).

Burnett, John (ed.), *Useful Toil: Autobiographies of working people from the 1820s to the 1920s* (Harmondsworth, 1984).

Bibliography

Charlesworth, Maria, *The Female Visitor to the Poor: or, Records of Female Parochial Visiting* (1846).

Cohen, Lucy, *Lady de Rothschild and her Daughters, 1821–1931* (1935).

The Confessions of an Old Almsgiver; or, Three Cheers for the Charity Organisation Society (1871).

Cousins, D.L., *Extracts from the Diary of a Workhouse Chaplain* (1847).

De Leine, M.A., *Lilian Adelaide Neilson. A Memorial Sketch, Personal and Critical* (1881).

Elson, George, *The Last of the Climbing Boys: An Autobiography* (1900).

Hanbidge, William, *The Memories of William Hanbidge, Aged 93. 1906. An Autobiography* (St Albans, 1939).

Hawkins, Frederick W., *The Life of Edmund Kean. From Published and Original Sources*, two vols (1869).

Hindley, Charles (ed.), *The Life and Adventures of a Cheap Jack. By One of the Fraternity* (1876).

The History of Betty Thomson, and Her Family and Neighbours; Being the First Part of a Practical Commentary On the Reports of the Society for bettering the Condition of the Poor (1808).

Holcroft, Thomas, *Memoirs of the Late Thomas Holcroft*, three vols (1816).

Hollingshead, John, *My Lifetime*, two vols (1895).

Holloway, Laura C., *Adelaide Neilson: A Souvenir* (1885).

Horsley, John William, *'I Remember': Memories of a 'Sky Pilot' in the Prison and the Slum* (1911).

Hudson, Derek (ed.), *Munby, Man of Two Worlds: The Life and Diaries of Arthur J. Munby, 1828–1910* (1972).

Humphreys, Charles, *The Life of Charles Humphreys (Bookseller)* (1928).

Love, David, *David Love's Journey to London, and his Return to Nottingham* (Nottingham, c. 1814).

Love, David, *The Life, Adventures, and Experience, of David Love. Written by Himself* (3rd edition, Nottingham, 1823).

Magee, John, *Some Account of the Travels of John Magee, Pedlar and Flying Stationer, in North & South Britain, in the Years 1806 and 1808* (Paisley, 1826).

Malvery, Olive Christian, *A Year and a Day* (1912).

Manton Smith, Joseph, *Stray Leaves from my Life Story* (1885).

Manton Smith, Joseph, *More Stray Leaves* (1889).

Memories of a Sister of Saint Saviour's Priory (2nd edition, 1912).

Miller, David Prince, *The Life of a Showman* (1849).

Nevinson, Margaret Wynne, *Life's Fitful Fever: A Volume of Memories* (1926).

O'Neill, John, 'Fifty Years' Experience of an Irish Shoemaker in London', *St. Crispin, A Weekly Journal* 1–3 (1869–70).

Pilkington, Ernest, *An Eton Playing Field: A Reminiscence of Happy Days spent at the Eton Mission* (1896).

Procter, W.B., *The Life of Edmund Kean*, two vols (1835).

Sanderson, Thomas, *Chips and Shavings of an Old Shipwright* (Darlington, 1873).

Selfe, Emily Rose, *Light Amid London Shadows* (1906).

Shakesby, Alfred, *From Street Arab to Evangelist: The Life Story of Albert Shakesby, a Converted Athlete* (Hull, 1910).

Snowden, R.F. (ed.), *Prodigal of the Seven Seas* (1949).

Southey, Robert (pseud. Manuel Alvarez Espriella), *Letters from England*, three vols (1814).

Speaight, George (ed.), *Professional & Literary Memoirs of Charles Dibdin the Younger* (1956).

Tallack, William, *Peter Bedford* (2nd edition, 1893).

Thomas, Edward W., *Twenty-Five Years' Labour among the Friendless and Fallen* (1886).

Tomes, Ann, *Memoirs of Miss Ann Tomes, Late of Hackney, Aged 19* (1832).

Turner, J. Arthur (ed.), *The Life of a Chimney Boy, Written by Himself* (1901).

Twining, Louisa, *Recollections of Life and Work* (1893).

Vaux, James Hardy, *Memoirs of James Hardy Vaux, a Swindler and Thief* (2nd edition, 1830).

Vaux, James Hardy, *Memoirs of James Hardy Vaux*, ed. Noel McLachlan (New edition, 1964).

Vincent, David (ed.), *Testaments of Radicalism: Memoirs of Working Class Politicians 1790–1885* (1977).

Weylland, John Matthias, *Valiant for the Truth* (1899).

Yeats, Grant David, pseud. Ἰατρός., *A Biographical Sketch of the Life and Writings of Patrick Colquhoun* (1818).

Fiction and Poetry

Badcock, John, *Real Life in London; or, the Rambles and Adventures of Bob Tallyho, Esq. and his cousin, the Hon. Tom Dashall, through the Metropolis*, two vols (1821).

Burrowes, John [John Freckleton], *Life in St. George's Fields, or, the Rambles and Adventures of Disconsolate William, Esq.* (1821).

Edgeworth, Maria, *The Ballad Singer; or, Memoirs of the Bristol Family: A Most Interesting Novel in Four Volumes*, four vols (1814).

Egan, Pierce, *Life in London, or, The Day and Night Scenes of Jerry Hawthorn, Esq.* (2nd edition, c. 1870).

Fatherless Fanny; or, The Little Mendicant (1850).

Gilbert, William, *James Duke, Costermonger: A Tale of the Social Deposits* (1879).

Kelly, Isabella, *Joscelina: or, the Rewards of Benevolence. A Novel*, two vols (2nd edition, 1798).

Mayhew, Augustus, *Paved with Gold, or, The Romance and Reality of the London Streets* (1858, 2nd edition 1971).

Murray, Henry, *The Ordeal of Thomas Taffler, Costermonger* (1896).

Nicholson, M.J., *The Sunbeam of Seven-Dials; and Other Stories of London Poor* (1874).

Ostlere, Edith, *From Seven Dials* (1898).

Robinson, Frederick William, *Owen: A Waif*, three vols (1862).

Smeeton, George, *Doings in London* (10th edition, 1828).

The Surprising History of a Ballad Singer (Falkirk, 1818).

Taylor, Jane and Taylor, Ann, *The New Cries of London, with Characteristic Engravings* (1803)

Plays

à Beckett, Gilbert Abbott, *Man-Fred: A Burlesque Ballet Opera, In One Act* (1835).

Almar, George, *Oliver Twist. A Serio-Comic Burletta, in Three Acts* (Leipzig, 1842).

Barnett, Charles Z., *Oliver Twist, or, The Parish Boy's Progress. A Domestic Drama, in Three Acts* (1838).

Mathews, Charles, *Othello, the Moor of Fleet Street* (1833, new edition Tübingen, 1993).

Moncrieff, William T., *Tom and Jerry; or, Life in London: An Operatic Extravaganza, in Three Acts* (2nd edition, 1828).

Moncrieff, William T., *Sam Weller or, The Pickwickians: A Drama in Three Acts* (1837).

Moncrieff, William T., *The Ballad Singer, in Three Acts* (1839), in British Library, Add. MS. 42952, ff. 248–327.

Moncrieff, William T., *The Scamps of London; Or, The Cross Roads of Life. A Drama of Manners and Characters, in three acts* (1843).

Sims, George Robert, *The Lights o' London: A New and Original Drama in Five Acts* (1881, new edition Oxford, 1995, ed. Michael R. Booth).

Miscellaneous Primary Material

Acton, William, *Prostitution, Considered in its Moral, Social, and Sanitary Aspects* (2nd edition, 1870).

'Aleph' [William Harvey], *London Scenes and London People* (1863).

Aubineau, Léon, *Historical Notice of the Little Sisters of the Poor* (1863).

Babbage, Charles, *A Chapter on Street Nuisances* (1864).

Barnardo, Thomas, *'Taken out of the Gutter.' A True Incident of Child Life on the Streets of London* (1881).

Barnardo, Thomas, *A City Waif: How I Fished for and Caught Her* (1880).

Barnardo, Thomas, *Kidnapped! A Narrative of Fact* (1885).

Barnardo, Thomas, *Rescued for Life: The True Story of a Young Thief* (1885).

Barnardo, Thomas, *Worse than Orphans: How I Stole Two Girls and Fought for a Boy* (1885).

Barnardo, Thomas, *'The Seed of the Righteous,' among the Children of the Poorest* (1886).

Barnardo, Thomas, *My First Arab; or, How I Began my Life Work* (1888).

Barnardo, Thomas, *Saved from a Crime: Incidents in the Life of a Waif and Stray* (1888).

Barnardo, Thomas, *Never Had a Home: A Very Commonplace History* (1890).

Bass, Michael T., *Street Music in the Metropolis. Correspondence and Observations on the Existing Law, and Proposed Amendments* (1864).

Beames, Thomas, *The Rookeries of London: Past, Present, and Prospective* (2nd edition, 1852).

Bee, John [John Badcock], *A Living Picture of London, for 1828* (1828).

Beggs, Thomas, *An Inquiry into the Extent and Causes of Juvenile Depravity* (1849).

Blackmore, John, *London By Moonlight Mission* (1869).

Bowles, Carington (ed.), *Bowles's Florist: Containing sixty plates of beautiful flowers, regularly disposed in their succession of blowing* (1777).

Brenton, Edward Pelham, *A Letter to the Committee of Management for the Suppression of Mendicity, in Red Lion Square* (1830).

Brenton, Edward Pelham, *Observations on the Training and Education of Children in Great Britain* (1834).

Brierley, Benjamin (ed.), *'Ab-O'Th'-Yate' in London; or, Southern Life from a Northern Point of View* (Manchester: 1868).

Busby, Thomas L., *Costume of the Lower Orders of London. Painted and Engraved from Nature* (1820).

The Cabinet of Curiosities: Or Wonders of the World Displayed (1824).

Carpenter, Mary, *Reformatory Schools, for the Children of the Perishing and Dangerous Classes, and for Juvenile Offenders* (1851).

Caulfield, James, *Blackguardiana: or, a dictionary of rogues* (c. 1793).

Chesney, Kellow, *The Victorian Underworld* (1970).

Cochrane, Charles, *How to Improve the Homes of the People!* (1849).

Colquhoun, Patrick, *The State of Indigence, and the Situation of the Casual Poor in the Metropolis, Explained* (1799).

Colquhoun, Patrick, *A Treatise on the Police of the Metropolis* (6th edition, 1800).

Colquhoun, Patrick, *A Treatise on the Functions and Duties of a Constable* (1803).

Colquhoun, Patrick, *A Treatise on Indigence* (1806).

The Dens of London Exposed (1835).

Bibliography

A Dictionary of Modern Slang, Cant, and Vulgar Words (1859).

Diprose, John, Some Account of the Parish of Saint Clement Danes (Westminster) Past and Present, two vols (1868).

Diprose, John, Diprose's Book about London and London Life (1872).

Fontane, Theodor, Journeys to England in Victoria's Early Days, 1844–1859, trans. Dorothy Harrison (1939).

Frost, Thomas, The Old Showmen, and the Old London Fairs (1874).

Garwood, John, The Million-Peopled City; or, One-Half of the People of London Made Known to the Other Half (1853).

Gascoigne, Henry Barnet, Suggestions for the Employment of the Poor of the Metropolis (1817).

Godwin, George, London Shadows; A Glance at the 'Homes' of the Thousands (1854).

Gore, Montague, On the Dwellings of the Poor, and the Means of Improving Them (3rd edition, 1851).

Grant, James, The Great Metropolis, two vols (1837).

Grant, James, Sketches in London (1838).

Greenwood, James, In Strange Company: Being the Experiences of a Roving Correspondent (2nd edition, 1883).

Greenwood, James, Unsentimental Journeys: or, Byways of the Modern Babylon (1867).

Greg, William, The Great Sin of Great Cities (1853).

Grego, Joseph, Rowlandson the Caricaturist: A Selection from his Works, two vols (1880).

Guthrie, Thomas, Seed-Time & Harvest of Ragged Schools, or A Third Plea with New Editions of the First & Second Pleas (Edinburgh, 1860).

Heads of the People: Being Portraits of the English, two vols (1840).

Highmore, Anthony, Pietas Londinensis: The History, Design, and Present State of the various Public Charities in and near London (2nd edition, 1814).

Hindley, Charles, A History of the Cries of London, Ancient and Modern (1881).

Hindley, Charles, The True History of Tom and Jerry (1888).

Hollingshead, John, Odd Journeys in and out of London (1860).

Hollingshead, John, Under Bow Bells: A City Book for all Readers (1860).

Hollingshead, John, Ragged London in 1861 (1861, reprinted 1986).

Hollingshead, John, Ways of Life (1861).

Hollingshead, John, To-day: Essays and Miscellanies, two vols (1865).

Hollingshead, John, According to my Lights (1900).

Hone, William, The Every-day Book and Table Book, three vols (1825–33).

Hopkins, Ellice, The Visitation of Dens. An Appeal to the Women of England (1874).

Hopkins, Ellice, Work Among the Lost (1874).

Hopkins, Ellice, 'God's Little Girl.' A Truthful Narrative of Facts Concerning a poor 'waif' admitted into 'Dr. Barnardo's Village Home' (1885).

Jerrold, Blanchard, *London: A Pilgrimage. Illustrated by Gustave Doré with an Introduction by Peter Ackroyd* (1872, new edition 2006).

Jerrold, Douglas, *The Essays of Douglas Jerrold. Edited by his Grandson Walter Jerrold with Illustrations by H.M. Brock* (1903).

Knight, Charles (ed.), *London*, six vols (1851).

Leighton, John, *London Cries & Public Edifices. By Luke Limner Esq.* (1847).

Lewis, Matthew, *Journal of a Residence Among the Negroes in the West Indies* (1845, reprinted Stroud, 2005).

Lhotsky, John, *Hunger and Revolution. By the Author of 'Daily Bread'* (1843).

Lockie, John, and Hatton, Edward, *Lockie's Topography of London* (1810).

Lowe, Clara M.S., *God's Answers: A Record of Miss Annie Macpherson's Work at the home of industry, Spitalfields, London, and in Canada* (1882).

Mackay, Charles, *Memoirs of Extraordinary Popular Delusions*, three vols (1841).

Macpherson, Annie, *The Little London Arabs* (1870).

Malcolm, James P., *Anecdotes of the Manners and Customs of London During the Eighteenth Century*, two vols (2nd edition, 1810).

Martin, Matthew, *Letter to the Right Hon. Lord Pelham, on the State of Mendicity in the Metropolis* (1803).

Mayhew, Henry, et al., *London Labour and the London Poor*, four vols (1861–62, new edition 1968).

The Mendicity Society Unmasked, in a letter to the managers (1825).

Metropolitan Grievances; or, a Serio-Comic Glance at Minor Mischiefs in London and its Vicinity (1812).

The Moving Market: Or, Cries of London. For the Amusement of Good Children. (Glasgow, 1815).

My Secret Life, eleven vols (c. 1888; new edition New York, 1966).

Nolan, Thomas, *Motives for Missions. A Series of Six Lectures delivered before the Church of England Young Men's Society in the autumn of 1852* (1853).

Parker, George, *Life's Painter of Variegated Characters in Public and Private Life* (1789).

Parker, George, *A View of Society and Manners in High and Low Life*, two vols (1791).

Parton, John, *Some Account of the Hospital and Parish of St. Giles in the Fields, Middlesex* (1822).

Phillips, Richard, *A Morning's Walk from London to Kew* (1817).

The Practice of the Mendicity Society. By 'One who knows it well' (1847).

'Rag, Jack' (ed.), *Streetology of London; or, the Metropolitan Papers of the Itinerant Club* (1837).

Ram, Abel, *The Little Sisters of the Poor* (1894).

Ranyard, Ellen (L.N.R.), *The Missing Link; or, Bible-Women in the Homes of the London Poor* (1859).

Bibliography

Reynolds, George W.M., *The Mysteries of London* (1850–6, New edition, Keele, 1996).

Reynolds, George, *Dr Barnardo's Homes* (1877).

Ribton-Turner, C.J., *A History of Vagrants and Vagrancy and Beggars and Begging* (1887).

Ritchie, J. Ewing, *The Night Side of London* (1857).

Rowlandson, Thomas, *Characteristic Sketches of the Lower Orders* (c. 1820).

Ryan, Michael, *Prostitution in London, with a Comparative View of that of Paris and New York* (1839).

Sala, George Augustus, *Twice Round the Clock; or the Hours of the Day and Night in London* (1861).

Sala, George Augustus, *Gaslight and Daylight* (New edition, 1872).

Schlesinger, Max, *Saunterings in and about London. The English Edition by Otto Wenckstern* (1853).

Sheppard, Emma, *An Out-Stretched Hand to the Fallen* (1850).

Slater, Michael (ed.), *Dickens' Journalism: Sketches by Boz and other Early Papers, 1833–39* (1996).

Smeeton, George, *Biographia Curiosa; or, Memoirs of Remarkable Characters of the Reign of George the Third* (1822).

Smith, Albert R. (ed.), *Gavarni in London, Sketches of Life and Character: With Illustrative Essays by Popular Writers* (1849).

Smith, Charles M., *Curiosities of London Life: or, Phases, Physiological and Social, of the Great Metropolis* (1853).

Smith, Charles M., *The Little World of London; or, Pictures in Little of London Life* (1857).

Smith, John T., *Antient Topography of London* (1810).

Smith, John T., *Etchings of Remarkable Beggars, Itinerant Traders, and other Persons of Notoriety in London and its Environs* (1815).

Smith, John T., *Vagabondiana; or, Anecdotes of Mendicant Wanderers through the Streets of London; with Portraits of the Most Remarkable Drawn from the Life* (1817).

Smith, John T., *The Cries of London: exhibiting several of the Itinerant Traders of Antient and Modern Times* (1839).

Stallard, Joshua H., *The Female Casual and her Lodging* (1866).

Stallard, Joshua H., *London Pauperism amongst Jews and Christians* (1867).

Stallard, Joshua H., *Pauperism, Charity, & Poor Laws* (1868).

Stanhope, Philip D., *Chesterfield Travestie: Or, School for Modern Manners* (1808).

Taine, Hyppolyte, *Taine's Notes on England*, trans. Edward Hyams (1957).

Talbot, James Beard, *The Miseries of Prostitution* (1844).

Tallis, John, *John Tallis's London Street Views: 1838–1840. Together with the revised and enlarged views of 1847 introducted and with a biographical essay by Peter Jackson* (New edition, 1969).

Tennant, Dorothy, *London Street Arabs* (1890).

The Swell's Night Guide: or, a Peep Through the Great Metropolis (New edition, 1846).

Thornbury, Walter, *Old and New London*, 5 vols (1873–78).

Timbs, John, *Curiosities of London* (New edition, 1867).

Toilers in London; or, Inquiries Concerning Female Labour in the Metropolis (1889).

Tuer, Alfred W., *Old London Street Cries* (1885).

Westmacott, Charles, *The English Spy*, two vols (1825–26).

Whitehorne, James C., *The Social Evil Practically Considered* (1858).

Wightman, Julia B., *Annals of the Rescued* (New York, 1861).

Wontner, Thomas, *Old Bailey Experience* (1833).

Wright, Thomas, *The Great Unwashed. By the Journeyman Engineer* (1868).

Secondary Material

Ackroyd, Peter, *London: The Biography* (2000).

Almeroth-Williams, Thomas, *City of Beasts: How Animals Shaped Georgian London* (Manchester, 2019).

Altick, Richard, *The Shows of London* (Harvard, 1978).

Amigoni, David (ed.), *Life Writing and Victorian Culture* (Aldershot, 2006).

Amy, Helen, *The Street Children of Dickens's London* (Stroud, 2012).

Anderson, Hugh, *Farewell to Judges & Juries: The Broadside Ballad & Convict Transportation to Australia, 1788–1868* (Victoria, 2000).

Andrews, Gavin, Kingsbury, Paul, and Kearns, Robin (eds), *Soundscapes of Wellbeing in Popular Music* (Farnham, 2014).

Atkins, Peter (ed.), *Animal Cities: Beastly Urban Histories* (Farnham, 2012).

Bailey, Peter, *Popular Culture and Performance in the Victorian City* (Cambridge, 1998).

Barringer, Tim, Forrester, Gillian, and Martinez-Ruiz, Barbaro (eds), *Art and Emancipation in Jamaica: Isaac Mendes Belisario and His Worlds* (New Haven, 2007).

Batts, John Stuart, *British Manuscript Diaries of the 19th Century: An Annotated Listing* (Fontwell, 1976).

Bayley, David H. (ed.), *Police and Society* (1977).

Beaumont, Matthew, *Nightwalking: A Nocturnal History of London* (2015).

Berlanstein, Lenard R., 'Vagrants, Beggars, and Thieves: Delinquent Boys in Mid-Nineteenth Century Paris', *Journal of Social History* 12 (1979): 531–52.

Bibliography

Berry, Helen, *Orphans of Empire: The Fate of London's Foundlings* (Oxford, 2019).

Bondeson, Jan, *The London Monster: A Sanguinary Tale* (2nd edition, Cambridge, M.A., 2002).

Boone, Troy, *Youth of Darkest England: Working-Class Children at the Heart of Victorian Empire* (Abingdon, 2005).

Botelho, Lynn, Connors, Richard, Hitchcock, Tim, Archer, Ian W., Fumerton, Patricia, and Griffiths, Paul, 'London Calling!', *Histoire Sociale/Social History* 43 (2010): 213–40.

Braddick, Michael J., and Innes, Joanna (eds), *Suffering and Happiness in England 1550–1850: Narratives and Representations* (Oxford, 2017).

Braddick, Michael J. and Walter, John (eds), *Negotiating Power in Early Modern Society: Order, Hierarchy and Subordination in Britain and Ireland* (Cambridge, 2001).

Brant, Clare and Whyman, Susan E. (eds), *Walking the Streets of Eighteenth-Century London: John Gay's Trivia (1716)* (Oxford, 2007).

Breton, Rob, 'Portraits of the Poor in Early Nineteenth-Century Radical Journalism', *Journal of Victorian Culture* 21 (2016): 168–83.

Burnett, John, Vincent, David, and Mayall, David (eds), *The Autobiography of the Working Class: An Annotated, Critical Bibliography*, three vols (Brighton, 1984–89).

Bywater, Michael, 'Performing Spaces: Street Music and Public Territory', *Twentieth-Century Music* 3 (2007): 97–120.

Calaresu, Melissa and van den Heuvel, Danielle (eds), *Food Hawkers: Selling in the Streets from Antiquity to the Present* (Abingdon, 2016).

Cannadine, David, and Reeder, David (eds), *Exploring the Urban Past: Essays in Urban History by H.J. Dyos* (Cambridge, 1982).

Carter, Paul and Whistance, Natalie, 'The Poor Law Commission: A New Digital Resource for Nineteenth-Century Domestic Historians', *History Workshop Journal* 71 (2011): 29–48.

Chambers, Eddie, 'Black British Artists: Celebrating Nelson's Ships', at theibtaurisblog.com/2014/07/02/black-british-artists-celebrating-nelsons-ship

Chandler, James and Gilmartin, Kevin (eds), *Romantic Metropolis: The Urban Scene of British Culture, 1780–1840* (Cambridge, 2005).

Charlesworth, Simon J., *A Phenomenology of Working-Class Experience* (Cambridge, 2000).

Chesney, Kellow, *The Victorian Underworld: A Fascinating Re-Creation* (1991, 1st edition 1970).

Chrisman-Campbell, Kimberley, *Fashion Victims: Dress at the Court of Louis XVI and Marie-Antoinette* (New Haven, 2015).

Clark, Glenn, Owens, Judith, and Smith, Greg T. (eds), *City Limits: Perspectives on the Historical European City* (Montreal, 2010).

Clarke, Candace, *Misery and Company: Sympathy in Everyday Life* (Chicago, 1997).

Clarke, Martin V., 'The *Illingworth Moor Singers' Book*: A Snapshot of Methodist Music in the Early Nineteenth Century', *Nineteenth-Century Music Review* 7 (2010): 81–103.

Clarke, Susanna, *Jonathan Strange & Mr Norrell* (2004).

Cook, Daniel and Culley, Amy (eds), *Women's Life Writing, 1700–1850: Gender, Genre and Authorship* (Basingstoke, 2012).

Corfield, Penelope J., 'Walking the City Streets: "The Urban Odyssey in Eighteenth-Century England"', *Journal of Urban History* 16 (1990): 132–74.

Corton, Christine L., *London Fog: The Biography* (Cambridge M.A., 2015).

Couser, G. Thomas, *Memoir: An Introduction* (Oxford, 2012).

Cox Jensen, Oskar, 'The Travels of John Magee: Tracing the geographies of Britain's itinerant print-sellers, 1789–1815', *Journal of Cultural and Social History* 11 (2014): 195–216.

Cox Jensen, Oskar, 'Joseph Johnson's Hat, or, The Storm on Tower Hill', *Studies in Romanticism* 58 (2019): 545–69.

Cox Jensen, Oskar, 'Of Ships and Spectacles: Maritime Identity in Regency London', *Nineteenth Century Theatre and Film* 46 (2019): 136–60.

Cox Jensen, Oskar, *The Ballad-Singer in Georgian and Victorian London* (Cambridge, 2021).

Culley, Amy, *British Women's Life Writing, 1760–1840* (Basingstoke, 2014).

Cuming, Emily, '"Home is home be it never so homely": Reading Mid-Victorian Slum Interiors', *Journal of Victorian Culture* 18 (2013): 368–86.

Cuming, Emily, 'At Home in the World? The Ornamental Life of Sailors in Victorian Sailortown', *Journal of Victorian Culture* 47 (2019): 463–85.

Cunningham, Hugh, *Leisure in the Industrial Revolution, c. 1780–c. 1880* (1980).

Cunningham, Hugh, *The Children of the Poor: Representations of Childhood since the Seventeenth Century* (Oxford, 1991).

Cunningham, Hugh, *Children & Childhood in Western Society since 1500* (Harlow, 1995).

Daly, Nicholas, *The Demographic Imagination and the Nineteenth-Century City: Paris, London, New York* (Cambridge, 2015).

Davin, Anna, 'Waif Stories in Late Nineteenth-Century England', *History Workshop Journal* 52 (2001): 67–98.

Dawes, Kwame, 'Negotiating the Ship on the Head: Black British Fiction', *Wasafiri* 14 (1999): 18–24.

Dillon, Elizabeth Maddock, *New World Drama: The Performative Commons in the Atlantic World, 1649–1849* (Durham & London, 2014).

Dixon, Thomas, *The Invention of Altruism: Making Moral Meanings in Victorian Britain* (Oxford, 2008).

Dolan, Alice, 'Touching Linen: Textiles, Emotion and Bodily Intimacy in England c. 1708–1818', *Cultural and Social History* 16 (2019): 145–64.

Donajgrodzki, A.P. (ed.), *Social Control in Nineteenth Century Britain* (1977).

Donald, Diana, '"Beastly Sights": The Treatment of Animals as a Moral Theme in Representations of London, c. 1820–1850', *Art History* 22 (1999): 514–44.

Dyos, H.J., *Exploring the Urban Past: Essays in Urban History*, ed. David Cannadine and David Reeder (Cambridge, 1982).

Dyos, H.J. and Wolff, Michael (eds), *The Victorian City: Images and Realities*, two vols (1999).

Eccles, Audrey, *Vagrancy in Law and Practice under the Old Poor Law* (Farnham, 2012).

Edwards, Paul, and Walvin, James, *Black Personalities in the Era of the Slave Trade* (Baton Rouge, 1983).

Epstein Nord, Deborah, *Walking the Victorian Streets: Women, Representation, and the City* (New York, 1995).

Esmail, Jennifer, '"The Little Dog is Only a Stage Property": The Blind Man's Dog in Victorian Culture', *Victorian Review* 40 (2014): 18–23.

Flanders, Judith, *The Victorian City: Everyday Life in Dickens' London* (2012, new edition 2013).

Fontaine, Laurence, *History of Pedlars in Europe*, trans. Vicki Whittaker (Cambridge, 1996).

Foster, Laura, 'Christmas in the Workhouse: Staging Philanthropy in the Nineteenth-Century Periodical', *Journal of Victorian Culture* 22 (2017): 553–78.

Freeman, Mark, '"Journeys into Poverty Kingdom": Complete Participation and the British Vagrant, 1866–1914', *History Workshop Journal* 52 (2001): 99–121.

Fulford, Tim, 'Fallen Ladies and Cruel Mothers: Ballad Singers and Ballad Heroines in the Eighteenth Century', *The Eighteenth Century: Theory and Interpretation* 47 (2006): 309–30.

Fumerton, Patricia, *Unsettled: The Culture of Mobility and the Working Poor in Early Modern England* (Chicago, 2006).

Gagnier, Regenia, *Subjectivities: A History of Self-Representation in Britain, 1832–1920* (Oxford, 1991).

Gatrell, Vic A.C., *The Hanging Tree: Execution and the English People, 1770–1868* (Oxford, 1994).

Gelder, Ken (ed.), *The Subcultures Reader* (2nd edition, Abingdon, 2005).

George Scharf: From the Regency Street to the Modern Metropolis: An Exhibition (2009).

Gibson, Ian, *The Erotomaniac: The Secret Life of Henry Spencer Ashbee* (2002).

Gikandi, Simon, *Slavery and the Culture of Taste* (Princeton, 2011).

Gilbert, Pamela K., *The Citizen's Body: Desire, Health, and the Social in Victorian England* (Columbus, 2007).

Grant, Charlotte, and Robinson, Alistair (eds), *Cultures of London: Legacies of Migration* (2022).

Green, Bryan S., 'Learning from Henry Mayhew: The Role of the Impartial Spectator in Mayhew's *London Labour and the London Poor*', *Journal of Contemporary Ethnography* 31, No. 2 (2002): 99–134.

Green, David, Brown, Douglas, McIlvenna, Kathleen, and Shelton, Nicola, '"The Postman Wears Out Fast": Retiring Sick in London's Victorian Post Office', *London Journal* (2019): 1–26.

Griffin, Emma, *Liberty's Dawn: A People's History of the Industrial Revolution* (Yale, 2014).

Hackman, Rowan, *Ships of the East India Company* (Gravesend, 2001).

Harris, Tim (ed.), *The Politics of the Excluded, c. 1500–1850* (Basingstoke, 2001).

Harte, Liam, *The Literature of the Irish in Britain: Autobiography and Memoir, 1725–2001* (Basingstoke, 2009).

Harriman-Smith, James, 'Representing the Poor: Charles Lamb and the *Vagabondiana*', *Studies in Romanticism* 54 (2015): 551–68.

Haworth, Catherine, and Colton, Lisa (eds), *Gender, Age and Musical Creativity* (Farnham, 2015).

Hayward, Sally, '"Those Who Cannot Work"', *Prose Studies: History, Theory, Criticism* 27 (2005): 53–71.

Hepburn, James, *A Book of Scattered Leaves: Poetry of Poverty in Broadside Ballads of Nineteenth-Century England*, 2 vols (Cranbury, 2000–1).

Hewitt, Martin (ed.), *The Victorian World* (Abingdon, 2012).

Himmelfarb, Gertrude, *The Idea of Poverty: England in the Early Industrial Age* (New York, 1983).

Hitchcock, David, *Vagrancy in English Society and Culture, 1650–1750* (2016).

Hitchcock, Tim, *Down and Out in Eighteenth-Century London* (2004).

Hitchcock, Tim, 'Begging on the Streets of Eighteenth-Century London', *Journal of British Studies* 44 (2005): 478–98.

Hitchcock, Tim, et al. (eds), *Chronicling Poverty: The Voices and Strategies of the English Poor, 1640–1840* (Basingstoke, 1997).

Hitchcock, Tim, and Shoemaker, Robert, *London Lives: Poverty, Crime and the Making of a Modern City, 1690–1800* (Cambridge, 2015).

Hitchcock, Tim, and Shore, Heather (eds), *The Streets of London: From the Great Fire to the Great Stink* (2003).

Hofer-Robinson, Joanna, *Dickens and Demolition: Literary Afterlives and Mid-Nineteenth-Century Urban Development* (Edinburgh, 2018).

Bibliography

Holmes, Vicky, 'Accommodating the Lodger: The Domestic Arrangements of Lodgers in Working-Class Dwellings in a Victorian Provincial Town', *Journal of Victorian Culture* 19 (2014): 314-31.

Huff, Cynthia (ed.), *Women's Life Writing and Imagined Communities* (Abingdon, 2005).

Humpherys, Anne (ed.), *Voices of the Poor: Selections from the Morning Chronicle 'Labour and the Poor' (1849-1850) by Henry Mayhew* (1971).

Humpherys, Anne, *Travels into the Poor Man's Country: The Work of Henry Mayhew* (Athens, Georgia, 1977).

Humphries, Jane, *Childhood and Child Labour in the British Industrial Revolution* (Cambridge, 2010).

Inglis, Lucy, *Georgian London: Into the Streets* (2014).

Jackson-Houlston, Caroline M., '"The Burial-Place of the Fashions": The Representation of the Dress of the Poor in Illustrated Serial Prose by Dickens and Hardy', *Textile History* 33 (2002): 98-111.

Jankiewicz, Stephen, 'A Dangerous Class: The Street Sellers of Nineteenth-Century London', *Journal of Social History* 46 (2012): 391-415.

Jones, Peter D., 'Clothing the Poor in Early-Nineteenth-Century England', *Textile History* 37 (2006): 17-37.

Jones, Peter D., '"I cannot keep my place without being deascent": Pauper Letters, Parish Clothing and Pragmatism in the South of England, 1750-1830', *Rural History* 20 (2009): 31-49.

Jones, Peter T.A., 'Redressing Reform Narratives: Victorian London's Street Markets and the Informal Supply Lines of Urban Modernity', *London Journal* 41 (2016): 60-81.

Joyce, Patrick, *Visions of the People: Industrial England and the question of class, 1848-1914* (Cambridge, 1991).

Joyce, Patrick, *Democratic Subjects: The self and the social in nineteenth-century England* (Cambridge, 1994).

Joyce, Patrick, 'What is the Social in Social History?', *Past and Present* 205 (2009): 175-210.

Keating, Peter J., *The Working Classes in Victorian Fiction* (1971, new edition Abingdon, 2016).

Kelley, Victoria, *Soap and Water: Cleanliness, Dirt and the Working Classes in Victorian and Edwardian Britain* (2010).

Kincaid, James R., *Child-Loving: The Erotic Child and Victorian Culture* (New York, 1992).

King, Steven, *Poverty and Welfare in England, 1700-1850: A Regional Perspective* (Manchester, 2000).

King, Steven, 'Reclothing the English Poor, 1750-1840', *Textile History* 33 (2002): 37-47.

King, Steven, *Writing the Lives of the English Poor, 1750s–1830s* (Montreal, 2019).

King, Steven and Payne, Christiana, 'The Dress of the Poor', *Textile History* 33 (2002): 1–8.

Koven, Seth, *Slumming: Sexual and Social Politics in Victorian London* (Princeton, 2006).

Laitinen, Riitta and Cohen, Thomas V. (eds), *Cultural History of Early Modern European Streets* (Leiden, 2009).

Lamb, Jonathan, *The Evolution of Sympathy in the Long Eighteenth Century* (2009).

Landes, Joan B., Lee, Paula Young, and Youngquist, Paul (eds), *Gorgeous Beasts: Animal Bodies in Historical Perspective* (University Park, P.A., 2012).

Lavery, Brian, *The Ship of the Line*, two vols (2003).

Lee, Ying S., *Masculinity and the English Working Class: Studies in Victorian Autobiography and Fiction* (Abingdon, 2007).

Lees, Lynn Hollen, *Exiles of Erin: Irish Migrants in Victorian London* (Manchester, 1979).

Lemire, Beverly, *The Business of Everyday Life: Gender, Practice and Social Politics in England, c. 1600–1900* (Manchester, 2005).

Loftus, Diana, 'Work, Poverty and Modernity in Mayhew's London', *Journal of Victorian Culture* 19 (2014): 507–19.

Longmore, Paul K., *Telethons: Spectacle, Disability, and the Business of Charity* (Oxford, 2016).

Louttit, Chris, 'The Novelistic Afterlife of Henry Mayhew', *Philological Quarterly* 85 (2006): 315–41.

Lydon, Jane, '"The Colonial Children Cry": Jo the Crossing-Sweep Goes to the Colonies', *Journal of Victorian Culture* 20 (2015): 308–25.

Maidment, Brian, *Dusty Bob: A Cultural History of Dustmen, 1780–1870* (Manchester, 2007).

Makdisi, Saree, *Making England Western: Occidentalism, Race, and Imperial Culture* (Chicago, 2014).

Mandler, Peter (ed.), *The Uses of Charity: The Poor on Relief in the Nineteenth-Century Metropolis* (Philadelphia, 1990).

Manton, Jo, *Mary Carpenter and the Children of the Streets* (1976).

Marcus, Laura, *Auto/biographical Discourses: Theory, Criticism, Practice* (Manchester, 1994).

Marshall, Nancy R., *City of Gold and Mud: Painting Victorian London* (New Haven, 2012).

Martin, Nancy, *A Man with a Vision: The Story of John Groom* (Oxford, 1983).

Matthews, William, *British Diaries: An Annotated Bibliography of British Diaries Written Between 1442 and 1942* (Berkeley and Los Angeles, 1950).

Bibliography

Matthews, William, *British Autobiographies: An Annotated Bibliography of British Autobiographies Published or Written Before 1951* (Berkeley and Los Angeles, 1955).

McClure, Ruth, *Coram's Children: The London Foundling Hospital in the Eighteenth Century* (New Haven, 1981).

McFarland, Sarah, and Hediger, Ryan (eds), *Animals and Agency: An Interdisciplinary Explanation* (Leiden, 2009).

McKechnie, Claire Charlotte, and Miller, John, 'Victorian Animals', *Journal of Victorian Culture* 17 (2012): 436–41.

McKellar, Elizabeth, 'Peripheral Visions: Alternative aspects and rural presences in mid-eighteenth-century London', *Art History* 22 (1999): 495–513.

Michals, Teresa, 'Invisible Amputation and Heroic Masculinity', *Studies in Eighteenth-Century Culture* 44 (2015): 17–39.

Miele, Kathryn, 'Horse-Sense: Understanding the Working Horse in Victorian London', *Victorian Literature and Culture* 37 (2009): 129–40.

Murdoch, Lydia, *Imagined Orphans: Poor Families, Child Welfare, and Contested Citizenship in London* (New Brunswick, 2006).

Myers, Norma, 'Servant, Sailor, Soldier, Tailor, Beggarman: Black Survival in White Society 1780–1830', *Immigrants and Minorities* 12 (1993): 47–74.

Naggar, Betty, *Jewish Pedlars and Hawkers, 1740–1940* (Camberley, 1992).

Nead, Lynda, *Victorian Babylon: People, Streets, and Images in Nineteenth-Century London* (New Haven, 2000).

Nead, Lynda, 'Fallen Women and Foundlings: Rethinking Victorian Sexuality', *History Workshop Journal* 82 (2016): 177–87.

'New Lights upon Old Tunes. "The Arethusa"', *Musical Times and Singing Class Circular* 35 (1894): 666–8.

Norcia, Megan A., '"Come Buy, Come Buy": Christina Rossetti's "Goblin Market" and the Cries of London', *Journal of Victorian Culture* 17 (2012): 24–45.

Nussbaum, Felicity, *The Autobiographical Subject: Gender and Ideology in Eighteenth-Century England* (Baltimore, 1989).

Nussbaum, Martha, *Frontiers of Justice: Disability, Nationality, Species Membership* (Harvard, 2006).

O'Byrne, Alison, 'The Art of Walking in London: Representing Pedestrianism in the Early Nineteenth Century', *Romanticism* 14, No .2 (2008): 94–107.

Ogborn, Miles, *Spaces of Modernity: London's Geographies, 1680–1780* (New York, 1998).

Owens, Alastair, Jeffries, Nigel, Wehner, Karen, and Featherby, Rupert, 'Fragments of the Modern City: Material Culture and the Rhythms of Everyday Life in Victorian London', *Journal of Victorian Culture* 15 (2010): 212–25.

Peltz, Lucy, 'Aestheticising the Ancestral City: Antiquarianism, topography and the representation of London in the long eighteenth century', *Art History* 22 (1999): 472-94.

Pemberton, Neil, 'The Rat-Catcher's Prank: Interspecies Cunningness and Scavenging in Henry Mayhew's London', *Journal of Victorian Culture* 19 (2014): 520-35.

Peterson, Linda H., *Traditions of Victorian Women's Autobiography: The Poetics and Politics of Life Writing* (Charlottesville, 1999).

Philo, Chris, and Wilbert, Chris (eds), *Animal Spaces, Beastly Places: New Geographies of Human-Animal Relations* (2000).

Picard, Liza, *Victorian London: The Life of a City, 1840-1870* (2005, new edition 2006).

Picker, John M., *Victorian Soundscapes* (Oxford, 2003).

Poovey, Mary, *Making a Social Body: British Cultural Formation, 1830-1864* (Chicago, 1995).

Porter, Roy, *London: A Social History* (1994, new edition 2000).

Prizel, Natalie, '"The Dead Man Come To Life Again": Edward Albert and the Strategies of Black Endurance', *Victorian Literature and Culture* 45 (2017): 293-320.

Prochaska, F.K., *Women and Philanthropy in Nineteenth-Century England* (Oxford, 1980).

Reed, Peter, '"There Was No Resisting John Canoe": Circum-Atlantic Transracial Performance', *Theatre History Studies* 27 (2007): 65-85.

Reed, Peter, *Rogue Performances: Staging the Underclasses in Early American Theatre Culture* (New York, 2009).

Reid, Douglas A., 'The Decline of Saint Monday 1766-1876', *Past & Present* 71 (1976): 76-101.

Renders, Hans, and de Haan, Binne (eds), *Theoretical Discussions of Biography: Approaches from History, Microhistory, and Life Writing* (Revised edition, Leiden, 2014).

Richardson, Ruth, *Death, Dissection and the Destitute* (2nd edition, 2001).

Richmond, Vivienne, *Clothing the Poor in Nineteenth-Century England* (Cambridge, 2013).

Ritvo, Harriet, *The Animal Estate: The English and Other Creatures in the Victorian Age* (Cambridge, M.A., 1987).

Roach, Joseph, *Cities of the Dead: Circum-Atlantic Performance* (New York, 1996).

Roberts, M.J.D., 'Reshaping the Gift Relationship: The London Mendicity Society and the Suppression of Begging in England, 1818-1869', *International Review of Social History* 36 (1991): 201-31.

Bibliography

Roddy, Sarah, Strange, Julie-Marie, and Taithe, Bertrand, 'Henry Mayhew at 200 – the "Other" Victorian Bicentenary', *Journal of Victorian Culture* 19 (2014): 481-96.

Rogers, Helen, and Cuming, Emily, 'Revealing Fragments: Close and Distant Reading of Working-Class Autobiography', *Family and Community History* 21 (2018): 180-201.

Rose, Lionel, *'Rogues and Vagabonds': Vagrant Underworld in Britain, 1815-1985* (1988).

Rose, Michael (ed.), *The Poor and the City: The English Poor Law in its Urban Context, 1834-1914* (Leicester: 1985).

Sabbagh, Karl (ed.), *The Wayward Genius of Henry Mayhew: Pioneering Reportage from Victorian London* (2012).

Salzberg, Rosa, '"Poverty Makes Me Invisible": Street Singers and Hard Times in Italian Renaissance Cities', *Italian Studies* 71 (2016): 212-24.

Saunders, Max, *Self Impression: Life-Writing, Autobiografiction, and the Forms of Modern Literature* (Oxford, 2010).

Scriven, Tom, 'The Jim Crow Craze in London's Press and Streets, 1836-39', *Journal of Victorian Culture* 19 (2014): 93-109.

Seed, John, 'Did the Subaltern Speak? Mayhew and the Coster Girl', *Journal of Victorian Culture* 19 (2014): 536-49.

Shannon, Mary, 'The Multiple Lives of Billy Waters: Dangerous Theatricality and Networked Illustrations in Nineteenth-Century Popular Culture', *Nineteenth Century Theatre and Film* 46 (2019): 161-89.

Shaw, David Gary, 'The Torturer's Horse: Agency and Animals in History', *History and Theory* 52, No. 4 (2013): 146-67.

Shesgreen, Sean, *Images of the Outcast: The Urban Poor in the Cries of London* (Manchester, 2002).

Shoemaker, Robert, *The London Mob: Violence and Disorder in Eighteenth-Century England* (2004).

Simons, John, *The Tiger that Swallowed the Boy: Exotic Animals in Victorian England* (Faringdon, 2012).

Simpson, Paul, 'Chronic Everyday Life: Rhythmanalysing Street Performance', *Social & Cultural Geography* 9 (2008): 807-29.

Simpson, Paul, 'Street Performance and the City: Public Space, Sociality, and Intervening in the Everyday', *Space and Culture* 14 (2011): 415-30.

Simpson, Paul, 'Apprehending Everyday Rhythms: Rhythmanalysis, Time-Lapse Photography, and the Space-Times of Street Performance', *Cultural Geographies* 19 (2012): 423-45.

Simpson, Paul, 'Ecologies of Experience: Materiality, Sociality, and the Embodied Experience of (Street) Performing', *Environment and Planning* 45 (2013): 180-96.

Simpson, Paul, 'Sonic Affects and the Production of Space: "Music by Handle" and the Politics of Street Music in Victorian London', *Cultural Geographies* 24 (2017): 89–109.

Smiles, Sam, 'Defying Comprehension: Resistance to Uniform Appearance in Depicting the Poor, 1770s to 1830s', *Textile History* 33 (2002): 22–36.

Smith, Linday, 'The Shoe-Black to the Crossing Sweeper: Victorian Street Arabs and Photography', *Textual Practice* 10 (2008): 29–55.

Smyth, Adam, *Autobiography in Early Modern England* (Cambridge, 2010).

Stedman Jones, Gareth, *Languages of Class: Studies in English Working Class History, 1832–1982* (Cambridge, 1983).

Stedman Jones, Gareth, *Outcast London: A Study in the Relationship between Classes in Victorian Society* (2nd edition, Harmondsworth, 1984).

Steedman, Carolyn, *Past Tenses: Essays on Writing, Autobiography and History* (1992).

Steedman, Carolyn, *Strange Dislocations: Childhood and the Idea of Human Interiority, 1780–1930* (1995).

Steedman, Carolyn, *Master and Servant: Love and Labour in the English Industrial Age* (Cambridge, 2007).

Steedman, Carolyn, 'Cries Unheard, Sights Unseen: Writing the Eighteenth-Century Metropolis', *Representations* 118 (2012): 28–71.

Steedman, Carolyn, *An Everyday Life of the English Working Class: Work, Self and Sociability in the Early Nineteenth Century* (Cambridge, 2013).

Steedman, Carolyn, 'Mayhew: On Reading, About Writing', *Journal of Victorian Culture* 19 (2014): 550–61.

Stein, Mark, *Black British Literature: Novels of Transformation* (Ohio, 2004), 103–4.

Stern, Walter M., *The Porters of London* (1960).

Stoddard Holmes, Martha, *Fictions of Affliction: Physical Disability in Victorian Culture* (Ann Arbor, 2004).

Storch, Robert D. (ed.), *Popular Culture and Custom in Nineteenth-Century England* (1982).

Suddaby, John, 'The Crossing Sweeper in Bleak House: Dickens and the Original Jo', *Dickensian* 8, No. 9 (1912): 246–50.

Taithe, Bertrand, *The Essential Mayhew: Representing and Communicating the Poor* (1996).

Taverner, Charlie, *Street Food: Hawkers and the History of London* (Oxford, 2022).

Thompson, E.P., and Yeo, Eileen, *The Unknown Mayhew* (1973).

Thurston, Gavin, *The Clerkenwell Riot: The Killing of Constable Culley* (1967).

Tindall, Gillian, *The Fields Beneath: The History of One London Village* (1977, new edition 2010).

Bibliography

Tomkins, Alannah, 'Poor Law Institutions through Working-Class Eyes: Autobiography, Emotion, and Family Context, 1834–1914', *Journal of British Studies* 60 (2021): 285–309.

Treadwell, James, *Autobiographical Writing and British Literature, 1783–1834* (Oxford, 2005).

Treble, James H., *Urban Poverty in Britain, 1830–1914* (1979).

Valladares, Susan, 'Afro-Creole Revelry and Rebellion on the British Stage: Jonkanoo in Obi; or, Three-Fingered Jack (1800)', *Review of English Studies*, New Series (2018): 1–21.

van der Linden, Marcel, and Lucassen, Leo (eds), *Working on Labor: Essays in Honor of Jan Lucassen* (Leiden, 2012).

Veder, Robin, 'Flowers in the Slums: Weavers' Floristry in the Age of Spitalfields' Decline', *Journal of Victorian Culture* 14 (2009): 261–81.

Velten, Hannah, *Beastly London: A History of Animals in the City* (2013).

Vincent, David, *Bread, Knowledge and Freedom: A Study of Nineteenth-Century Working Class Autobiography* (1981).

Wagner, Gillian, *Barnardo* (1979).

Walkowitz, Judith, *Prostitution and Victorian Society: Women, Class, and the State* (Cambridge, 1980).

Walkowitz, Judith, *City of Dreadful Delight: Narratives of Sexual Danger in Late-Victorian London* (Chicago, 1992).

Walkowitz, Judith, 'The Politics of Prostitution and Sexual Labour', *History Workshop Journal* 82 (2016): 188–98.

Waller, John, *The Real Oliver Twist* (Thriplow, 2005).

Weisbrod, Bernd, 'How to Become a Good Foundling in Early Victorian London', *Social History* 10 (1985): 193–209.

Wendelin, Greta Kristian, 'The Genealogy of the Prostitute: Defining and Disciplining Prostitution through Journalism in Victorian England, 1809–1886' (PhD dissertation, University of Kansas, 2012).

Weygand, Zina, *The Blind in French Society from the Middle Ages to the Century of Louis Braille* (Stanford, 2009).

White, Jerry, *London in the Nineteenth Century* (2008).

White, Jerry, 'Pain and Degradation in Georgian London: Life in the Marshalsea Prison', *History Workshop Journal* 68 (2009): 69–98.

Williams, Karel, *From Pauperism to Poverty* (1981).

Williams, Raymond, *The Country and the City* (New edition, Nottingham, 2011).

Wilson, James C., and Lewiecki-Wilson, Cynthia (eds), *Embodied Rhetorics: Disability in Language and Culture* (Carbondale and Edwardsville, 2001).

Wilson, Kathleen, *The Island Race: Englishness, Empire and Gender in the Eighteenth Century* (2003).

Wilson, Kathleen (ed.), *A New Imperial History: Culture, Identity, and Modernity in Britain and the Empire, 1660–1840* (Cambridge, 2004).

Winfield, Rif, *British Warships in the Age of Sail 1793–1817* (Barnsley, 2008).

Winter, James, *London's Teeming Streets, 1830–1914* (1993).

Wise, Sarah, *The Italian Boy: Murder and Grave-Robbery in 1830s London* (2005).

Wise, Sarah, *The Blackest Streets: The Life and Death of a Victorian Slum* (2009).

Wohl, Anthony S., *The Victorian Family: Structure and Stresses* (1978).

Wood, Richard, *A Day in the Life of a Victorian Street Seller* (Hove, 1999).

Woolf, Stuart, *The Poor in Western Europe in the Eighteenth and Nineteenth Centuries* (1986).

Wynne, Deborah, 'Reading Victorian Rags: Recycling, Redemption, and Dickens's Ragged Children', *Journal of Victorian Culture* 20 (2015): 34–49.

Young, Arlene, 'Comprehending the Slum-Dweller: Affect and "A Child of the Jago"', *Victorian Review* 40 (2014): 39–43.

Zimmer, Oliver, *Remaking the Rhythms of Life: German Communities in the Age of the Nation-State* (Oxford, 2013).

Zucchi, John E., *The Little Slaves of the Harp : Italian Child Street Musicians in Nineteenth-Century Paris, London, and New York* (Quebec, 1992).

List of Images

Acknowledgments

This book owes its existence to a three-year Early Career Fellowship jointly funded by the Leverhulme Trust and Queen Mary University of London, and I am deeply indebted to both institutions for their interest and their generosity. I'd like to thank all my colleagues, both in Queen Mary's history department and elsewhere, for advice, encouragement, suggestions, drinks and general bonhomie – and none more so than my official mentor, Colin Jones, a great inspiration and a stalwart supporter. I finished writing *Vagabonds* at the University of East Anglia, thanks to the inestimable kindness of my boss there, John Street; UEA's Humanities Faculty Research Awards Committee was also generous enough to fund this book's final four image permissions. Thanks, too, to all the staff of my old haunt, the British Library's Rare Books and Music room, as well as to those institutions whose holdings have found their way into this book in the form of words and pictures – and in particular to the enlightened attitude of the New York Public Library, Yale's Lewis Walpole Library and the J. Paul Getty Museum when it comes to sharing their collections gratis.

A number of people's thoughts, provocations and responses have found their way directly or indirectly into *Vagabonds* – thank you Jo, other Jo, Joe, Ken, Matthew, Robyn and the rest! Thanks, now as always, to my family – for everything. Emma Whipday read it all over, made the book better and endured many walks full of half-formed thoughts, tumbled out back and forth along Folkestone's Leas Promenade. Joanna Swainson continued to be the best agent on earth and brought the book to the perfect home: thank you Matt and Pete for taking the punt and being so keen, Danny for tying things together, Sarah for the scrupulous scrutinising, David for putting everything in its right place, Andrew for the peerless design, Dusty for lighting the fires, and as for my editor, Rowan Cope – there are no words sufficient to express my thanks, but if there were, you'd find them (and then convince me, correctly, to cut about half).

Index

Index

About the Author

OSKAR JENSEN is an author and academic with a doctorate in history from Oxford University. He was named a BBC New Generation Thinker for 2022, and his previous books on British and European history have been published by Oxford and Cambridge University Presses. He is currently an arts and humanities fellow at Newcastle University.

oskarcoxjensen.com